D1174952

*Cultivating Gentlemen*

# *Cultivating Gentlemen*

## The Meaning of
## Country Life among the
## Boston Elite
## 1785–1860

*Tamara Plakins Thornton*

*Yale University Press*   *New Haven & London*

Designed by James J. Johnson
and set in Monticello types by
Keystone Typesetting, Inc.
Printed in the United States of America by
Vail-Ballou Press, Binghamton, New York.


*Library of Congress Cataloging-in-Publication Data*

Thornton, Tamara Plakins, 1957–
Cultivating gentlemen : the meaning of country life among the Boston elite, 1785–1860
/ Tamara Plakins Thornton.
p. cm.
Bibliography: p.
Includes index.
ISBN 0–300–04256–6 (alk. paper)

1. Boston (Mass.)—Social life and customs. 2. Elite (Social
sciences)—Massachusetts—Boston—History—19th century. 3. Elite
(Social sciences)—Massachusetts—Boston—History—18th century.
4. Agriculture—Massachusetts—History—19th century.
5. Agriculture—Massachusetts—History—18th century. 6. Country
life—Massachusetts—History—19th century. 7. Country life—
Massachusetts—History—18th century. I. Title.
F73.44.T48 1989
974.4'6103'0880621—dc19                                  89-30108
                                                          CIP

The paper in this book meets the guidelines for
permanence and durability of the Committee on
Production Guidelines for Book Longevity of the
Council on Library Resources.
2 4 6 8 10 9 7 5 3 1

For Jonathan
*With love and devotion*

# Contents

List of Illustrations  ix
Acknowledgments  xi
Introduction  1

*Part I: The Postrevolutionary Elite*
Introduction  15
Chapter 1: The Private Man in Pursuit of the Rural  21
Chapter 2: The Public Man and the Agricultural Society  57

*Part II: Between Generations*
Introduction  81
Chapter 3: The Agricultural Society Revitalized  85
Chapter 4: Agricultural Reform and the Aging of New England  106

*Part III: The Consolidated Elite*
Introduction  141
Chapter 5: The Moral Dimensions of Horticulture  147
Chapter 6: Agriculture in an Age of Ornament and Nostalgia  174

Epilogue  201
Appendix: Rural Biographies of Selected Elite Bostonians  213
Bibliographical Essay: Rural Pursuits in Boston  233
Index  241

# Illustrations

1. *The Vale, Seat of Theodore Lyman* 23
2. *Forcing Garden, in Winter* 25
3. *Christopher Gore* 28
4. *Woburn Sheepshearing* 30
5. *The Dinner* 34
6. *Trolling for Pike* 35
7. *Allerton Hall, Seat of William Roscoe* 37
8. *John Adams's Seat in Braintree* 38
9. *Pleasant Hill, Seat of Joseph Barrell* 41
10. *Thomson's "Summer"* 47
11. *Temple of Modern Virtue, Stowe* 50
12. *Fisher Ames* 53
13. *John Lowell (1743–1802)* 59
14. *Boxes for Conveying Plants by Sea* 65
15. *Estate of Moses Gill* 72
16. *Grove Hill, Seat of John Coakley Lettsom* 76
17. *Sir Joseph Banks* 88
18. *Downton Castle, Seat of Thomas Andrew Knight* 90
19. *Hotchkiss' Improved Patent Straw Cutter* 93
20. *Merino Ram* 94
21. *Road Scene in Brighton. Driving to Market* 96
22. *A Bird Eye View of Smithfield Market* 97
23. *Oakes's Prize Cow* 101

24. *Oakley, Seat of Harrison Gray Otis* 107
25. *John Lowell (1769–1840)* 109
26. *West India Docks* 112
27. *Josiah Quincy* 115
28. *The Farm of Ezekiel Hersey Derby* 120
29. *Josiah Quincy's Seat in Braintree* 127
30. *The Horrors of the West Exposed* 133
31. *Thomas Handasyd Perkins* 149
32. *Belmont, Seat of John Perkins Cushing* 152
33. *Gardens at the Hunnewell Estate* 154
34. *Marshall Pinckney Wilder* 156
35. *Horticultural Hall* 158
36. *Massachusetts Horticultural Society Dinner, Faneuil Hall* 160
37. *Map of Mount Auburn Cemetery* 161
38. *Scene at Mount Auburn* 167
39. Enkianthus quinqueflorus 173
40. *The Champion Trotting Stallion* SMUGGLER 182
41. *Alice, Jersey Cow Owned by the State* 183
42. *Green Harbor, Seat of Daniel Webster* 196
43. *The Marshfield Farmer* 199
44. Lilium parkmanni 209

# Acknowledgments

In acknowledging the many institutions and individuals that have aided me in this undertaking, I begin with the very subjects of this book—those members of the Boston elite who lived between the Revolution and the Civil War. To study these men is to study the history of the overarticulate. Here were people whose sense of self-importance caused them to commit everything from personal expenses to personal philosophies into writing, to save these records, and then to found the Massachusetts Historical Society in order to preserve them for a grateful posterity. And grateful I am. The Massachusetts Historical Society, with its many collections of personal and institutional papers, has been invaluable in my research. Of course, the literary and visual traces of the Boston elite can be found elsewhere, and so, for their aid in conducting research and gathering illustrations, I would like to note my appreciation for the staffs of the American Antiquarian Society; the Boston Athenaeum; the Connecticut Historical Society; the Dedham Historical Society; the Frick Art Reference Library; the Harvard University Art Museums; Houghton Library, Harvard University; the Library of Congress; the Massachusetts Horticultural Society; the Museum of Fine Arts, Boston; the New-York Historical Society; the Newberry Library; the Society for the Preservation of New England Antiquities; the Yale Center for British Art; the Yale University Art Gallery; and the Sterling and Beinecke libraries of Yale University. Nor can I forget the Lindley Library of the Royal Horticultural Society in London. In reading the manuscript minutes of this society's early meetings, I found "Mr. Lowel of Mombry, near Boston, Massachusets," whom I recognized as John Lowell of Roxbury, near Boston, Massachusetts. I was thrilled to discover a friend from home, even if he was wearing a disguise.

I would also like to thank the Idlewild Foundation for its support of my attendance at the 1983 Attingham Trust Summer School in Britain and the Mrs. Giles Whiting Foundation for its award of a 1985–86 fellowship for research and writing. I am obliged as well to the *New England Quarterly* for permission to incorporate two articles I previously published in that journal into this present work.

My gratitude goes also to Elizabeth Blackmar, Judith Colton, George Hersey, Alan Taylor, and, most especially, John R. Stilgoe for their aid in my study of landscape history and for their comments on earlier versions of portions of this manuscript. I go beyond the usual academic acknowledgments in thanking Sydney E. Ahlstrom, Edmund S. Morgan, and David B. Davis, for they have been models to me not only of historians but of human beings. Professor Ahlstrom died in the middle of my graduate school career, but not before having transmitted some of his mischievous intimacy with the characters of American history, and not before having literally sung at my wedding. Professor Morgan especially impressed me with his humility before those same characters of history. Studying with him taught me a great deal about listening respectfully to the past; reading his works has been a lesson in how to transmit with eloquence the voices that have emerged. Professor Davis always amazes me with his insight, but he has also touched me with his generosity and kindness. Those familiar with his ideas will understand what an inspiring experience it was to study with Professor Davis, but I must add that it was also a moving one.

Finally, I thank the members of my family. This book would not be complete without remembering the men, women, and children of the Fischgrund family. I have never met them, but their lives have convinced me of the power of the human mind and soul to rise above, to shape, to transcend, and to endure. I know I bring that conviction to the study of history; I probably will never know just how much they had to do with my decision to become a student of the past. I have my parents to thank for supporting me in that decision, and simply for being the fascinating and loving people they are. My sisters, Ava and Naomi, have participated in the excitement I have felt for my studies; as women with active and creative minds, they have added to that excitement. It is hard for me to express how lucky I feel to have them as lifelong companions. It must also be luck that brought me Jonathan, my husband. Here I thank him for the sincere interest and—I am embarrassed but pleased to add—the pride he has taken in my work, but there is everything else to thank him for as well. Finally, we are both thankful for jolly little Lydia, who first saw this world just days after the first draft of this book and who needs no revisions whatsoever.

# Introduction

It is a curious fact of history that the same men directly responsible for changing the Massachusetts economy from a farming to a commercial and industrial one—merchants, financiers, manufacturers, and their legal and political advocates—should have endeavored so assiduously to identify themselves with things rural and agrarian. Between the Revolution and the Civil War, many of Boston's elite settled on country estates, took up gentleman farming, and made a stab at horticultural experimentation. Even more identified themselves with what contemporaries termed "rural pursuits" through active membership in agricultural and horticultural societies.

Just when we believe we know all there is to know about this class of much-studied men, just when we think that antiquarians and historians have sketched a comprehensive picture of the Boston elite, just when we are convinced we have been quite sufficiently Lowelled and Caboted, the proper Bostonians surprise us once more. We had thought these men constituted the ultimate business aristocracy. They held sway over the New England economy, sounded the voice of mercantile and manufacturing interests in government, and, in their private bearing, strove to embody the entrepreneurial virtues of industry, frugality, and temperance. Yet see what new and unexpected pictures we must contemplate: George Cabot, the quintessential Federalist merchant and statesman, attending to his potatoes on his secluded Brookline farm; Josiah Quincy, remembered as a congressman, Boston mayor, and Harvard president, calculating the yields of carrots on his Braintree estate; Nathaniel Ingersoll, an East India merchant, enthusiastically reporting the design of his model piggery to a Boston agricultural periodical; Thomas Handasyd Perkins, prince of the China

I

trade, pursuing exotic fruit varieties around the world with as much zeal as he acquired opium from Smyrna.

To comprehend just what function an identification with rural pursuits served for individuals within the commercial-industrial elite and for the elite as a social class, we must understand the symbolic tensions that existed between trade, manufacturing, and agriculture. What we may define merely as different kinds of economic enterprise were, for Americans of the early Republic and antebellum decades, morally charged categories freighted with symbolic significance. None of this added up to anything favorable to elite Bostonians, because the connotations of urban commerce and manufacturing were in the main negative, whereas those of rural life and agriculture were largely positive. Major strands of American thought—the legacy of the Puritan ethic, economic theory, republican ideology, and contemporary notions of historical progress and decline—agreed in their suspicion of urban commerce (and later of manufacturing) as illegitimate, destructive, and debilitating, and in their identification of a rural, agricultural society with the maintenance of a virtuous and flourishing society. Here were the negative associations the Boston elite tried to shake; here were the positive ones they hoped to tap.

Bostonians of the late eighteenth century were not Puritans, but neither had they managed to discard the intellectual legacy bequeathed to them by their Puritan forefathers. Included in this heritage was the notion of calling, one's service to God through service to the community in the world of work. Although by the Revolution the concept of calling had been largely secularized, by no means had it lost its ethical content. Work was still a moral matter, a social not an economic function; it still involved the subordination of selfish concerns to those of society. If idleness and luxury came to be understood more as social vices than as sins against God, it was nonetheless the duty of each human being to fulfill his or her duties in the world of work by laboring diligently and without succumbing to the temptations of material prosperity.[1]

In light of the doctrine of the calling, not all forms of work were judged ethically equal. Productivity and usefulness were the criteria by which

1. J. E. Crowley, *This Sheba, Self: The Conceptualization of Economic Life in Eighteenth-Century America* (Baltimore: Johns Hopkins University Press, 1974), pp. 50–85; Edmund S. Morgan, "The Puritan Ethic and the American Revolution," *William and Mary Quarterly* (hereafter *WMQ*), 3d ser., 24 (January 1967):3–7.

occupations were evaluated, while the people engaged in those occupations were judged according to standards of industry and frugality. In this scheme of things, commerce fared poorly, while manufacturing and agriculture ranked among the ethically desirable. The problem with trade was that it consisted of the mere exchange of goods; nothing was actually produced. Then too much of the merchant's business involved encouraging people to buy things they did not really need, thereby promoting luxury and extravagance. By contrast were the true productivity and obvious utility of manufacturing, which, in the prefactory era, denoted domestic production. The products of home manufactures had only the best of moral overtones, for they bespoke of household and societal self-sufficiency and the shunning of imported luxury items and hence, in a larger sense of commerce altogether, for simple but adequate necessities.[2]

Agriculture stood out as an even more clearly productive and useful calling. What after all could be of greater importance to mankind than the production of food and fiber?[3] There was more than just a moral argument here. One influential strand of economic thought, the physiocratic school of political economy advanced by the Frenchman François Quesnay, identified agriculture as the sole, true source of national wealth and greatness. According to Quesnay and such economic thinkers as Adam Smith, whom he influenced, international trade and the production of luxury manufactures only appeared to underly the economic might and glory of the great European nations. In fact, commerce and manufacturing were artificially stimulated by government policy into their state of prosperity and power; under a more natural arrangement, agriculture would emerge as the real foundation of national wealth and might. As Drew McCoy has pointed out, few Americans shared the specific political agenda of Quesnay or Smith or adopted the physiocratic philosophy in any systematic fashion, but physiocracy nonetheless held relevance for American thinkers. For one, it appeared as something of a scientific codification of a familiar literary tradition that characterized agriculture as the most ancient and noble of employments. Then, too, in the relatively underdeveloped New World, the identification of agriculture as the source of national wealth may simply have corresponded with commonsense observation. Finally, as McCoy further notes, the "cluster of fears and concerns" that characterized physiocracy

2. Morgan, "Puritan Ethic," pp. 11–13, 34–41; Crowley, *Sheba,* pp. 125–46; John F. Kasson, *Civilizing the Machine: Technology and Republican Values in America, 1776–1900* (New York: Viking Press, 1976), pp. 8–21; Drew R. McCoy, *The Elusive Republic: Political Economy in Jeffersonian America* (New York: W. W. Norton, 1980), pp. 63–67.

3. Morgan, "Puritan Ethic," pp. 4–5.

resonated with a similar set of anxieties expressed in the political ideology current in revolutionary America and the new nation, republicanism.[4]

Republican theory held that republics were fragile things, threatened by the constant attempts of power to encroach on liberty.[5] History was a dismal record of power's ultimate success against liberty; one need only look at the ancient republics of Greece and Rome, or what induced even greater pessimism because of its greater immediacy, at the example of Britain, fatally weakened by corruption, doomed to endure the death of liberty. A republic's only defense against the aggression of power—and therefore the ultimate source of its strength or weakness—was the character of its citizenry. A republic might retain its integrity only so long as its citizens retained their virtue, that is, so long as they placed the public good before private gain.

The farmer, it was believed, was the uniquely ideal republican type. The private virtues engendered by the practice of husbandry, most notably industry and frugality, nourished the public virtue vital to a republic's continuance. Even more critically, the degree of economic autonomy enjoyed by the farmer insured such disinterestedness, inasmuch as the man who controlled his own economic destiny was free to concern himself with the common good. By contrast was the man who by virtue of his lack of autonomy was forced to pursue the narrow interests of those on whom he depended for a livelihood. Clearly, such dependents as the army officer, the government pensioner, and the speculator in public funds could not be trusted to look out for the common good. All these characters were creatures of an emerging modern order characterized by unprecedented state power and supported by an increasingly complex financial structure. At least in its early stages, republicanism reacted against financialism rather than commerce, but if we understand republicanism more broadly as an ideological resistance to modernization, we might well expect the objects of

4. McCoy, *Elusive Republic,* pp. 41–46. On the classical literary tradition "In Praise of Husbandry," see Paul H. Johnstone's article of that name in *Agricultural History* 11 (April 1937):80–95.

5. The literature on republican theory is voluminous. Among the most useful sources are Bernard Bailyn, *The Ideological Origins of the American Revolution* (Cambridge: Harvard University Press, 1967); Gordon S. Wood, *The Creation of the American Republic, 1776–1787* (New York: W. W. Norton, 1969), pp. 3–70; J. G. A. Pocock, "Civic Humanism and Its Role in Anglo-American Thought," in *Politics, Language and Time: Essays on Political Thought and History* (New York: Atheneum, 1971), pp. 80–103; Pocock, "Virtue and Commerce in the Eighteenth Century," *Journal of Interdisciplinary History* 3 (Summer 1972): 119–34; Pocock, *The Machiavellian Moment: Florentine Political Thought and the Atlantic Republican Tradition* (Princeton, N.J.: Princeton University Press, 1975); and Robert E. Shalhope, "Toward a Republican Synthesis: The Emergence of an Understanding of Republicanism in American Historiography," *WMQ,* 3d ser., 29 (January 1972):49–80.

resistance to change as the modern order unfolded. Thus as the commercial revolution followed the financial revolution, we may expect to see the merchant join the stockjobber in the rogues' gallery of republicanism.

Republican ideology, then, exhibited a tendency to regard historical change as corruption and decline. This outlook, and the associated attitude toward agriculture as a moment to be captured, was reinforced by contemporary understandings of the process of history. The cyclical theory of history, which held that all societies "age" through a "life cycle" of infant barbarism, mature civilization, senile corruption, and final decline, posited inevitable moral transformation and decay. Societies begin in simplicity, frugality, and industry. As they mature they acquire such laudable aspects of civilization as perfection in arts and sciences, military might, and economic prosperity. Just at this apex of greatness, the society begins to self-destruct, as prosperity breeds avarice and idleness, luxury and extravagance, portending the ultimate ruin of civilization.[6] "Will you tell me how to prevent riches from becoming the effects of temperance and industry?" asked John Adams of his old rival Jefferson in 1819. "Will you tell me how to prevent riches from producing luxury? Will you tell me how to prevent luxury from producing effeminacy intoxication extravagance Vice and folly?"[7]

The linkage of this moral cycle to the progression from an agricultural to a commercial society was even more explicit in a concept of history originally articulated by mid-eighteenth-century French and Scottish social theorists and eventually informing popular thought in Europe and North America. According to this version of historical change, societies pass through successive stages, each defined by a mode of subsistence—hunting, pasturage, agriculture, and commerce—and each characterized by distinctive concepts of property, law, and government, and, even more critically, by a distinctive set of virtues and vices. The commerical stage, the theory held ominously, is characterized by luxury, a debilitating and corrupting influence that threatens personal and national autonomy and thus foretells the end of liberty and virtue, the total decay of morals, and the decline of civilization.[8] If, therefore, to enter that fourth stage of history

6. Stow Persons, "The Cyclical Theory of History in Eighteenth Century America," *American Quarterly* 6 (Summer 1954): 147–63.

7. Adams to Jefferson, 21 December 1819, *The Adams-Jefferson Letters: The Complete Correspondence between Thomas Jefferson and Abigail and John Adams,* ed. Lester J. Cappon, 2 vols. (Chapel Hill: University of North Carolina Press, 1959), 2:551.

8. McCoy, *Elusive Republic,* pp. 5–40; Ronald L. Meek, *Social Science and the Ignoble Savage* (Cambridge: Cambridge University Press, 1976). On the currency of the four-stages theory of history in turn-of-the-century Boston, see Joseph Barrell, "Reflections on Agricul-

would mean that the ultimate downfall of the republic was only a matter of time—a prediction only reinforced by republican ideology and the cyclical theory of history—then the nation's ability to step out of the historical process of moral declension, in effect to step out of time, hinged on its continuance as an agricultural republic. The yeoman, of course, was the man who made time stand still.[9]

But perhaps we must halt here and question the continued relevance of these strands of thought, decades old, foreign in origin, to America of the late eighteenth and early nineteenth centuries. Could it be that a pro-agricultural, anticommercial bias survived into an era that witnessed the economic and social modernization of America? Surely Americans would have to adjust to changing realities. The Jacksonian era, for example, was a time in which every American seemed to be in hot pursuit of the main chance, looking for, in Tocqueville's words, "the shortest cut to happiness."[10] This was an age of canals, wharves, factories, cities. Even agriculture could not be clearly distinguished from land speculation, or the yeoman from the businessman. If Americans were to go forward in this direction, it would seem they must have jettisoned their inconvenient

---

ture," *Massachusetts Magazine* 1 (June, July 1789): 357–61, 411–14, and the *Monthly Anthology and Boston Review* 2 (May 1806): 235–36. The latter summarized the "PROGRESS OF THE ARTS" as follows: "First the necessary arts are practised, afterward those which are convenient and pleasurable. First hunting, then fowling, then fishing. First pasturage, then agriculture, then gardening. First thatched houses, then log . . . framed . . . brick . . . stone . . . marble. First besmearing the body, then skins . . . coarse cloths . . . dyed cloths . . . linens . . . muslins . . . bleaching . . . washing . . . and all the tinkling ornaments of a Parisian belle." The ellipsis points are original to the passage. We may also recognize the four-stages theory in some of the British and French sources reprinted by Americans (including Barrell) in Boston and quoted by Chester E. Eisinger in "The Influence of Natural Rights and Physiocratic Doctrines on American Thought during the Revolutionary Period," *Agricultural History* 21 (January 1947): 15.

9. The suspension in time represented by the agricultural stage of civilization had its parallel in space, the "middle landscape" described by Leo Marx in *The Machine in the Garden: Technology and the Pastoral Ideal in America* (London: Oxford University Press, 1964). We should note that those attitudes that invested a rural setting with moral significance overlap considerably with those that credited agriculture and the farmer with a special moral status, but they are not one and the same. The pastoral ideal, to use Marx's phrase, represented a moral appreciation of the countryside quite apart from that landscape's economic function. See also Perry Miller, "Nature and the National Ego," in *Errand into the Wilderness* (1956; New York: Harper and Row, 1964), pp. 204–16, and Barbara Novak, *Nature and Culture: American Landscape and Painting, 1825–1875* (New York: Oxford University Press, 1980), pp. 3–17, for further discussion of the moral significance invested in the natural landscape in nineteenth-century America.

10. Alexis de Tocqueville, *Democracy in America*, trans. Henry Reeve, rev. Francis Bowen and Phillips Bradley, 2 vols. (New York: Vintage Books, 1945), 2:145.

notions about agriculture, farmers, and the continuance of the nation somewhere along the line.

Recently, historians have sought to correct what they regard as an oversimplified understanding of American ideology in the era between the Revolution and the Civil War.[11] The notion that Americans adopted republican thought in its classical form—nostalgic, conservative, fearful of modernizing tendencies—in a wholesale manner is being disputed. Some historians have sought to demonstrate how Americans poured new wine into old bottles, that is, how they made room for commerce in an essentially agrarian ideology. Drew McCoy, for example, has demonstrated that the political economy of Jeffersonian America granted commerce a critical role in preserving the Republic. By providing an outlet for agricultural products, foreign commerce acted as a spur to the farmer's industry, thus helping to maintain his private virtue. It also insured that the United States would maintain its identity as a primarily agricultural nation, thereby staving off the dreaded fate of nations dominated by commerce.[12]

Other historians suggest a more fundamental revision. They argue that the antimodernist bent of American thought has been exaggerated and its liberal content ignored, that the entire standard by which societies were evaluated changed in the aftermath of the Revolution. The idea that the world of work must be evaluated in strictly moral terms, as it sustained the common good and a communal order, was replaced with an endorsement of an economic order characterized by amoral market relations. The ideal of the virtuous citizen, subordinating considerations of private gain to the public good—for the two were perceived as necessarily opposed—was replaced with the ideal of economic man, merrily pursuing purely private interests, a process in no way incompatible with the common good.[13] Under these circumstances, national prosperity, once suspect as the first step in the dreaded process of moral declension, reemerged as proof of national success, a sign that America must be doing something right. Some Americans even suggested that general prosperity was particularly condu-

11. For an overview of recent historiography, see Joyce Appleby, "What Is Still American in the Political Philosophy of Thomas Jefferson?" *WMQ*, 3d ser., 39 (April 1982): 287–309; Appleby, "Republicanism in Old and New Contexts," ibid. 43 (January 1986): 20–34; and Lance Banning, "Jeffersonian Ideology Revisited: Liberal and Classical Ideas in the New American Republic," ibid.: 3–19.

12. McCoy, *Elusive Republic,* pp. 76–85, 121–32.

13. See, especially, Joyce Appleby, *Capitalism and a New Social Order: The Republican Vision of the 1790s* (New York: New York University Press, 1984), and Ralph Lerner, "Commerce and Character: The Anglo-American as New-Model Man," *WMQ*, 3d ser., 36 (January 1979): 3–26.

cive to popular virtue and that economic progress engendered moral and intellectual progress.[14]

Our understanding of American ideology of the early republic apparently needs to be broadened and refined. Intellectual tools were indeed available to establish a legitimate place for economic man and his new economic activities.[15] Yet we must not dismiss republican anxieties for the fate of the nation as mere figments of the historian's imagination, for at the same time as modern notions legitimizing the new market society gained acceptance—and even more pointedly, as the conditions of modernity became the overwhelming reality of social and economic life—older notions of the links between work and morality, prosperity and corruption, commerce and luxury, and virtue and agriculture persisted. Did Americans adapt their ideology to changing economic and social conditions? Did they jettison rhetoric to keep pace with reality? Not completely.

Antebellum America was marked by an increase in both the enthusiasm for prosperity and the fear of prosperity. Even as Americans prided themselves on the unprecedented growth of their economy and on what they regarded as the individual's unrestrained ability to take advantage of this growth, they feared the effects of wealth and opportunity. Social commentators, ranging from highbrow European travelers to evangelical preachers, lambasted Americans as a people peculiarly absorbed in a feverish pursuit of material gain, and many Americans were ready to admit the truth of that characterization.[16] Americans fretted over the decline of virtue in the face of prosperity even as they applied themselves to realizing that prosperity in earnest.

Indeed, we cannot separate the two. We must understand this anxiety as part of a broader phenomenon, the inability to adjust to rapid and massive change. The condemnation of luxury and materialism was just one symptom of a widespread cultural malaise that induced Americans to hold onto patently anachronistic ideas, to persist in a rhetoric clearly at odds with their changing society. Robert E. Shalhope has commented that "as the gap widened between classical ideals and social realities in the nineteenth

14. Kasson, *Civilizing the Machine*, pp. 38–41; Fred Somkin, *Unquiet Eagle: Memory and Desire in the Idea of American Freedom, 1815–1860* (Ithaca, N.Y.: Cornell University Press, 1967), pp. 11–16, 23, 27–31; Daniel Walker Howe, *The Political Culture of the American Whigs* (Chicago: University of Chicago Press, 1979), p. 101.

15. As J. E. Crowley has shown, these tools had in fact been in place during the eighteenth century, and it is a measure of just how resistant colonial Americans were not to modern market conditions and relations but to the image of themselves as an amoral, modern, market society, that they by and large refused to avail themselves of these tools (*Sheba*, pp. 75, 96–124).

16. Somkin, *Unquiet Eagle*, 16–23, 31–34.

century, Americans grasped more urgently the republican view of themselves that obscured the actual ramifications of accelerated economic development."[17] The persistence of the jeremiad tradition into the antebellum decades is good evidence of this kind of anachronistic thinking. So too is Jacksonian ideology. Here the hero is the self-sufficient yeoman farmer, a character idealized from the start, and never more than in this age of land speculation and international markets for agricultural products, and the villain is the "money power" exemplified by the Bank of the United States, a thinly disguised update of the stockjobbers of classical republican rhetoric.[18] Even when antebellum Americans did adapt their ideology to new social realities, it was often by characterizing those realities in republican terms, not by discarding those terms as anachronistic. Thus, for example, the independence that classical republicanism had pinpointed as the basis of civic virtue came to be identified with the spirit of free enterprise.[19] If there was irony in equating the individual's acquisitive impulses with what had once been defined as the ability to subordinate considerations of private gain to the public good, that irony was lost on antebellum Americans. This way, they might continue to think of themselves as adhering to the values of the revolutionary generation, even as they joined in the postrevolutionary scramble for wealth.

How did Boston's merchant-industrialist elite fit into all of this? Surely they had a vested interest in embracing modernity; in their corner of the world, they were largely responsible for it. We do find wealthy and prominent Bostonians taking advantage of arguments that portrayed commerce and manufacturing in a positive light. Sometimes their claims were modest, as when they accepted a secondary role in society as fair exchange for a moral blessing, albeit a limited one, of commerce and manufacturing.[20] More often, members of the Boston elite championed the moral legitimacy

17. Robert E. Shalhope, "Republicanism and Early American Historiography," *WMQ*, 3d ser., 39 (April 1982): 347–48. See also Somkin, *Unquiet Eagle*, pp. 6–7.

18. Marvin Meyers, *The Jacksonian Persuasion: Politics and Belief*, 2d ed. (New York: Vintage Books, 1960), pp. 3–32.

19. Rowland Berthoff, "Independence and Attachment, Virtue and Interest: From Republican Citizen to Free Enterpriser, 1787–1837," in Richard L. Bushman et al., *Uprooted Americans: Essays to Honor Oscar Handlin* (Boston: Little, Brown, 1979), pp. 97–124. See also Rowland Berthoff and John M. Murrin, "Feudalism, Communalism, and the Yeoman Freeholder: The American Revolution Considered as a Social Accident," in Stephen G. Kurtz and James H. Hutson, eds., *Essays on the American Revolution* (Chapel Hill: University of North Carolina Press, 1973), pp. 256–88.

20. See, for example, John Lowell, "Address Delivered before the Massachusetts Agricultural Society at the Brighton Cattle Show, October 13, 1818," *Massachusetts Agricultural Repository and Journal* 5 (January 1819): 222, and I. H. Wright, "The Position of Agriculture," an address to the Middlesex South [Agricultural] Society, in Charles L. Flint, ed., *The*

of commerce and later manufacturing in a more aggressive manner. They did so by exploiting the ambiguities inherent in the concept of luxury. The usual understanding of luxury was decidedly negative.[21] If, however, one could break the connection between luxury and corruption, then luxury could be understood not as the prelude to cultural decline but as the triumphant emergence from primitive society. It could be defined, in other words, as the laudable essence of civilized life. When in 1785 some Bostonians criticized the dandyish Sans Souci club as a distressing manifestation of opulence, those who defended the club responded with just such a redefinition. The alternative, they pointed out, was nothing less than barbaric primitivism. Opponents of the club would have its members "refuse all connection with the arts and sciences which live under the patronage of commerce and retire to the woods." They would have them "cut each other's throats without remorse, and even with satisfaction, for the inestimable reward of a garland of parsley, or a wreath of pine."[22] A generation later, another Bostonian presented this opposition of commerce and barbarism even more forcefully. "Some have regretted that America has interfered in foreign trade," wrote James Savage in the high-toned *Monthly Anthology and Boston Review,* but it would be a cultural disaster for the United States to devote itself exclusively to agriculture. "If all are constrained to daily labour with their hands," he explained, "there can be no cultivation of mind; and without intelligence there will be few delights of society and little interchange of benevolence. Man in such a state ceases to be sociable, and becomes only gregarious. *So that from gradual degeneration to barbarism we shall best be preserved by commerce.*"[23]

To those who, looking back at the decline and fall of ancient commercial civilizations, continued to insist on a necessary connection between commerce and corruption, there was another argument to consider. Chris-

*Agriculture of Massachusetts, as Shown in Returns of the Agricultural Societies, 1854* (Boston: William White, 1855), p. 453.

21. For relevant discussions of this concept, see John Sekora, *Luxury: The Concept in Western Thought, Eden to Smollett* (Baltimore: Johns Hopkins University Press, 1977), pp. 63–131, and McCoy, *Elusive Republic,* pp. 21–32.

22. *Massachusetts Centinel,* 19 January 1785. On the Sans Souci controversy, see Wood, *American Republic,* pp. 422–25, and McCoy, *Elusive Republic,* p. 98.

23. James Savage, "The Remarker, No. 27," *Monthly Anthology and Boston Review* 4 (November 1807): 576–77, emphasis in original. Savage's concern about degeneration reflects the scientific theory, still the subject of international controversy in the early nineteenth century, that Old World life forms, including human beings, degenerate in the New World environment, as well as a broader cultural assumption that the transition from Old World civilization to the New World wilderness involves moral and cultural regression. See Gilbert Chinard, "Eighteenth-Century Theories on America as a Human Habitat," *American Philosophical Society Proceedings* 91 (February 1947): 27–57.

tianity, it was asserted, made all the difference between moral degeneration and moral superiority. "Tell me not of Tyre, and Sidon, and Corinth, and Carthage," stated the Reverend Joseph Buckminster of Boston, "I know they were commercial and corrupt. But let it be remembered that they flourished long before the true principles of honorable trade were understood, before the introduction of Christianity had given any stability to those virtues of conscientious integrity, and strict fidelity in trusts, which are not indispensable to commercial prosperity."[24] Under these circumstances, commerce actually became an agent of moral and cultural uplift, and the merchant, something of a missionary. The trading vessel brought not only goods—that was the least of it—but religion and morals, knowledge, *civilization* to foreign lands. This characterization of international trade found advocates from the first years of the American Republic, but by the mid-nineteenth century it had developed into a full-fledged mercantile propaganda campaign.[25] "The friendly intercourse created by commerce is slowly but surely revolutionizing the earth," wrote one Boston merchant in 1856. "Nations are forgetting that they have met as foes," he continued, for "the familiarity of commercial intercourse has given them new impulses, and taught them that there are higher glories than those of the battle-field."[26]

Meanwhile, a parallel campaign on behalf of industrial enterprises and entrepreneurs was being waged. When manufacturing ceased to denote household production and involved instead factory production in cities and mill towns, it was feared that along with this Old World system of manufacturing would come Old World social conditions—poverty, vice, crime, disease, ignorance—and, ultimately, Old World corruption and cultural decline. To counter this view of manufacturing, early advocates of industry insisted that by building model mill towns in rural locations and hiring virtuous young women as operatives, factory production could be placed on a thoroughly republican social basis in America. This was the rationale behind the development of Lowell, Massachusetts, by that select group of industrialists known as the Boston Associates. As factory production settled into its role as cornerstone of the regional economy, spokesmen for industrial interests went beyond their essentially defensive line of argument and grew more expansive in their claims. Thus Edward Everett and Daniel

24. Henry Ware, Jr., ed., *The Works of Joseph S. Buckminster, with Memoirs of His Life,* 2 vols. (Boston: James Munroe, 1839), 2:382.

25. McCoy, *Elusive Republic,* pp. 86–90; Somkin, *Unquiet Eagle,* pp. 23–24.

26. George R. Russell, "Introductory Essay," in Freeman Hunt, ed., *Lives of American Merchants,* 2 vols. (New York: Office of Hunt's Merchants' Magazine, 1856; Derby and Jackson, 1858), 1:xxxvi, xl.

Webster represented Boston manufacturers not only as they wielded power in the federal government but also as they used their oratorical talents to portray machine technology as a man-made wonder attesting to the glory of the human mind and manufacturers as heroic leaders in the inspiring march of human progress.[27].

These Boston merchants and manufacturers no doubt held their heads up with pride. But it would be surprising if they were in some way immune to the ambivalence that characterized most Americans' attitudes toward economic and social change, particularly in light of their direct responsibility for that change. It would be odd if they were not forced at least to react to that ambivalence, even if by some chance they managed to escape it themselves. Although we can accept their procommercial, promanufacturing rhetoric at face value, we must also accept the undeniable evidence that the rural and agricultural remained compellingly attractive to members of the Boston elite throughout the antebellum period. Cabot's potatoes, Quincy's carrots, Ingersoll's pigs, and Perkins's fruits constitute a second body of statements made by prominent Bostonians. What lies ahead is a close reading of rural pursuits among the Boston elite.

27. Kasson, *Civilizing the Machine,* pp. 39–51, 55–86; Howe, *American Whigs,* pp. 98–103; Thomas Bender, *Toward an Urban Vision: Ideas and Institutions in Nineteenth-Century America* (1975; Baltimore: Johns Hopkins University Press, 1982), pp. 3–93.

# PART ONE

## The Postrevolutionary Elite

# Introduction

O N the morning of 17 March 1776, 170 ships set sail for Halifax from Boston Harbor, taking not only British troops but also about one thousand American Loyalists. Away went many of the most prominent men of the prerevolutionary city, men like Chief Justice Peter Oliver and merchant Harrison Gray. Many leading families remained behind, of course, to reappear in the postrevolutionary elite:[1] Endicotts, Saltonstalls, and Winthrops traced their prominence back to the seventeenth century, whereas other families that survived the Revolution intact—the Quincys, Amorys, and Otises, for example—had entered the colonial elite only a few generations before the break with Britain. During and immediately following the Revolution many provincial families of power and wealth, particularly those from the Essex County towns of Newburyport, Salem, and Beverly, moved into Boston to take advantage of the many new economic opportunities. For the merchants and lawyers of

1. I use the term *elite* in a general sense, to denote those individuals and families who by virtue of wealth, power, and/or some major cultural accomplishment, such as advanced scholarship, recognized by the wealthy and powerful as carrying status, constituted the uppermost stratum of society and exercised a regional influence. There was no single test of elite status in Boston between the Revolution and the Civil War. Wealth by itself, for example, did not guarantee membership in the elite, though it did form the basis of most elite families' prominence. Furthermore, the criteria for membership changed over time. Thus, for example, individuals entered the elite by virtue of their personal achievements well into the nineteenth century, but by the end of the antebellum era, something akin to a true patriciate, a hereditary class, had taken shape. I avoid the term *aristocracy* as charged with meaning throughout the period under study. *Upper class,* as suggesting a Great Chain forged of infinite gradations of status (middle, upper-middle, etc.), impresses me as too indefinite to denote individuals that had no difficulty recognizing themselves as strikingly distinct from those who did not share elite status.

the Lee, Higginson, Lowell, Cabot, and Jackson families, a good deal of money and many a reputation could be made from privateering, army contracts, and the adjudication of confiscated estate and maritime spoils cases. Others also profited from the rapidly changing fortunes of war, including many who rose from comparative obscurity, geographical as well as social and economic, into the postwar elite.[2]

It was, then, a vastly changed group of men who emerged as the power and wealth of Boston in the wake of revolution, a group, furthermore, that could not take its internal cohesion for granted. Yet it was not long before the forty or so families who made up the postwar elite had achieved a unified identity and outlook. Through intermarriage, distinctive testamentary practices, collaborative business enterprises, and association with elite institutions (many of which, such as Harvard College, extended over from colonial days), members of the postwar elite emerged as a well-integrated body, mercantile in orientation, Federalist in loyalty.[3] They strengthened this elite status by including in their class a select group of intelligentsia— Unitarian ministers, Harvard scholars, and miscellaneous literati. Through their participation in and leadership of such institutions as Harvard, the Boston Athenaeum, and the *Monthly Anthology and Boston Review,* these men functioned as cultural ornaments to mercantile society. A certain amount of tension existed between the merchants and their literary wards—

2. Lorenzo Sabine, *The American Loyalists* (Boston: Charles C. Little and James Brown, 1847), pp. 334, 491–92; E. Alfred Jones, *The Loyalists of Massachusetts: Their Memorials, Petitions and Claims* (London: Saint Catherine Press, 1930), pp. 151–52, 223–24; Janice Potter, *The Liberty We Seek: Loyalist Ideology in Colonial New York and Massachusetts* (Cambridge: Harvard University Press, 1983), p. vii; Frederic Cople Jaher, *The Urban Establishment: Upper Strata in Boston, New York, Charleston, Chicago, and Los Angeles* (Urbana: University of Illinois Press, 1982), pp. 19–21; Robert A. East, *Business Enterprise in the American Revolutionary Era* (New York: Columbia University Press, 1938), pp. 49–79, 218–20, 224–25, 231–32.

3. A number of relatively recent secondary sources go into more detail on this process of class formation. Jaher's *Urban Establishment,* pp. 121–44, provides a general overview of this early period. In *The Organization of American Culture, 1700–1900: Private Institutions, Elites, and the Origins of American Nationality* (New York: New York University Press, 1984), pp. 55–75, Peter Dobkin Hall stresses (perhaps overly so) the degree to which elite cultural patterns were shaped by such mundane business concerns as the consolidation of capital and the spread of risk. Ronald Story's analysis of class cohesion in *The Forging of an Aristocracy: Harvard and the Boston Upper Class, 1800–1870* (Middletown, Conn.: Wesleyan University Press, 1980), pp. 3–23, is probably the closest to mine in its emphasis on elite institutions as the focus of elite identity. I would further argue that not institutions per se, but the cultural resonance these institutions struck through their larger associations with individual and collective character ideals, was the key to their utility. Thus, collective habits, such as country estate living, could effectively function as institutions quite apart from specific institutional settings.

the *Monthly Anthology* became an outlet for the condemnation of commercial materialism and philistinism—but even these critics paid obeisance to the essential high-mindedness of a mercantile class so willing to ally itself with and celebrate learning and literary accomplishment.[4]

But for all their wealth and power, members of this same elite found themselves in an awkward position. They were convinced of their own legitimacy as a ruling class but increasingly discovered that the citizenry of their state did not necessarily concur. In colonial days, it was understood that men of education, broad experience, habits of command, and historical sense of public responsibility—in other words, rich and prominent men— were the obvious choices to lead society and government. What had changed with the Revolution were the criteria that determined a legitimate ruling class. Now public virtue, the ability to place the public good before private gain, was the operative criterion; nothing was said about social or economic standing.[5] It was all very difficult for the elite to accept.

Not that the Boston elite advocated a ruling class based on hereditary privilege. As republicans, they rejected that sort of aristocracy as contrary to the meaning of the American political system. The type they had in mind was a "natural aristocracy," an "aristocracy of experience," an "aristocracy of talents."[6] If their Jeffersonian opponents insisted on branding Federalists as aristocratic in the undesirable, Old World sense, Federalists regarded themselves as a legitimate republican aristocracy; as for Jefferson and his cohorts, it was *they* who constituted an "aristocracy of the southern nabobs."[7] According to the Bostonians, much of what separated the worthy

4. Lewis P. Simpson, ed., *The Federalist Literary Mind: Selections from the Monthly Anthology and Boston Review, 1803–1811* (Baton Rouge: Louisiana State University Press, 1962), esp. pp. 47–74, and Simpson, *The Man of Letters in New England and the South: Essays on the History of the Literary Vocation in America* (Baton Rouge: Louisiana State University Press, 1973), pp. 3–61.

5. David Hackett Fischer, *The Revolution of American Conservatism: The Federalist Party in the Era of Jeffersonian Democracy* (New York: Harper and Row, 1965), pp. xii–xiv; Gordon S. Wood, *The Creation of the American Republic, 1776–1787* (New York: W. W. Norton, 1969), pp. 475–83; Richard D. Brown, "Who Should Rule at Home? The Establishment of the Brahmin Upper Class," *Reviews in American History* 9 (March 1981): 55–57.

6. [Jonathan Jackson], *Thoughts upon the Political Situation of the United States of America* . . . (Worcester, Mass.: Isaiah Thomas, 1788), p. 57; Fisher Ames, "American Literature," in Seth Ames, ed., *Works of Fisher Ames*, 2 vols. (Boston: Little, Brown, 1854), 2:441; James M. Banner, Jr., *To the Hartford Convention: The Federalists and the Origins of Party Politics in Massachusetts, 1789–1815* (New York: Alfred A. Knopf, 1970), pp. 127–28; Fischer, *Revolution of American Conservatism*, p. 19; John W. Malsberger, "The Political Thought of Fisher Ames," *Journal of the Early Republic* 2 (April 1982): 5–7.

7. Fisher Ames to George Richards Minot, 9 July 1789, in Ames, *Works of Fisher Ames*, 1:62.

aristocracy of Massachusetts from the "unrestrained aristocracy"[8] of Virginia was the moral gulf that yawned between merchant and planter. They contrasted the mercantile virtues of frugality, industry, and sobriety with the vices engendered by a slave society: luxurious living, laziness, and a brutality conditioned by years of unchecked power.[9]

Yet for all their claims that the only legitimate type of ruling class was one based on talent, virtue, and experience, Massachusetts Federalists firmly believed that these republican qualifications naturally coincided with such traditional criteria as genteel education and manners, membership in a well-established family, high social position, and, yes, wealth. Furthermore, they never subscribed to the idea of equality of condition among men. Of course human beings occupied different levels in the social and economic scale; to deny the reality of that situation was foolish, utopian, and—the ultimate condemnation—democratic. Any leveling tendencies in society, whether from Jacobins in France or their collaborators at home, the Jeffersonians, were dangerous. According to the Federalist conception of society, men accepted their places in society. For those at the top of the scale, this meant the responsibilities of stewardship, most notably the duty to rule. For those below them, this meant deference to their rulers. It was government by consent to be sure, but consent to the men in power and not to the measures they might take.[10]

It came, then, as a rude shock to elite sensibilities when in 1786 heavily indebted farmers of the state's western counties threatened violence, closed law courts, and published demands under the leadership of one Daniel Shays. In these developments, elite Boston saw the fearsome results— social chaos, anarchy, mobs—of a democratic spirit that threatened the downfall of the Republic.[11] Shays's Rebellion appeared all the more significant in the context of what were perceived as other signs of a leveling tendency in Massachusetts. From 1793, for example, there appeared "Jacobin" clubs, sure to bring a Reign of Terror to the peaceful and law-abiding Commonwealth.[12] More intangible but no less real was the decline in

8. Oliver Wolcott to Ames, 24 January 1803, Wolcott Papers, Connecticut Historical Society, Hartford.

9. Linda K. Kerber, *Federalists in Dissent: Imagery and Ideology in Jeffersonian America* (Ithaca, N.Y.: Cornell University Press, 1970), pp. 23–32; Banner, *Hartford Convention,* pp. 84–89.

10. Fischer, *Revolution of American Conservatism,* pp. 1–10, 29; Banner, *Hartford Convention,* pp. 53–58, 60–65.

11. For a reaction to Shays's Rebellion typical of the Boston elite, see Winfred E. A. Bernhard, *Fisher Ames: Federalist and Statesman, 1758–1808* (Chapel Hill: University of North Carolina Press, 1965), pp. 47–52.

12. Banner, *Hartford Convention,* p. 19; Bernhard, *Fisher Ames,* pp. 235–37, 242–44.

habits of deference among the state's citizenry. Concrete evidence of that decline was seen in the diminishing control of Massachusetts Federalists over their own state and the parallel growth in popularity of the Jeffersonians.[13]

To understand Federalist opposition to the party of Jefferson, we must first understand that this was no mere political disagreement, for according to the ideology shared by both Federalists and Jeffersonians in the 1790s, there really was no such thing. The very existence of rival political parties was dreaded as evidence of the pernicious spirit of faction, the division of society into competing groups promoting narrow and selfish interests. Since Federalists were convinced that their policies represented the public good, any contrary views, such as those held by their political rivals, must represent the sacrifice of the public good to private advantage. And in the tense atmosphere of the postrevolutionary world, in which the very survival of that inherently frail entity, the American Republic, seemed to hang in the balance, the differences between Federalists and Jeffersonians assumed a moral significance of Manichaean proportions. Thus Federalists regarded Jeffersonians as something even more sinister than an alternate (and therefore dangerous) philosophy. As James Banner has pointed out, they represented an alternate personality—irresponsibly visionary, popularity seeking, morally unscrupulous.[14]

The Federalists could only watch the progress of their society with trepidation and a sense of doom. Probably the most famous of these pessimists, and the main spokesmen for this high Federalist outlook in Massachusetts, were the members of the so-called Essex Junto—a group of lawyers and merchants, many of whom migrated from Essex County towns into Boston during the revolutionary era. In this group we may count Fisher Ames, George Cabot, Francis Dana, Nathan Dane, Benjamin Goodhue, Stephen Higginson, Jonathan Jackson, John Lowell, Theophilus Parsons, Timothy Pickering, Israel Thorndike, and Nathaniel Tracy. Although long regarded as a kind of Federalist politburo, it now seems more likely that members of the Essex Junto had less effectual power than was once believed. Nevertheless, they did define Massachusetts Federalist orthodoxy, and they did retain their positions as grand old men of the Boston elite. They epitomized the elite in at least one other critical manner—that is, in the way that their professional outlook and political orienta-

13. Fischer, *Revolution of American Conservatism,* pp. 25–28, 33–35.
14. John R. Howe, Jr., "Republican Thought and the Political Violence of the 1790s," *American Quarterly* 19 (Summer 1967): 147–65; Banner, *Hartford Convention,* pp. 25–46, 72–83. On the Federalist image of the Jeffersonians, see also Kerber, *Federalists in Dissent,* pp. 1–94.

tion merged indistinguishably into a unified world view. No clear line separated those whose primary occupation was merchant and those who counted themselves lawyers. Many merchants assumed elected or appointed posts in government, while many attorneys, also sometime statesmen, concentrated in the practice of commercial and admiralty law. More important, Federalism stood for the interests of an urban, mercantile class, just as that same class identified strongly with the Federalist principles of order, stability, and hierarchy.[15]

The Boston elite rejected Old World concepts of aristocracy, yet they lived on country seats in the manner of the British landed gentry. They were mercantile in outlook, yet many were avid gentleman farmers. If they regarded themselves as polar opposites of their political opponents the Jeffersonians, it is hard to ignore that in their estate living and experimental farming they might almost be confused for the master of Monticello himself. If we are to understand why many of the postwar Boston elite identified themselves with rural pursuits, we must constantly bear in mind the problems these men faced in the aftermath of revolution. In a new nation, cut loose from Old World standards and traditions, what forms of distinction could be expected to characterize a New World elite? And in republican America, what made these men a legitimate ruling class?

---

15. David H. Fischer, "The Myth of the Essex Junto," *William and Mary Quarterly,* 3d ser., 21 (April 1964): 191–234. For capsule intellectual biographies of these men, see Fischer, *Revolution of American Conservatism,* app. 2, pp. 245–62.

# ONE

## The Private Man in Pursuit of the Rural

"*I* go to town scarcely once in a month," wrote George Cabot, merchant and senator from Massachusetts, in September 1796.[1] In the warmer months, Cabot, with many of his fellow merchants and statesmen, retired to country seats scattered around Boston, there to enjoy the pleasures of rural living—conversation with like-minded friends, companionship with books, gardening, and gentleman farming. The phenomenon of the country seat was by no means new—wealthy Bostonians had acquired suburban estates in the colonial era as well—but it did change after the Revolution. For one, the interest in experimental agriculture was a new development. Perhaps more important, rural pursuits took on new meanings in postrevolutionary Boston, as they had to in a world in which everything had to be redefined and reoriented. Country estates were things of the elite, and what was the role of an elite in the Republic? Estates were also cultural artifacts of the British social system, and how much and what parts of that system had a place in the new nation? And they figured prominently in British literary tradition, but how did that tradition remain relevant to America?

In acquiring country estates and practicing gentleman farming, prominent Bostonians confronted these questions and in so doing defined what it meant to be members of an American elite. Rural pursuits turned out to be a powerful means of self-characterization. There was, however, no single image that country seat owners wished to project. In fact rural pursuits

1. Cabot to Rufus King, 24 September 1796, in Charles R. King, ed., *The Life and Correspondence of Rufus King,* 6 vols. (1894–1900; reprint ed., New York: DaCapo Press, 1971), 2:91.

were so potent precisely because they acted as a rich and varied reservoir of associations, conjuring images laden with meanings of the aristocrat, the squire, the landed merchant, the yeoman, and the statesman retired from the world. Elite Bostonians hoped to tap this reservoir in all its wealth.

Most obvious was the association of the country seat with the British aristocracy.[2] Of course, the Boston elite and its counterpart across the Atlantic differed significantly. For one, Boston estates came nowhere near British properties in scale and elegance. If the Bostonian might measure landholdings in tens or at most hundreds of acres, British counterparts reckoned theirs in the tens and even hundreds of thousands. His country house might be nothing more than a largish version of a substantial Federalist period residence, or it might have some pretension to architectural distinction and sophistication, but in no case was it a Blenheim or a Stowe—room upon opulent room of the most splendid in European art and craftsmanship. These differences reflect larger political, social, and economic realities. For the British aristocrat, land formed the basis of power, prestige, and wealth, whereas for the Bostonian, land was a trapping of power, prestige, and wealth acquired elsewhere, most likely in maritime commerce or subsidiary professions. The thousands of acres constituting a British estate meant rental income—the aristocrat was above all a landlord—whereas the modest acreages of Boston estates held no economic import. But all this is only to say that Boston "aristocrats" were not true aristocrats in the European sense; they were men of commerce at the top of the social scale. Nevertheless, nothing prevented these landed merchants from patterning if not their substance then at least their style of living after that of a British baronet.

Let us look at Theodore Lyman's estate, the Vale (fig. 1). In 1793 Lyman, a Federalist merchant heavily involved in the East Indies and China trade, purchased a thirty-acre parcel of land in suburban Waltham and proceeded to turn it into an estate reminiscent of a proper English seat. The Salem craftsman and architect Samuel McIntire was hired to design the dwelling. In many ways, the house could not have been more provincial

2. For the purposes of this discussion, I am using the term *aristocracy* to denote the great landowners of Britain, both titled (nobility or peerage) and untitled, who by virtue of their landholdings and consequent wealth, occupied the apex of British landed society. As historian F. M. L. Thompson points out, legal status is a less meaningful criterion in understanding this society than estate size and wealth; surely, he insists, Thomas Coke, esq., was the equal of many peers in wealth and power even before receiving the title earl of Leicester. Below the aristocracy ranked the gentry (including the "greater" county notables, the "lesser" squirearchy, and "gentlemen"), and below the gentry ranked the freeholders. (Thompson, "The Social Distribution of Landed Property in England since the Sixteenth Century," *Economic History Review*, 2d ser., 19 [December 1966]: 506–7.)

1. *The Vale, Seat of Theodore Lyman.* Painting by Alvan Fisher. (Courtesy Society for the Preservation of New England Antiquities.)

New England: built of wood, characteristically Federalist in its hip roof and balustrade, a stolid, self-confident box of a house. McIntire gave the house some sophistication, however, in an oval drawing room—a typically French shape—known as the bow parlor. But outside, the Vale was neither New England nor France; it was pure England. Lyman hired an English gardener named William Bell to lay out the Waltham landscape in the Picturesque style as then advanced by the English landscape gardener and theoretician Sir Humphrey Repton. Bell had precious little to work with; the point of the Picturesque was to engender mental variety through aesthetic variety, but the Vale landscape was almost unrelievedly uniform. Nevertheless, Bell's final product was admirably, suitably Reptonian. Workaday Beaver Brook was transformed into a serpentine canal spanned by a three-arched bridge of white granite. Below the bridge, the brook was dammed to create ponds and a waterfall. Bell also created a classically English park, planted with English limes, elms, and oaks and stocked with forty Bengal deer.[3]

3. Samuel Ripley, "A Topographical and Historical Description of Waltham, in the County of Middlesex, Jan. 1, 1815," *Massachusetts Historical Society Collections,* 2d ser., 3

Repton's particular brand of the Picturesque catered to the new passion for horticulture that had seized his aristocratic clientele. His designs included flower gardens, terraces, conservatories, and pleached trellises (fig. 2).[4] Only at the turn of the century was the new vogue manifested institutionally in horticultural societies and periodicals,[5] but already in the eighteenth century, a greenhouse might vie with a grotto or temple as the pride of the estate.[6] Bell's plans for the Vale, which included flower beds, fruit trees, a peach wall, kitchen garden, and two greenhouses heated for the benefit of resident banana trees and pineapple plants, were right in contemporary British style.[7] Lyman himself conformed to the British mold by designing the Vale not only as a country house, garden, and park but as a working farm suitable for experimental agriculture.[8]

It was in the late eighteenth century that what has been referred to as the Agricultural Revolution was launched in Britain.[9] Although the actual

(January 1815): 272; *Gardener's Magazine* [London] 1 (1826): 205; A. J. Downing, *A Treatise on the Theory and Practice of Landscape Gardening, Adapted to North America; with a View to the Improvement of Country Residences,* 2d ed. (New York: Wiley and Putnam, 1844), p. 33; Gordon Allen, "The Vale," *Old Time New England* (hereafter *OTNE*) 42 (April–June 1952): 81–87; R. Newton Mayall, "Country Seat of a Gentleman: 'The Vale,'" *OTNE* 43 (October–December 1952): 37–41; Bertram K. Little, "A McIntire Country House," *Antiques* 63 (June 1953): 506–8; Abbott L. Cummings, "Theodore Lyman's Country Seat, 'The Vale,' Waltham, Massachusetts," *Ellis Memorial Antiques Show Catalogue* (Boston, 1964), pp. 17–24. For an introduction to Picturesque gardening and to Repton, see John Dixon Hunt and Peter Willis, eds., *The Genius of the Place: The English Landscape Garden, 1620–1820* (New York: Harper and Row, 1975), pp. 318–79.

4. Hunt and Willis, *Genius of the Place,* p. 358.

5. The first British horticultural society was established in London in 1804; the first periodical, in 1787. Harold R. Fletcher, *The Story of the Royal Horticultural Society, 1804–1968* (London: Oxford University Press, 1969); Ray Desmond, "British Nineteenth-Century Gardening Periodicals: A Chronological List," in Elisabeth B. Macdougall, ed., *John Claudius Loudon and the Early Nineteenth Century in Great Britain,* Dumbarton Oaks Colloquium on the History of Landscape Architecture 6 (Washington, D.C.: Trustees for Harvard University, Dumbarton Oaks, 1980), p. 101. Horticulture in both Britain and America is discussed in greater detail in chapter 5.

6. Sir Robert Barker's seat in Surrey, for example, was famous for its 171-foot-long greenhouse and for the date palm, allegedly the only one in Britain in 1787, that fruited within. [William Angus], *Seats of the Nobility and Gentry in Great Britain and Wales* (Islington: W. Angus, 1787), pl. 6 and accompanying description.

7. Ripley, "Description of Waltham," p. 272; Mayall, "'The Vale,'" pp. 39–41; Ann E. Compton, "The Lyman Greenhouses," *OTNE* 50 (Winter 1960): 83, iv.

8. Although we know little about Lyman's early involvement in agriculture, his later interest in stockbreeding is more amply documented. See, for example, Lyman to Timothy Pickering, 19 January 1825, Timothy Pickering Papers, reel 45, frame 305, Massachusetts Historical Society (hereafter MHS), Boston.

9. The discussion of the Agricultural Revolution is based on the following sources: J. D. Chambers and G. E. Mingay, *The Agricultural Revolution, 1750–1880* (New York:

2. *Forcing Garden, in Winter.* Reprinted from Humphrey Repton, *Fragments on the Theory and Practice of Landscape Gardening* (London, 1816). (Courtesy Beinecke Rare Book and Manuscript Library, Yale University.)

era of reform may have been far more extended and responsibility for reform far more diffused than historians once thought, the revolution as a dramatic change retains its integrity in at least one critical sense. There can be no doubt of a greatly increased interest in agricultural reform among the British landed classes dating from this period. The landlord reformers represented their motives as disinterested and patriotic. In practicing experimental farming, it was claimed, they hoped to increase the body of scientific agricultural knowledge and, by the success of their operations, to set an example for the farmers of Britain. Through this all-important process of emulation, agriculture would acquire a new vigor, and, the argument continued, since agriculture is the ultimate source of national wealth and power, an era of unprecedented prosperity and greatness would follow. Thus gentleman reformers were praised as public servants and their

Schocken Books, 1966); G. E. Mingay, *English Landed Society in the Eighteenth Century* (London: Routledge and Kegan Paul, 1963), pp. 163–88; F. M. L. Thompson, *English Landed Society in the Nineteenth Century* (London: Routledge and Kegan Paul, 1963), pp. 151–83, 212–37, 247–55; Kenneth Hudson, *Patriotism with Profit: British Agricultural Societies in the Eighteenth and Nineteenth Centuries* (London: Hugh Evelyn, 1972); Hudson, *The Bath and West: A Bicentenary History* (Bradford-on-Avon: Moonraker Press, 1976); R. A. C. Parker, "Coke of Norfolk and the Agrarian Revolution," *Economic History Review,* 2d ser., 8 (August 1956): 156–66.

agricultural societies as "publick-spirited institutions" promoting "the safety, independence, and prosperity of their country."[10]

Although agricultural reform in Britain was infused with the rhetoric of unselfish patriotism and benevolence, the reformers themselves were characterized by less disinterested motives. These men were above all landlords, and so above all else improvements in agriculture meant higher rents. One agricultural society official stated the case clearly:

> A taste for experiment now animates the minds of most country gentlemen, and perhaps there are few things operate to encourage this taste more than the luxury of the times. A country gentleman, who some years since kept his carriage and his respectable table for 700£ or 800£ per annum, now finds himself in a straitened situation. He must either reduce his establishment, or have recourse to some means of increasing his income. Agriculture, therefore, naturally suggests itself as an honourable and effectual mode of increasing his funds. He takes upon him the task of a farmer, occupies in whole or in part his own estate, makes agriculture his study, and pursues it with unremitting ardour.[11]

The situation was very different in Massachusetts. Although their position in society may have been roughly analagous to that of the 800£ per annum gentlemen, elite Bostonians were not motivated by pecuniary considerations when it came to agricultural improvement. When Boston country seat owners took on tenant farmers, as they often did, it was to carry out their improvement programs; any rental they received thereby was tiny compared with other sources of profit, therefore incidental. But if members of the Boston elite did not face the same economic stimulus as their counterparts across the Atlantic, they nonetheless inherited the vogue for agricultural improvement.[12] In the period between the Revolution and the War of 1812, they adopted both the latest British ideas in agricultural improve-

10. *Letters and Papers of the Bath Society* 6 (1792) and 12 (1810), quoted in Hudson, *Bath and West*, pp. 33, 64.

11. John Billingsley, quoted in Hudson, *Bath and West*, pp. 52–53. Chambers and Mingay point out that landlords pushed for enclosure not so much to improve agriculture as to make money; rents on enclosed farms, they estimate, doubled, and the return on the investment of enclosure was on the order of 15 to 20 percent, as opposed to 5 to 6 percent on Funds (*Agricultural Revolution*, pp. 82–88). Elsewhere, Mingay summarizes the situation succinctly when he remarks that "when landlords spoke of 'improvement,' it was usually an 'improved rental' they had in mind" (*Landed Society in the Eighteenth Century*, p. 172).

12. For a general discussion of the importation of the English Agricultural Revolution into America, see Rodney C. Loehr, "The Influence of English Agriculture on American Agriculture, 1775–1825," *Agricultural History* (hereafter *AH*) 11 (January 1937): 3–15. See also Loehr, "Arthur Young and American Agriculture," ibid. 43 (January 1969): 43–56.

ment and the rhetoric of patriotism and benevolence that informed those innovations.

A prime example of just such a Boston improver was the lawyer and statesman Christopher Gore (fig. 3), whose country seat in Waltham, erected in 1804, stood not a mile from Theodore Lyman's Vale.[13] Like Lyman, Gore erected a splendid dwelling. He described it modestly as "a convenient and comfortable Mansion," while the Reverend Samuel Ripley more accurately characterized it as "a spacious and noble building, of brick, after the plan"—for like the Vale, Gore Place incorporated an elliptical salon—"of some of the best houses in Europe."[14] As at the Vale, the house was set in a landscape designed according to the latest aesthetic precepts: broad expanses of lawn, a deer park, plantations of forest trees, as well as a thriving kitchen garden, two greenhouses, and a large variety of fruit trees.[15] The estate was also a true experimental farm, agricultural land interspersed with pleasure grounds. Radiating from the library was the "Straight Walk," a raised path that acted as a viewing platform for agricultural operations in nearby fields. Over the almost quarter-century in which he lived at Waltham (quitting the country only in winter), Gore experi-

13. Gore had acquired the Waltham property in 1789, shortly thereafter expanding his holdings from fifty to three hundred acres, and finally building a residence in 1793. This first mansion burned down in 1799, during Gore's absence in London. Until his departure for England in 1796, Gore undertook experimental farming on the estate. He received, for example, a gift of an English bull, the foundation of what became known as the Gore breed. Helen R. Pinkney, *Christopher Gore: Federalist of Massachusetts, 1758–1827* (Waltham, Mass.: Gore Place Society, 1969), pp. 49–50; George F. Lemmer, "The Spread of Improved Cattle through the Eastern United States to 1850," *AH* 21 (April 1947): 80; Gore to Timothy Pickering, 11 March 1825, Pickering Papers, 32:139.

14. Gore to Rufus King, 26 March 1806, Rufus King Papers, New-York Historical Society, New York; Ripley, "Description of Waltham," pp. 272–73. On the architecture of Gore Place, see Pinkney, *Christopher Gore,* pp. 84–89; Charles Arthur Hammond, "'Where the Arts and the Virtues Unite': Country Life near Boston, 1637–1864" (Ph.D. diss., Boston University, 1982), pp. 117–28; and "Gore Place," *Antiques* 47 (April 1945): 213, 217–19. The Gore-King correspondence at the New-York Historical Society also contains numerous references to the construction of the dwelling.

15. Pinkney, *Christopher Gore,* pp. 88, 140–41; Hammond, "Country Life near Boston," pp. 237–38; John Lowell, "Remarks on the Gradual Diminution of the Forests of Massachusetts," *Massachusetts Agricultural Repository and Journal* 5 (January 1818): 37. Gore's correspondence with King includes many reports of the progress and yields of fruits and vegetables at Gore Place. In autumn 1805, for example, Gore reported sadly that a mere two barrels of apples were left from that season's crop, due to the ravages of a July hailstorm and the hefty appetites of the many workmen erecting his house. On the other hand, in a letter of 1816, Gore proudly noted the hundreds of bunches of grapes growing in his greenhouse. Gore to King, 9 November 1805, 1 August 1816, King Papers. For references to Gore's British gardener, Mr. Heathcot, see Gore to King, 13 January 1806, 14 June 1818, 21 April 1819, and 15 November 1822, King Papers.

3. *Christopher Gore*. Portrait by John Trumbull. (Courtesy Harvard University Portrait Collection. Gift of Dr. William E. Paine, 1834.)

mented with new crop rotations and fertilizers, planted test plots of various field crops, tried out the latest in farm implements, and bred livestock.[16]

There can be no doubt that in his enthusiasm for gentleman farming, Gore was heavily influenced by British agricultural improvers. As one of the U.S. commissioners appointed under the terms of Jay's Treaty to negotiate claims on behalf of American citizens, Gore lived in London from 1796 to 1804. Here he made the acquaintance of a number of the most famous of the British improvers. His major accomplishment in this regard was probably his attendance at two world-renowned agricultural events, the sheepshearings—conventions of aristocrats interested in agricultural improvement, really—given by Thomas Coke, later earl of Leicester, and the duke of Bedford. "Shortly after your departure," wrote Gore to his closest friend, Rufus King, in July 1803, "Mr. Coke visited me. He invited me to his sheep shearing at Holkam [*sic*], and the Duke [of Bedford] sent me a note, inviting me to his at Woburn [fig. 4]. I went to both these places, & was highly gratified." Gore's "jaunt" lasted a week, and, he reported, "I would have remained longer, but for my attending my duty at the Board." At the sheepshearings, Gore was a conscientious student of agricultural improvement, going so far as to take notes on what he had learned. He rubbed shoulders with Lord Somerville and Lord Talbot, listening to their discussions over the relative merits of Devonshire and long-horned Leicester cows.[17] Even after his return home, Gore continued to look to Britain for agricultural intelligence. He imported English spring wheat for trial on his estate; kept abreast of the writings of Arthur Young, the most influential of English agricultural reformers; and, having read an updated account of Coke's sheepshearing, did his best to obtain a new farming implement Coke used at Holkham.[18]

England may have provided the model, but just what provided the motivation for this prominent lawyer, this powerful statesman, this wealthy investor in Boston transportation and manufacturing enterprises to become a gentleman farmer? The answer given by Gore's contemporaries, of course, was disinterested benevolence, a desire to improve agricultural techniques and thereby the lot of yeoman neighbors. Here the rhetoric is similar to that characterizing British agricultural reform. "The grounds [of Gore Place]," wrote the Reverend Ripley in 1815, "are not improved

16. Pinkney, *Christopher Gore,* pp. 88, 140–41; Hammond, "Country Life near Boston," pp. 145–53. Gore's correspondence with King, especially after his retirement from public affairs in 1816, contains much of an agricultural nature.

17. Gore to King, 2 July 1803, 10, 23 July 1817, King Papers.

18. Gore to King, 9 October 1816, 23 October 1817, 29 February, 20 May, 6 August 1820, 14 June 1821, King Papers.

4. *Woburn Sheepshearing.* Included in the scene are the Duke of Bedford, on his horse, inspecting merino sheep broadcloth; such noted agricultural reformers as Thomas Coke, Sir John Sinclair, and Arthur Young; and numerous miscellaneous dukes, lords, marquises, esquires, and reverends. Engraving by M. N. Bate, J. C. Stadtler, and T. Morris, after a painting by George Garrard, 1811. (Courtesy Yale Center for British Art, Paul Mellon Collection.)

merely to gratify personal feelings, or attract observation and receive applause; but they are devoted to the raising of every variety of horticulture, grass, corn, wheat, barley, &c.:—and while this variety itself delights the eye of the beholder, it makes him feel, that utility is the main design of the exertions there displayed, and that it is compatible with the highest rank and most exalted mind, to study the convenience and supply the wants of society."[19] In his funeral sermon for Gore, the Reverend F. W. P. Greenwood concurred. "Sensible of the value of a judicious system of agriculture," he preached of the late statesman, "he endeavoured to bring others to a sense of it by his example." Greenwood characterized Gore as an "active, tasteful, improving agriculturist" and therefore "a public benefactor."[20]

If Gore was so serious in his desire to aid his fellow man through agricultural improvement, one may wonder why he did so little to publicize the results of his farming experiments. Gore's fields were left to speak for themselves. Who but his close friends, fellow gentleman farmers, would know that English wheat proved unsatisfactory in the Waltham soil and climate? In fact, for Christopher Gore, experimental farming was an act not of public benevolence but of private self-characterization.

Before he returned from England, Gore asked his friend Fisher Ames for advice. Once back in Boston, should he take up the law once more or

19. Ripley, "Description of Waltham," p. 273.
20. F. W. P. Greenwood, *Funeral Sermon on the Late Hon. Christopher Gore, Formerly Governor of Massachusetts* (Boston: Wells and Lilly, 1827), p. 14.

retire to his Waltham estate? Pecuniary considerations—to maintain a proper style of living in London, Gore had been forced to outspend his salary[21]—probably lent a certain urgency to the question. When Ames urged Gore to "'open shop' again," it was for reasons both financial and otherwise. Sequestered on a suburban estate, Gore might well be forgotten by the public and therefore passed over for positions of public responsibility. The bar would keep his mind occupied and his "social affections" engaged. And a law practice would make financial sense, since retirement to Waltham would entail fifteen hundred or even two thousand dollars of expenditures. "Every southern visitor," wrote Ames with his usual bias, "must see your improvements, show them to his wife, and eat and drink you ten guineas' worth." The final reckoning, according to Ames, was that "$2000 saved, and $2000 got is $4000, enough to meet all the demands on your treasury." It was not wealth per se that Ames regarded as critical— even he admitted that Gore might have to settle for some "not very lucrative fagging at the bar"—so much as the responsibility Gore had to himself to keep up the appearances of a style of living appropriate to a Boston gentleman. "A man may not incline to take a certain degree on the scale of genteel living," insisted Ames, "but having once taken it he must maintain it."[22]

Gore did "open shop" again, but he also retained his country seat. What seems to have been pivotal in Gore's decision to practice law was precisely the desire to maintain an aristocratic style of living, one that ironically had little to do with being an attorney. For him, a law practice was largely a means to an end, and that end was the life of a landed gentleman. No sooner did Gore return to his Boston law practice and Waltham estate than he was looking for ways to quit the former in favor of the latter. He hoped that by investing in foreign trade he might make a quick killing and retire from the bar. He fretted over the huge cost of building Gore Place, for, as he wrote King, the expense "will keep me longer at the Bar, than will suit my Love for Indulgence." "My occupation & views . . . ," he summarized for King in 1805, "are bounded by the Desire of obtaining an easy Independance, and a Power of retirement from Business, with the means of indulging those Habits of Living, to which I have been accustomed."[23]

21. John Codman to Catherine Amory Codman, 20 July, 15 October 1800, Codman Family Manuscripts Collection (hereafter CFMC), Society for the Preservation of New England Antiquities, Boston, Mass.

22. Ames to Gore, 5 October 1802, in Seth Ames, ed., *Works of Fisher Ames,* 2 vols. (Boston: Little, Brown, 1854), 1:302–3.

23. Gore to King, 8 May, 10 December 1805, 26 March 1806, King Papers. On Gore's investments, most of which were made not in foreign trade but in Boston insurance, banking, transportation, and textile manufactures, see Pinkney, *Christopher Gore,* pp. 89–92.

Those habits of living were distinctly British and aristocratic in tone. They included, for example, Gore's use of a richly upholstered open carriage, pulled by four long-tailed bays and attended by liveried coachmen and outriders. Regarding then Governor Gore's tour of Massachusetts in such equipage in 1809, Federalist newspapers proudly compared him to an English nobleman meeting with his tenants before an election. Gore's political opponents made the same comparison, but with disapproval not pride. "Whose carriage is that, that rolls so majestically thro the street, decked in scarlet and gold?" inquired the *Independent Chronicle.* "One might as well elect the Duke of York."[24]

Fancy carriages were only the most obvious sign of Gore's interest in an aristocratic style of living. So too were his membership in such genteel learned societies as the Massachusetts Historical Society and the American Academy of Arts and Sciences, his collection of an extensive gentleman's library, his residence on a country estate and simultaneous ownership of a town house (suitable for the Boston equivalent of the "London season"), and, not least of all, his avid pursuit of experimental agriculture.[25] Gore became a gentleman farmer because, through a kind of cultural intuition, he knew it to be appropriate to a man of his station and pretensions. Scientific farming was something that proper gentlemen, British and American, did. Gore both wished to characterize himself as and knew himself to be just such a gentleman. Hence, English wheat.

It would be a mistake, however, to regard Boston's estate owners as would-be copies of British aristocrats. Certainly the prestige and power of the aristocracy appealed to them, and aristocratic longings must be counted among their motives for country living, but by no means did elite Bostonians subscribe unquestioningly to Britain's social system. Recall that Boston's Federalists rejected a system that granted power solely on the basis of hereditary privilege in favor of one that looked toward a "natural aristocracy" of talent and virtue for leadership. If these republican aristocrats happened to coincide with the wealthy and educated classes in America—as the Boston elite had every expectation they would—that still did

24. Pinkney, *Christopher Gore,* pp. 115–18; *Independent Chronicle,* 3 April 1809, quoted in ibid., pp. 115–16. Gore, even more than most Federalists, was vulnerable to the charge of advocating a British-style aristocracy in America; his father's Toryism was a lifelong stigma. Greenwood, *Christopher Gore,* p. 11.

25. Pinkney, *Christopher Gore,* pp. 48–49, 88–89, 92–93. Regarding the necessity of an urban residence for the winter season, Gore wrote King: "I must build or purchase a Town House, before I can have the means of living according to the style I have been accustomed to" (Gore to King, 26 March 1806, King Papers).

not mean that upper-crust Bostonians hoped to duplicate the British class system in the new nation.

Furthermore, if Britain's landed interest was not an automatic model for elite Bostonians, it was also because that interest was by no means monolithic. Even in Britain, significant differences—economic, social, and even moral—were recognized as separating the great landlords from the gentry. In 1790 the former group comprised perhaps four hundred families, including most peers and many baronets, who belonged to the uppermost crust by virtue of the amount of land they owned, the rental income they received from that land, and their ability to sustain a style of living that included not only six months on the great estate but also a month at some fashionable spa, a month of travel, and the all-important, four-month social season in London. The last criterion—the London social season—is perhaps most significant, for it represented the great landlords' attachment to metropolitan life and, conversely, their weak identification with rural values. Small wonder that they had acquired the reputation of decadent living. These were the men who squandered their fantastic wealth on horse racing at Newmarket and expensive social diversions in London and who even on their estates shunned the rustic for the refined (fig. 5).[26]

In contrast with the decadent aristocracy—again, even in the British understanding—was the landed gentry, men of middling means and moderate habits, rural tastes and loyalties. This group, numbering in the thousands, comprised the wealthy gentry, squires, and "gentlemen," none of whom could afford either the costs of campaigns for national office or the expense of a London social season. Accordingly, in contrast to the aristocracy, their outlook was decidedly provincial and rural. If the aristocracy enjoyed the artifice and ostentation of the fox hunt, the gentry preferred the rural pastimes of game shooting and fishing (fig. 6). While their wealthier neighbors were living the high life in the metropolis, members of the gentry were planning next season's agricultural improvements.[27] Even

26. Mingay, *Landed Society in the Eighteenth Century,* pp. 6–10, 19–26, 131–62; Thompson, *Landed Society in the Nineteenth Century,* pp. 22–25, 76–108, 134–36; Mark Girouard, *Life in the English Country House: A Social and Architectural History* (New Haven and London: Yale University Press, 1978), pp. 5–9.

27. Mingay, *Landed Society in the Eighteenth Century,* pp. 6–10, 19–26, 131–62; Thompson, *Landed Society in the Nineteenth Century,* pp. 22–25, 109–50. In spite of the fame of such great landlords interested in agricultural reform as the duke of Bedford [Woburn] and the earl of Leicester [Holkham], it appears that the gentry were actually more involved in experimental farming. Arthur Young was in fact the spokesman for these more modest country gentlemen and not for the more famous aristocrat-reformers. Mingay, *Landed Society*

5. *The Dinner.* Engraving by Thomas Rowlandson, 1787. From a series entitled "Fox Hunting." (Courtesy Yale Center for British Art, Paul Mellon Collection.)

among the gentry itself, there were those who translated these sorts of differences into moral ones, contrasting the hollowness and decadence of the aristocratic social whirl with the moral sturdiness of country living. Especially as they lost economic ground under the burdens of increased taxation while the aristocracy absorbed the extra load in stride, members of the gentry insisted on their moral advantage over those above them.[28] Probably an even more significant spur to the insistence on the moral superiority of plain living (all terms are relative, of course!) was the rising economic power of the nouveaux riches, the merchants, bankers, and lawyers with their newly acquired fortunes—and country estates.[29]

Although longtime estate owners might dismiss the newly landed

in the Eighteenth Century, pp. 163–88; Chambers and Mingay, *Agricultural Revolution,* pp. 73–75.

28. Mingay, *Landed Society in the Eighteenth Century,* pp. 81–85; Thompson, *Landed Society in the Nineteenth Century,* pp. 134–35.

29. Mingay, *Landed Society in the Eighteenth Century,* pp. 101–7, 216; Thompson, *Landed Society in the Nineteenth Century,* pp. 21, 122–23, 129, 187–88.

6. *Trolling for Pike*. Aquatint by George Hunt, after James Pollard. (Courtesy Yale Center for British Art, Paul Mellon Collection.)

merchants and professionals as arrivistes, others began to regard them seriously as models of breeding and benevolence. We might look, for example—as the Bostonians may well have—at the character of Sir Andrew Freeport, merchant, as portrayed in the pages of Joseph Addison's *Spectator*. Sir Andrew defended his fellow merchants against charges of greed and praised them for their many public acts of benevolence as well as private virtues of thrift and hard work. Indeed, in the banker-baronet's estimation merchants compared favorably to landed gentlemen on both accounts. "It is the fortune of many . . . gentlemen," he remarked caustically, "to turn out of the seats of their ancestors, to make way for such new masters as have been more exact in their accounts than themselves; and certainly he deserves the estate a great deal better who has got it by his industry, than he who has lost it by his negligence."[30]

Freeport, of course, was just one such new master. Having made a

30. *Spectator* no. 174, 19 September 1711. On Freeport, see N. S. B. Gras, "Sir Andrew Freeport, a Merchant of London," *Bulletin of the Business Historical Society* 19 (November 1945): 159–62.

fortune in commerce, he removed his riches from "the uncertainty of stocks, winds, and waves" and purchased a country estate. Here he was determined to enjoy his possessions by "making . . . them useful to the public"; to improve his agricultural lands, in the process providing employment to "a great many indigent persons"; and to live a life of rural self-sufficiency, subsisting on "mutton of my own feeding," on "fish out of my own ponds," and on "fruit out of my own gardens."[31] Surely this was a man who avoided both extremes of aristocratic indolence and mercantile boorishness, whose choice of rural living identified him as a man of refinement and whose manner of rural living showed him to be a man of public and private virtue alike.

Elite Bostonians did not need to consult the *Spectator* to find other examples of landed merchants and professionals. Many such men were subjects of their own acquaintance: Liverpool merchant William Roscoe, civic benefactor, historian, agricultural improver, and estate owner (fig. 7);[32] Sir Francis Baring, a London merchant and an owner of an estate in Kent, whose American business correspondents included John Codman and Stephen Higginson;[33] and John Coakley Lettsom, a wealthy Quaker physician who undertook botanical and agricultural experiments at his suburban seat.[34]

From the point of view of elite Bostonians, what all this meant was that the rustic gentry and the enlightened merchant class might be embraced as models for country living even as the decadent aristocracy was rejected. Of course, not all Bostonians saw fit to make these distinctions. When in 1786, for example, John Adams (fig. 8) visited numerous English estates, he had harsh words for aristocracy, gentry, and landed merchants alike. Having viewed such great estates as Stowe, Hagley, Blenheim, and Woburn, Adams remarked, "It will be long, I hope before Ridings, Parks, Pleasure Grounds, Gardens and ornamented Farms grow so much in fashion in America." Noting that Mr. Hopkins, the owner of Paines Hill in Surrey,

31. *Spectator* no. 549, 29 November 1712.
32. Henry Roscoe, *The Life of William Roscoe*, 2 vols. (Boston: Russell, Odiorne, 1833), esp. 1:150–53, 178–83, 186–96, 2:38–39, 54–76; *Dictionary of National Biography* (hereafter *DNB*), s.v. "Roscoe, William." On Roscoe as a model for Boston's elite, see Ronald Story, "Class and Culture in Boston: The Athenaeum, 1807–1860," *American Quarterly* 27 (May 1975): 184–86.
33. *DNB*, s.v. "Baring, Sir Francis"; Ralph W. Hidy, *The House of Baring in American Trade and Finance: English Merchant Bankers at Work, 1763–1861* (Cambridge: Harvard University Press, 1949), pp. 3–54.
34. Thomas Joseph Pettigrew, *Memoirs of the Life and Writings of the Late John Coakley Lettsom*, 3 vols. (London: Longman, Hurst, Rees, Orme, and Brown, 1817); *DNB*, s.v. "Lettsom, John Coakley."

7. *Allerton Hall, Seat of William Roscoe*. Reprinted from J. P. Neale, *Views of the Seats of Noblemen and Gentlemen, in England, Wales, Scotland, and Ireland*, 2d ser. (London, 1824). (Courtesy Yale University Library.)

"rides by it, but never stops," Adams remarked that "the owners of these enchanting Seats are very indifferent to their Beauties." He admired the gardens and greenhouses of Osterly, the suburban London seat of a wealthy banking family, but once again insisted that "the Beauty, Convenience, and Utility of these Country Seats, are not appreciated by the owners. They are mere Ostentations of Vanity. Races, Cocking, Gambling draw away their attention." And when it came to Mill Hill, seat of another London banker, Adams regretted that the owner had "spoiled it." "They are very good, civil People," he wrote of the banker and his family, "but have no Taste."[35]

But Adams *would* be uncompromisingly harsh in his assessment. This is the same man, after all, who steadfastly refused to acknowledge the letters and packets of the Scottish agricultural reformer Sir John Sinclair and who consistently declined membership in British learned societies.[36]

35. John Adams, *The Adams Papers*, ed. L. H. Butterfield, ser. 1: *Diary and Autobiography of John Adams*, 4 vols. (Cambridge: Harvard University Press, 1961–62), vol. 3: *Diary 1782–1804, Autobiography Part One to October 1776*, pp. 184–86, 189–91, 199.

36. John Adams to Timothy Pickering, Pickering Papers, 21:227; Edward Handler, "'Nature Itself Is All Arcanum': The Scientific Outlook of John Adams," *Proceedings of the American Philosophical Society* 120 (June 1976): 226–28.

8. *John Adams's Seat in Braintree.* Drawing by Eliza Susan Quincy, 1822. (Courtesy Massachusetts Historical Society.)

Most Bostonians were not likely to be such thorough curmudgeons, though we must not go to the other extreme and accept the Jeffersonian view of Boston Federalist merchants as "Anglomen," obsequious quasi-subjects of Britain. The experiences and attitudes of John Codman, a Boston merchant abroad in England at the turn of the century, are probably representative of his class. Codman resented being given the cold shoulder by his English business associates in the House of Baring. "I have seen the Barings often," he reported to his wife, "though none have been to my lodgings to pay me a visit. . . . They really do not know how to be attentive to a stranger." He strongly suspected that the politeness with which he was treated on the rare occasion when he did catch their attention—this time at Leigh, Sir Francis Baring's country estate—was insincere and self-interested. "The fact is," Codman wrote of Sir Francis, ". . . that he finds I have been a profitable customer & shall be a valuable one in the future, [and] that such an object is worth cultivation. I understand all these things. Interest is all that governs here, money is all that is sought for." Codman wrote with particular resentment that evening, for, as he noted, "Sir F. did not press me to stay and dine." But the story by no means ends with a boardinghouse dinner and mutual insult, for Codman immediately went on to sing the praises of the Baring estate. "Sir Francis's place at Leigh is a delightful one," he wrote. He admired the lawns and woods, gardens and greenhouses, the "calm soft sweet scenes," and set about thinking how he might transform his own estate in Lincoln on the model of Leigh.[37] The lonely meal in his lodgings had been forgotten.

Thus, when forced to deal with them in a social context, Americans found British merchants, bankers, and lawyers almost as exclusive as any aristocrat, but once back in Boston, with memories of hurt pride faded and of mercantile splendor magnified, these same men might reappear as especially attractive and appropriate models. At least the monied classes sidestepped many of the moral objections raised against titled classes, especially those at the apex of the social pyramid. If the choice of a decadent duke as a model for rural living might be questionable, the same might not be true of the simple-living gentry or, even more relevant, landed men of commerce and the professions. This is not to say that a desire to imitate the English aristocracy played no role in the choice of a rural life among the Boston elite; rural pursuits probably involved many clusters of different and even contradictory associations, all of which might be used at one time or another. To the extent that the British landed aristocracy proved attractive to the Boston elite—in the power and prestige their landedness engendered and the permanency and stability it represented—Bostonians may have patterned themselves after the aristocracy. But given those aspects of the British aristocracy less commendable in republican America, those same Bostonians may have looked to other sectors of British landed society, notably the gentry and the estate-owning merchants and professionals, as additional models. Never mind the inconsistencies here. Why shouldn't the elite Bostonian want to be now the aristocrat, simultaneously the country squire, and then, for a time, the enlightened landed merchant? After all, a major part of the tremendous attractiveness of rural pursuits was the very wealth of associations they engendered.

Thus it may have been either the duke of Devonshire or Sir Andrew Freeport—more likely, it was both—who acted as a model for Boston

37. John Codman to Catherine Amory Codman, 24 August 1800, CFMC. Codman reported that the Gores were similarly snubbed: "Their situation is elevated but not pleasant. They see few of the people of this country except by cards of compliment once or twice a year" (20 July 1800, CFMC).

merchant Joseph Barrell when in 1792 he erected Pleasant Hill, a magnificent estate overlooking the Charles River (fig. 9).[38] "It was Mr. Barrell's ambition," wrote an early chronicler of the estate's history, "to create an ideal country-seat."[39] The dwelling itself, designed by Charles Bulfinch, was the latest in fashion, built on a French oval-on-axis plan, ornamented with Corinthian capitals ordered from London, and outfitted with wallpaper, carpets, tapestries, silver, porcelain, and glass imported from Europe. The gardens, said to have cost fifty thousand dollars, featured stone cupids, dovecotes, and a fountain stocked with goldfish and trout. And Barrell was known to commute from his estate into Boston on a barge manned by liveried boatmen.[40] He might have been any one of the many London merchants who, as one British contemporary described them, "retreat from the industrious Labours of the Compting-house to share their well-earned Wealth with their Friends, in the hospitality of their Country Seats" along the banks of the Thames.[41]

Pleasant Hill was also a farm, and Barrell was keenly aware of his position as not only an estate owner but also a gentleman farmer. "In the improvement of the land," he wrote in 1794, "I hope to find employment as long as I live."[42] Some of Barrell's agricultural interests were relatively ornamental; he lavished attention, for example, on his orchards and hothouses, importing not only trees and plants from Europe but also competent gardeners.[43] But Barrell's farming activities also turned to the more prosaic. In the first years of the nineteenth century, for example, the results of his experiments with potato cultivation appeared in the publications of

38. On Barrell, see his obituary in the *Monthly Anthology and Boston Review* 1 (October 1804): 571–72, and Dean A. Fales, Jr., "Joseph Barrell's Pleasant Hill," *Publications of the Colonial Society of Massachusetts* 43 (1966): 374–76.

39. Edward G. Porter, "Demolition of the McLean Asylum at Somerville," *Proceedings of the Massachusetts Historical Society*, 2d ser., 10 (April 1896): 549. In 1816, twelve years after Barrell's death, Pleasant Hill was sold to the Massachusetts General Hospital.

40. Ibid., pp. 549–51; Fales, "Pleasant Hill," pp. 376–88; Frank Chouteau Brown, "The Joseph Barrell Estate, Somerville, Massachusetts: Charles Bulfinch's First Country House," *OTNE* 38 (January 1948): 54–58; Marshall Pinckney Wilder, "The Horticulture of Boston and Vicinity," in Justin Winsor, ed., *The Memorial History of Boston, including Suffolk County, Massachusetts, 1630–1880*, 4 vols. (Boston: James R. Osgood, 1881), 4:636; Harold Kirker, *The Architecture of Charles Bulfinch* (Cambridge: Harvard University Press, 1969), pp. 45–53; Hammond, "Country Life near Boston," pp. 78–83, 89–111.

41. [Angus], *Seats of the Nobility and Gentry*, pl. 60 and accompanying description.

42. Barrell to John Webb, 3 February 1794, Letter Book (hereafter LB):105, MHS.

43. Barrell's Letter Book is filled with references to his garden activities. See, for example, Barrell to John Horshand & Co. (London), 28 June 1793, LB:61–62; Barrell to T. Dickinson & Co. (London), 15 November 1793, LB:78–79; Barrell to Mr. Pringle (London), 19 December 1793, LB:93–94. See also Fales, "Pleasant Hill," pp. 386–88.

9. *Pleasant Hill, Seat of Joseph Barrell.* (Courtesy Society for the Preservation of New England Antiquities.)

the Massachusetts Society for Promoting Agriculture.[44] And Pleasant Hill contained not only fish ponds and stables but also a poultry yard and dairy.[45]

Barrell's commitment to experimental agriculture was part of his larger outlook on what it meant to be a gentleman. "There is no other kind of life," he wrote in an essay entitled "Reflections on Agriculture" in 1789, "that can furnish a panegyrist with such an inexhaustible subject of eulogy." He cited the "universal utility" of agriculture and "the innocence and plea-sure," the "antiquity and dignity" of farming employments. As agriculture is the most useful of arts, it is also the source of all "the pleasures and

44. Barrell, "Experiment on Potatoes," *Papers on Agriculture, Consisting of Communications Made to the Massachusetts Agricultural Society, with Extracts from Various Publications* (Boston: Young and Minns, 1801), pp. 81–82; Barrell, "Culture of Potatoes," *Papers on Agriculture, Consisting of Communications Made to the Massachusetts Society for Promoting Agriculture* (Boston: Young and Minns, 1803), pp. 76–77; Barrell, "On Potatoes," *Papers on Agriculture; Consisting of Communications Made to the Massachusetts Society for Promoting Agriculture, with Extracts from Various Publications* (Boston: Young and Minns, 1804), pp. 12–14.

45. Porter, "McLean Asylum," p. 549; Barrell to Messrs. Shaler and Hall, 3 April 1794, LB:110.

elegancies of life." The life of a gentleman farmer is thus simultaneously one of utility and refinement, avoiding the dreaded extremes of frivolity and boorishness alike. Small wonder that "this art has been cultivated by many of the greatest men among the ancients" and therefore, by extension, modern men of ancient virtue.[46]

In Barrell's mind, the four-stages theory of history reinforced this line of thinking. To agriculture, wrote Barrell, "we owe the first foundation of society and order; the establishment of property; the consequent introduction of civilization, and all the humanizing arts of life."[47] It is only farming that has ushered mankind out of a state of hunting and gathering barbarism. But if agriculture is the starting point of civilization, it is also the end point. "It is a fact somewhat remarkable," wrote Barrell, " . . . that men should have returned to the exercise of Agriculture, the first of the arts, only after they had successively tried all the rest." Having left agriculture to pursue the "false and delusive" track of "commerce and the enjoyment of luxury," human beings eventually return to rural pursuits.[48] On a less abstract level, of course, Barrell was talking about himself, specifically, his retirement from the East India trade to a genteel life of hothouse management and spud cultivation. Barrell was quick to point out (and congratulate himself on) the moral transition the shift from urban commerce to rural husbandry entailed. There in the country, he wrote, are "the vast and noble scenes of nature," and "the light and open ways of the divine bounty"; here in the city are only "the confined and perishing works of art" and "the dark and intricate labyrinths of human policy and malice."[49] Continued Barrell: "*There* Pleasure appears, like a beautiful, virtuous, and endearing wife, in all the native charms of simplicity and truth: *Here* she assumes the form of the fickle, mercenary, and painted harlot, whose obtruding beauties glitter a while in the gaudy but fading colors of seduction, and leave disgust, remorse and misery behind."[50]

Barrell's ideas were highly stylized, of course. The exalted place of agriculture in the history of human society, the praise of agriculture and the life of rural retirement, and the moral condemnation of urban existence

46. Joseph Barrell, "Reflections on Agriculture," *Massachusetts Magazine* 1 (June 1789): 357, 360–61.

47. Ibid., p. 357. Barrell follows this statement with an unattributed excerpt, identified by Chester E. Eisinger as a reprint from the English *Universal Magazine* ("The Influence of Natural Rights and Physiocratic Doctrines on American Agrarian Thought during the Revolutionary Era," *AH* 21 [January 1947]: 15).

48. Barrell, "Reflections on Agriculture," *Massachusetts Magazine* 1 (July 1789): 411–12. The July essay was a continuation of the one published in June.

49. Ibid., pp. 412–13.

50. Ibid., p. 413.

were standard for the time; indeed, Barrell was not shy to quote extensively from "authorities" in his essay. But a stylized response is not the same thing as an insincere one. Obviously these ideas had real meaning for Barrell; he did, after all, build a country estate and practice experimental husbandry. Somehow the role of gentleman farmer struck Barrell as suitable for a man of his station. Likely as not, it was because that role symbolized both virtue and elegance, the perfect way station between aristocratic decadence and commercial crudity for a republican elite.

❧   ❧   ❧

If recent historians have called the existence of an all-powerful Essex Junto into question, the reality of a Boston Federalist agricultural junto cannot be doubted. Living on country estates and practicing some form of gentleman farming in this period were Stephen Higginson, Jonathan Jackson, Jonathan Mason, John Lowell, Christopher Gore, Timothy Pickering, George Cabot, and Fisher Ames.[51] Mixed in with the political correspondence these men held with one another—and by extension such other Federalist statesmen-gentleman farmers as Oliver Wolcott and Rufus King—are letters on agricultural matters, not to mention packets of seed and packages of plant cuttings. In 1799 Pickering sends seeds from Marseilles to George Cabot, Fisher Ames, and Judge Lowell.[52] Cabot reciprocates with two volumes of agricultural treatises,[53] Ames with detailed responses to Pickering's many queries on the Dedham farmer's agricultural

51. On Higginson's Brookline estate, see Thomas Wentworth Higginson, *Life and Times of Stephen Higginson* (Boston: Houghton Mifflin, 1907), pp. 233–35; John Gould Curtis, *History of the Town of Brookline Massachusetts* (Boston: Houghton Mifflin, 1933), p. 210; Theodore F. Jones and Charles F. White, *Land Ownership in Brookline from the First Settlement* (Brookline, Mass.: Riverdale Press, 1923), p. 33, map 6; and Samuel Aspinwall Goddard, *Recollections of Brookline, Being an Account of the Houses, the Families, and the Roads, in Brookline, in the Years 1800 to 1810* (Birmingham, Eng.: E. C. Osborne, 1873), p. 16. On the estates of Jonathan Jackson and Jonathan Mason in the same town, see Jones and White, *Brookline,* pp. 32–33, map 6, and Goddard, *Brookline,* p. 8. On Lowell's Roxbury estate, see Ferris Greenslet, *The Lowells and Their Seven Worlds* (Boston: Houghton Mifflin, 1946), pp. 76–78; Harrison Gray Otis, "Letter Relating to the Character and Services of the Hon. J. Lowell," *Historical Magazine* 1 (September 1857): 263; and Francis S. Drake, *The Town of Roxbury: Its Memorable Persons and Places, Its History and Antiquities* (Roxbury, Mass.: privately published, 1878), p. 394. Gore, Pickering, Cabot, and Ames are discussed at greater length elsewhere in this chapter.

52. Pickering to George Cabot, 26 February 1799, Pickering Papers, 10:417; Ames to Pickering, 12 March 1799, in Ames, *Works of Fisher Ames,* 1:253. In his letter, Ames wrote Pickering that he intended to forward the seeds to friends, explaining that "seeds from a rank democratic soil would not thrive in my garden, but the South of France is, I suppose, far from democratic." Referring to an opposition newspaper, he added: "Besides, the Aurora would maintain, that they are the seeds of aristocracy which *you* delight to spread."

53. Cabot to Pickering, 13 June 1802, Pickering Papers, 26:293.

practices.[54] By 1806 we find the Federalist network enlisted in the task of procuring grafts of Swaar apples for Fisher Ames. Pickering is the lead man here, requesting Henry Livingston of New York to forward the scions to Oliver Wolcott of Connecticut, who will then send them on to Ames.[55] Meanwhile in London Christopher Gore is kept abreast of agricultural developments on his Boston friends' farms.[56]

Among the many motives that induced men of this Federalist clan to settle on country estates, we cannot rule out the financial one. Rural retirement in response to business failure was nothing new; many wealthy merchants of Newburyport, for example, financially humbled by postrevolutionary economic conditions, traded town mansions for more modest country seats in the twilights of their lives.[57] Estate living was relatively cheap but still respectable, even genteel. Such considerations appear to have influenced Timothy Pickering in his decision to become a gentleman farmer.

In 1800, having been dismissed from his position as John Adams's secretary of state, Pickering considered settling on land he had purchased in the Pennsylvania wilderness fifteen years earlier. George Cabot disagreed with the plan. "I have convened with Judge Dana & some other friends on this topic & all agree that you ought not to withdraw from the world until fair experiment shall prove it to be necessary," he wrote Pickering in May 1800, then added tellingly: "This it is believed will never happen." Pickering's friends had good reason to believe otherwise; in 1801, they bought his Pennsylvania land, essentially as a gift, and then proceeded to look around for a suitable farm for the retiring statesman. In 1802 Pickering leased a farm in Danvers that his friends had procured for him. In 1804, now a U.S. senator, he moved to a farm in Upper Beverly.[58] Picker-

54. Pickering to Ames, 16 October 1805, Pickering Papers, 14:132–33; Ames to Pickering, 26 October 1805, Pickering Papers, 27:142.

55. Ames to Pickering, 24 February 1806, Pickering Papers, 27:237; Pickering to Wolcott, 16 March 1806, Wolcott Papers, 20:89, Connecticut Historical Society, Hartford; Pickering to Ames, 11 March, 7 April 1806, Pickering Papers, 14:152g, 156 1/2; Henry W. Livingston to Pickering, 28 March 1806, Pickering Papers, 45:105.

56. Fisher Ames to Gore, 11 January 1799, 7 November 1802, in Ames, *Works of Fisher Ames,* 1:249–51, 303–8. In the second letter, Ames reported that "against the dignity of the Royal Society, and their Botanical Garden, and in contempt of the common law, and of the Encyclopaedia," his cows, "with the voracious appetite of ignorance," had eaten a type of grass that all these authorities insisted was refused by cattle.

57. Benjamin W. Labaree, *Patriots and Partisans: The Merchants of Newburyport, 1764–1815* (Cambridge: Harvard University Press, 1962), pp. 213–14, 218–19.

58. Octavius Pickering and Charles W. Upham, *The Life of Timothy Pickering,* 4 vols. (Boston: Little, Brown, 1867–73), 2:179–82, 4:34–36, 42, 72; Gerard H. Clarfield, *Timothy Pickering and the American Republic* (Pittsburgh: University of Pittsburgh Press, 1980),

ing enjoyed experimental agriculture—"It was ever my desire to be an improving farmer," he wrote Ames in 1805[59]—but resented the Beverly farm as too small for the purpose, and more important, the Beverly accommodations as too mean for a man of his station. "I cannot endure it much longer," he wrote in a letter to his wife, Rebecca. The tiny "Beverly strip" and "that cabin, in which I have hardly room to breathe" had become unbearable. What he wanted now was a farm of his own. "A Farm somewhere I must have," he insisted, "because it is an object which has always been peculiarly grateful to me, because my attachment to husbandry has suffered no abatement, and because I do not know of any other employment in which I can reputably engage." And then, "if I do not get a farm *now*," he asked Rebecca rhetorically, "what am I to do five years hence, when my term as a Senator will expire?" How would he maintain his stature as a gentleman then? He was thrilled then when in 1806 he exchanged "the box" at Beverly for a more spacious estate of his own in nearby Wenham.[60]

Thus gentleman farming on a small estate was a relatively inexpensive way to live that was still, as Pickering stated so unequivocally, "reputable." But what made it reputable? Why did elite Bostonians share the sense that this style of life, this set of pastimes were somehow suitable to men of their class? As we have seen, the association of country estate living and gentleman farming with the British aristocracy, gentry, and landed commercial-professional class lent tremendous symbolic power to the practice of rural pursuits in America. But the reservoir of associations was by no means exhausted with British landowners as they existed in reality. Also influential, particularly with the educated statesmen of Boston, was the British literary tradition of rural retirement.

The ideal of rural retirement, as it appeared in British literature, was

pp. 214–16; George Cabot to Pickering, 26 May 1800, March 1801, Pickering Papers, 26:133, 42:282; George Cabot to Oliver Wolcott, 26 May 1800, Wolcott Papers, 18:44.

59. Pickering to Ames, 16 October 1805, Pickering Papers, 14:132. Still resident on the small Beverly farm, Pickering rued that whatever his desire regarding the life of a gentleman farmer, "it has been my fate never to attain the accomplishment of my wishes. Still I take great pleasure in Agricultural disquisitions; and have not yet abandoned the hope of being really a farmer." Pickering was hardly inactive in farming affairs. In 1803, for example, we find him ordering field crop and garden seeds from a London firm, and in 1805, communicating the results of his experiments with potatoes. Receipt, Warner & Seaman, Seedsmen, No. 28 Cornhill, London, 28 February 1803, Pickering Papers, 45:78; Pickering to George Cabot, 8 October 1805, Pickering Papers, 14:129.

60. Upham, *Life of Timothy Pickering,* 4:96–99; Pickering to Rebecca Pickering, 29 March 1806 [?], quoted in ibid., 4:96–97; Pickering to Rebecca Pickering, 29 March 1806, Pickering Papers, 3:36. Although Upham dates the letter he quotes as above, it is not the same letter of the same date and addressee in the Pickering Papers.

hardly static.[61] It continually acquired new meanings and was in fact based on earlier notions articulated by such classical authors as Horace and Virgil. By the early eighteenth century such Whig essayists and poets as Addison, Steele, Pope, and Thomson forwarded a version that stressed moderation, virtuous habits, and piety. The man of rural retirement was a man immersed in the study of nature, and therefore of God; a man whose contemplation of rural scenes had not only exalted but also tranquilized him, thereby allowing his rational faculties rather than his passions to dominate while at the same time softening his heart and engendering new feelings of benevolence; a man who had proven his refined sensibilities and exquisite taste through the choice of a rural existence. In all of this was a contrast, sometimes made explicit, with the world left behind, a world of shallow pomp and luxury often identified as urban and commercial.

We know that members of the Boston elite were aware of this literary tradition. They were familiar with the sources of the ideal of rural retirement through study of Greek and Roman classics, an education Boston's Federalists insisted was critical to achieve any degree of civilization in the new Republic.[62] And they were equally versed in the British literature of rural retirement. When Joseph Barrell published his 1789 essay on agriculture, for example, he saw fit to preface it with an excerpt from Thomson's *Seasons*. And when in 1806 John Lowell toured the English countryside, he remarked: "Thomson's Summer [fig. 10] is a perpetual commentary upon the road I have been travelling."[63]

Just as significant were the Boston contributions to this literature. If Boston could not boast of a Thomson, it did have "Alcadour," whose poem "Rural Retirement" appeared in the *Massachusetts Magazine* in 1794, complete with epigraph by Horace; or "Henry," author of "A Rural Scene," published in an 1804 issue of the *Monthly Anthology and Boston Review;* or "Peter Pastoral," who, having quoted Virgil on the "fortunate Agricola,"

61. The following discussion of the literary tradition of rural retirement is based on Maren-Sofie Røstvig, *The Happy Man: Studies in the Metamorphoses of a Classical Ideal,* vol. 2: *1700–1760,* 2d ed., 2 vols. (Oslo: Universitetsforlaget, 1977; New York: Humanities Press, 1971); Basil Willey, *The Eighteenth-Century Background: Studies on the Idea of Nature in the Thought of the Period* (Boston: Beacon Press, 1961); Paul H. Johnstone, "In Praise of Husbandry," *AH* 11 (April 1937): 80–95; and Johnstone, "Turnips and Romanticism," ibid. 12 (July 1938): 244–55.

62. Linda K. Kerber, *Federalists in Dissent: Imagery and Ideology in Jeffersonian America* (Ithaca, N.Y.: Cornell University Press, 1970), pp. 95–134.

63. Barrell, "Reflections on Agriculture," p. 357; [Lowell], *Monthly Anthology and Boston Review* 3 (August 1806): 403. Here, as elsewhere, attributions of articles appearing in the *Monthly Anthology and Boston Review* without the author's name are from M. A. DeWolfe Howe, ed., *Journal of the Proceedings of the Society Which Conducts the Monthly Anthology and Boston Review* (Boston: Boston Athenaeum, 1910).

10. *Thomson's "Summer."* Reprinted from *The Works of James Thomson, with His Last Corrections and Improvements* (London, 1862). (Courtesy Yale University Library.)

proceeded to relate his own "Pastoral," again in the *Monthly Anthology*.[64] The Boston poets reiterated many of the themes found in the classical and British literature of rural retirement. There is the stark contrast of the "noisome world," the "buzzing crowd," the "maddening multitude," the "rat'ling wheels," and the "sound of business" with the beauty and serenity of the countryside. There is the wisdom of the decision to retire to a rural

64. *Massachusetts Magazine* 6 (May 1794): 312–13; *Monthly Anthology and Boston Review* 1 (June, July 1804): 370, 424; ibid. 3 (October 1806): 522–23. All quotations in this paragraph are from these three poems. On eighteenth-century American pastoral poetry, see Chester E. Eisinger, "The Farmer in the Eighteenth-Century Almanac," *AH* 28 (July 1954): 107–12; Edwin T. Bowden, "Benjamin Church's *Choice* and American Colonial Poetry," *New England Quarterly* 32 (June 1959): 170–84; and Richard Bridgman, "Jefferson's Farmer before Jefferson," *American Quarterly* 14 (Winter 1962): 567–77.

paradise in favor of a life of "folly and wealth" practiced by such characters as "the *sop*, that round the mall gallants the fair; / The *clerk*, that glitters at a play or ball; / The *shoe-black coxcomb* with his powder'd hair, / And *rake*, that glories in a virgin's fall." There is the envy of the simple farmer, "remov'd from noisy fame and publick view," whose life flows with the rhythms of nature, "harmonious, tranquil, clear." There is the effect of rural scenes on the country dweller, calming "each conflicting, rude, ambitious thought," softening the "feeling" heart to beauty and virtue.

Many of the ideas involved in the literary tradition of rural retirement— retreat from the world, indulgence of rational pleasures, the growth of benevolent feelings—found fertile ground in the men of the Essex Junto.[65] Even Christopher Gore, known for his sophisticated style of living, characterized his life in Waltham as "the Shady Bower, or rural seclusion." He insisted that the Boston social whirl and the outside world of political intrigue held no true attraction for him, that the company of a few dear friends and good books was more to his liking. "I remain a silent observer," he wrote in the tumultuous year of 1812, "knowing little of Politicks, nothing of the Interiour, and interesting myself in my books, & my Farm."[66] George Cabot expressed similar sentiments, living as a "recluse," "abstracted from the political world" on a farm in Brookline "as retired in appearance as in the bosom of a Wilderness." Cabot welcomed the visits of his close friends, but "when I have no living company," he explained to Oliver Wolcott, "I call upon the Dead who are always ready to come from my Library & entertain me." Otherwise, he occupied himself with his farm. "I have much more to say," he closed a letter to Rufus King on Jay's Treaty, "but my Potatoes need hoeing & must not be neglected."[67] We hear the same from Fisher Ames. "My concern is now more to improve my tranquility," he wrote Wolcott in 1803, "than to rub off the rust from my

65. Of course, Junto members were not the only Bostonians influenced by this tradition. When John Codman visited Sir Francis Baring's seat in Kent, he was especially taken with the estate's isolation from the world. "Retirement is the object in this Country," he wrote his wife. "To be alone in the world as Adam & Eve were seems to be the taste." Here and elsewhere in England, he noted approvingly how estates were laid out so that country house and signs of human habitation and activity were mutually invisible. Codman himself hoped to retire to his Lincoln estate, there "to devote the residue of life to those rational domestic enjoyments which I am convinced contribute our greatest felicity here." Codman to Catherine Amory Codman, 20 or 21 July, 24 August 1800, 28 June [1801], CFMC.

66. Gore to Rufus King, 22 September 1803, 15 April 1806, 7 February 1812, King Papers.

67. Cabot to Oliver Wolcott, 26 March 1798, in Henry Cabot Lodge, *Life and Letters of George Cabot* (Boston: Little, Brown, 1877), p. 150; Cabot to Rufus King, 25 July 1795, 24 July 1796, in King, *Correspondence of Rufus King*, 2:19, 66; Cabot to Wolcott, 3 August 1801, Wolcott Papers, 18:57.

fame. . . . A little business at the bar, more on my farm, some pleasure sought in books, more with friends, and my affections, plans, and hopes chiefly concentrated in my family afford a substitute for the rewards and a refuge from the terrors & vexations of politics."[68]

All these men subscribed to the positive ideal of rural retirement—the rational pleasures of conversation, reading, and farming—but in the shadows lurks a negative presence urging them on to seclusion, what both Fisher Ames and George Cabot called the "vortex of politics."[69] To be sure, literary tradition had always presented rural retirement as an alternative to a more decadent, wicked world, but not necessarily a specifically political one. It is entirely possible that the men of the Essex Junto were tapping into a particularly resonant, historical tradition, the phenomenon of Opposition retirement.

The ideal of rural retirement took on a specifically political twist in the 1730s, when many prominent English statesmen interpreted their own residence on country estates as a further extension and manifestation of their Opposition politics. According to such Country party statesmen as Lord Cobham of Stowe and Lord Lyttleton of Hagley, together with such literary allies as Alexander Pope and James Thomson, English liberties were being threatened and the constitutional balance of power subverted by the Court party then in power.[70] For them, the country estate acquired a special political significance as the place where true patriots retreated to protest the corruption of the world, perhaps biding their time until they might once more lead their nation onto the proper path. What happened on Lord Cobham's estate in the 1730s, a center of Opposition politics and a showpiece of landscape architecture, was that these political overtones were made explicit in the design of the estate gardens. Thus we have the Temple of Modern Virtue, built as a ruin and crowned with a headless statue of Robert Walpole, the arch villain of the Court (fig. 11); the Temple of British Worthies, housing busts of men, each in some way relevant to the Opposition case against Walpole, with inscriptions composed by Lord Lyttleton; the Temple of Friendship, containing busts of Cobham and his Opposition friends; and the Gothic Temple, hearkening back to the sup-

68. Ames to Wolcott, 4 April 1803, Wolcott Papers, 18:98.
69. Ames to Thomas Dwight, 8 August 1794, in Ames, *Works of Fisher Ames,* 1:147; Cabot to Timothy Pickering, 2 April 1808, Pickering Papers, 28:269.
70. Perez Zagorin, *The Court and the Country: The Beginning of the English Revolution* (New York: Atheneum, 1970); J. G. A. Pocock, *The Machiavellian Moment: Florentine Political Thought and the Atlantic Republican Tradition* (Princeton, N.J.: Princeton University Press, 1975), pp. 462–505; Isaac F. Kramnick, *Bolingbroke and His Circle: The Politics of Nostalgia in the Age of Walpole* (Cambridge: Harvard University Press, 1968).

11. *Temple of Modern Virtue, Stowe.* Reprinted from George Bickham, *The Beauties of Stow* (London, 1750). (Courtesy Newberry Library.)

posed roots of the English constitution, English liberties, and even the sturdy English character. To stroll through Stowe was to hear the Opposition argue its case, to see Pope's satire writ large in the landscape.[71]

Recent historians have seen in the fierce ideological struggles of late eighteenth- and early nineteenth-century America a replay of the Country versus Court struggle in England. Jeffersonians have been identified as the equivalent of the Country party, drawing inspiration from the writings of English Opposition statesmen, resisting such phenomena as a funded national debt, a system of public credit, and a standing army as dangers to liberty. Federalists, especially in the person of Alexander Hamilton (the American Walpole), have been identified as the American Court party, anxious to establish an interdependence among government, financial interests, and the army. Although historians have taken pains to insist that

71. George Clarke, "Grecian Taste and Gothic Virtue: Lord Cobham's Gardening Programme and Its Iconography," *Apollo* 97 (June 1973): 566–71; Laurence Whistler, Michael Gibbon, and George Clarke, *Stowe: A Guide to the Gardens* (n.p., 1974). On Lyttleton's Hagley as an Opposition estate, see James Thomson's *Seasons*. Thomson writes: "O LYTTLETON, THE FRIEND! thy Passions thus / And Meditations vary, as at large, / Courting the Muse, thro' HAGLEY PARK you stray, / . . . / And oft, conducted by Historic Truth, / You tread the long Extent of backward Time: / Planning, with warm benevolence of Mind, / And honest Zeal unwarp'd by Party-Rage, / *Britannia's* Weal; how from the venal Gulph / To raise her Virtue, and her Arts revive." See also Maynard Mack, *The Garden and the City: Retirement and Politics in the Later Poetry of Pope, 1731–1743* (Toronto: University of Toronto Press, 1969).

the Country party feared not merchants but financiers, speculators, and stockjobbers, commercial interests have usually been lined up with the Court party and agrarian interests with the Country.[72]

What then do we do with members of the Boston elite, Federalists to the last, merchants to the core—*and* men of country tastes and pursuits? However it might violate the Country-Court schema, prominent Boston Federalists may well have regarded their rural occupations as analagous to those of England's Country Opposition. They were familiar with the history and literature of the Opposition,[73] as well as with, of course, their ideology. They saw their era as the equivalent of the Augustan age in England, and in their high cultural aspirations, cynical and even sneering attitudes toward the general populace, and pessimistic interpretation of contemporary society and politics, shared much in common with the English Augustans.[74] Perhaps most critically, Boston's high Federalists regarded themselves as the true patriots in a battle against corruption, selfishness, and evil design, and after 1800, with the election of Jefferson, they were true patriots out of power, the American Opposition. If their gardens did not feature the complex iconography of a Stowe, perhaps the very fact of retirement to an estate resonated with the meaning of the earlier, English tradition, a tradition long since abstracted from a specific political agenda and representing only the moral high ground in an ideological struggle. We should not be surprised that Boston's Federalists seized the high ground, wherever it lay. This is not to say that Fisher Ames was an American Lord Cobham and his Springfield Hall a Stowe on the Charles, only that when the Essex Junto settled on country estates, Opposition retirement was one more source of associations—and an especially piquant one—into which

72. Pocock, *Machiavellian Moment,* pp. 506–52; Pocock, "Virtue and Commerce in the Eighteenth Century," *Journal of Interdisciplinary History* 3 (Summer 1972): 119–34; James H. Hutson, "Country, Court, and Constitution: Antifederalism and the Historians," *William and Mary Quarterly,* 3d ser., 38 (July 1981): 337–68; John M. Murrin, "The Great Inversion, or Court versus Country: A Comparison of the Revolution Settlements in England (1688–1721) and America (1776–1818)," in Pocock, ed., *Three British Revolutions: 1641, 1688, 1776* (Princeton, N.J.: Princeton University Press, 1980), pp. 368–453; Lance Banning, *The Jeffersonian Persuasion: Evolution of a Party Ideology* (Ithaca, N.Y.: Cornell University Press, 1978).

73. When, for example, John Adams visited Stowe in 1786, he wrote in his diary: "I mounted Ld. Cobhams Pillar 120 feet high, with pleasure as his Lordships Name was familiar to me, from Popes Works." Adams noted of his visit to Hagley that "Ld. Littletons Seat interested me, from a recollection of his Works, as well as the Grandeur and Beauty of the Scaenes. Popes Pavillion and Thompsons [Thomson's] Seat, made the Excursion poetical." Adams, *Diary and Autobiography,* 3:186.

74. On the Federalist identification with Augustan England, see Kerber, *Federalists in Dissent,* pp. 1–22, and Lewis P. Simpson, "Federalism and the Crisis of Literary Order," *American Literature* 32 (November 1960): 253–66.

they tapped. To appreciate the entire complex of associations, let us look more closely at Congressman Ames (fig. 12).

In autumn 1794 Fisher Ames visited what he described as "Mr. Gore's palace" in Waltham. "I do not expect to build a smarter one myself," he commented.[75] What Ames did build was unostentatious but solid, a two-story house with a massive, old-fashioned center chimney, on twenty-five acres of land bordering the Charles River in Dedham. Surrounding the house were not only a formal garden but all the features of a working farm—pastures, meadows, and cropland, a large orchard, barns, a piggery, a dairy, and, what was quite a novelty in those days, an icehouse. Ames was a serious gentleman farmer, concentrating on the production of meat, vegetables, and dairy products for the Boston market (hence the icehouse to keep the butter fresh) but dabbling as well in swine husbandry and fruit cultivation. He corresponded frequently on farming and gardening matters, kept abreast of foreign agricultural intelligence, and undertook occasional agricultural experiments.[76]

His interest in agriculture and horticulture had not always been so serious. Even before Springfield Hall was built, Ames tried his hand at fruit cultivation but had to admit that "the weeds alone seem to grow well in my garden." His lack of success was probably of little account to him; gardening was really just a socially acceptable way for an educated statesman to wile away a long congressional vacation. "I begin to feel some spirit in the undertaking," he wrote his brother-in-law Thomas Dwight of his gardening activities in September 1793, "though conscious of a want of taste and industry. Yet even the lazy will work for an hobby horse. I begin to count the weeks which are left of the recess." Almost precisely a year later, Ames found himself in the same situation. "My fruit trees . . . are *pro tempore* my

75. Ames to Thomas Dwight, 3 September 1794, Fisher Ames Papers, Dedham Historical Society, Dedham, Mass. This was Gore's earlier residence on the Waltham estate that burned down in 1799 and was replaced in 1804 with Gore Hall.

76. Winfred E. A. Bernhard, *Fisher Ames: Federalist and Statesman, 1758–1808* (Chapel Hill: University of North Carolina Press, 1965), pp. 43, 234, 306–7; *Homes of American Statesmen: With Anecdotal, Personal, and Descriptive Sketches* (New York: Alfred W. Upham, 1860), pp. 287–92. An invaluable source of information on the details of Ames's agricultural activities are the dozens of letters he exchanged with his brother-in-law Thomas Dwight, now in the Ames Papers at the Dedham Historical Society. Ames's farm account book, spanning the years 1801 to 1807, is another useful source in the same collection. Other valuable correspondence includes Ames to Christopher Gore, 11 January 1799, 7 November 1802, in Ames, *Works of Fisher Ames,* 1:249–50, 303–8; Ames to Timothy Pickering, 12 March 1799, in ibid., 1:253; Ames to Pickering, 28 April 1804, 26 October 1805, 24 February 1806, Pickering Papers, 27:91, 142, 237; and Ames to John Worthington Ames, 27 February 1808, Ames Papers. The letter of 1805 to Pickering is an especially detailed account of the Dedham farm operations.

12. *Fisher Ames*. Portrait by Gilbert Stuart, 1810. (Courtesy Harvard University Portrait Collection. Gift of Isaac P. Davis and other Gentlemen of Boston, 1810.)

hobby-horse," he wrote Dwight, adding that he suspected that his enthusiasm for horticulture would wear out long before his trees bore fruit. And in November 1795 he confessed to Dwight that "my farming zeal has so far abated, that I prefer getting experiments made by others, to making them myself." Accordingly, he gave up the idea of breeding sheep for experimenting with potato cultivation. "The labor and expense of this petty operation," he explained, "suit my laziness, as well as my economy."[77]

It was really only with his retirement from Congress in March 1797, occasioned by failing health, that Ames began to take gentleman farming and gardening more seriously. From this date, we see truly directed efforts to operate a farm at once scientific and profitable—the keeping of careful accounts, for example, the expansion of acreage and acquisition of more livestock, and the erection of a model icehouse. By 1802 he was able to report to Christopher Gore that he was "full of zeal about farming," adding that "cattle and fruit trees are my themes, in prose," and that "poetry, if I had any, I would devote to my pigsty and politics—two scurvy subjects, that should be coupled together."[78] It is also after his retirement that the tone of Ames's letters shifts from a somewhat jaunty commentary on the folly of the world to a more dour, even depressed view of the decline of the Republic. Several factors were no doubt responsible for this change in mood. Certainly one was Ames's ill health; though he lived until 1808, to Ames, death was always lurking around the corner. Another was his natural love of politics; much as he might insist that his only ambition was "to rear pigs and calves, and feed chickens at Dedham—to the world forgetting, by the world forgot,"[79] Ames desperately missed taking an active role in the affairs of government. He complained of being a "cabbage stump," fated "to vegetate" in Dedham.[80] But when all is said and done, Ames did not sound terribly different from any other Massachusetts Federalist of the time. All saw the Republic deteriorating right before their eyes, as popularity-seeking politicians, Jacobin infidels to the core, pandered to an ignorant populace. It was enough to make even the healthiest and most active Federalist despair.

Given these factors, it was easy for Ames to fit himself into the tradition

77. Ames to Thomas Dwight, 26 June, 16 September 1793, 11 September 1794, 18 November 1795, Ames Papers.
78. Ames to Gore, 7 November 1802, in Ames, *Works of Fisher Ames,* 1:304.
79. Ames to Jeremiah Smith, 13 March 1798, in Ames, *Works of Fisher Ames,* 1:222.
80. Ames to Dwight Foster, 24 June 1797, in ibid., 1:216. Five years later he wrote Oliver Wolcott: "I am fated to grow, like a peach tree, in my garden, with a vigor that wastes the root, to yield fruits that soon perish, and to give place in a few years to a cabbage stump." 2 December 1802, Wolcott Papers, 18:96.

of rural retirement, particularly those parts of the tradition that characterized the world "back there" as irretrievably wicked. He would no longer
"play the Quixote for the reformation of this perverse generation," he wrote
fellow Federalist Oliver Wolcott in 1803. "Let the world slide, as it must,
downhill. I will not be disturbed because I foresee there will be a crash at
the bottom." For several years he had in fact attempted to arrest the
Republic's descent by contributing essays to Boston's Federalist newspapers. Now he was ready to recognize such efforts as futile. "Zeal is a bad
sleeper," he wrote Christopher Gore in London, "and I will try opium with
the rest of them. Expect me then, in future, to write about pruning apple
trees, or breeding cattle." And to Wolcott, he insisted on being glad of his ill
success. "I am unyoked from the team, and instead of working I may be
stall-fed." When he learned that Wolcott too would soon be retiring from
government, he applauded their mutual "transmigration from political
worms to . . . agricultural butterflies."[81] Ames never did entirely resign
himself to a life of political seclusion, but the literary and historical tradition
of rural retirement at least gave him a way to interpret his new life. It
provided him with a recognized stance in keeping with the dark times and
appropriate to a wise and virtuous man powerless to prevent the darkness
from falling.

Members of the postrevolutionary generation commonly bifurcated the
world of human affairs into public and private spheres. The two were
related but nevertheless mutually exclusive. Thus the yeoman's private
virtues—industry, simplicity, and thrift—were the foundation of his public
virtue, the ability to place the common good above selfish gain, but the two
were not one and the same. Similarly, the leaders of society could be
expected to have both a private and a public character, in effect, to have two
corresponding but separate identities.

Through the associations they generated, residence on a country estate
and the pursuit of gentleman farming were essentially private acts for the
Boston elite. Although these activities might be appropriate to men active
in the public sphere, they really spoke to such aspects of the individual's
private character as personal refinement, the preference for rational over
luxurious pleasures, and the rejection of worldly vanities. To be sure, the
impulse toward experimental agriculture was often ascribed to a civic
concern for the public welfare, but at least in this early period, the gentle-

81. Ames to Wolcott, 9 March, 4 April 1803, Wolcott Papers, 18:98; Ames to Gore, 24
February 1803, Ames Papers.

man farmers themselves made little effort to support this interpretation of their agricultural activities. We may look long and hard before finding any evidence of attempts to inspire the much-touted "spirit of emulation" among the Massachusetts yeomanry. "The labor of my Farm," wrote George Cabot in 1801, "is performed altogether by a Tenant to whom I give specific benefits that he may have no control over the management." Similarly, Fisher Ames seemed content to provide his tenant farmer with no more than annual wages of two hundred dollars, lodging, and two quarts of milk a day in the summertime.[82] Where was the attempt to disseminate knowledge among the Commonwealth's farmers? Boston's gentleman farmers reserved this knowledge almost exclusively for themselves, trading advice, exchanging experimental results, forwarding seeds and scions in a kind of agricultural round-robin.

For elite Bostonians, gentleman farming was simply part of an entire complex of activities—building an elegant house in a fashionable landscape, studying the classics, belonging to learned societies—that constituted a style of living rich with cultural associations and therefore with possibilities for self-characterization. The repertoire of rural pursuits, however, did not stop with estate living and gentleman farming. Membership in an agricultural society was something else altogether, and as such it entailed completely new symbolic possibilities. If country seats and experimental agriculture attested to the private character of the elite Bostonian, membership in the Massachusetts Society for Promoting Agriculture established his public character. Let us turn then to the public man.

82. Cabot to Wolcott, 3 August 1801, Wolcott Papers, 18:57; Ames, Account Book, 11 February 1807, Ames Papers.

# *TWO*

# *The Public Man and the Agricultural Society*

W HEN the Massachusetts Society for Promoting Agriculture was established in 1792, it was the third such organization in the United States and one of the few in the world.[1] Even the greatest of the British agricultural societies, the Bath and West, dated back only to 1777.[2] Before the formation of the MSPA, agricultural concerns were addressed to some extent by the American Academy of Arts and Sciences, established in Boston in 1780. But with only three hundred dollars subscribed to an agricultural premium fund and, more critically, with so many other areas of knowledge competing for members' attention, little was accomplished beyond the occasional publication of an agricultural essay.[3] The twenty-eight men who petitioned the state legislature for incorpora-

1. Brooke Hindle, *The Pursuit of Science in Revolutionary America, 1735–1789* (1956; reprint ed., New York: W. W. Norton, 1974), pp. 359–63; Margaret W. Rossiter, "The Organization of Agricultural Improvement in the United States, 1785–1865," in Alexandra Oleson and Sanborn C. Brown, eds., *The Pursuit of Knowledge in the Early American Republic: American Scientific and Learned Societies from Colonial Times to the Civil War* (Baltimore: Johns Hopkins University Press, 1976), pp. 279–87. Agricultural societies were established in Philadelphia and Charleston, S.C., in 1785. On the former, see Simon Baatz, *"Venerate the Plough": A History of the Philadelphia Society for Promoting Agriculture, 1785–1985* (Philadelphia: Philadelphia Society for Promoting Agriculture, 1985), and Lucius F. Ellsworth, "The Philadelphia Society for the Promotion of Agriculture and Agricultural Reform," *Agricultural History* 42 (July 1968): 189–99.

2. Kenneth Hudson, *The Bath and West: A Bicentenary History* (Bradford-on-Avon: Moonraker Press, 1976).

3. Walter Muir Whitehill, "Early Learned Societies in Boston and Vicinity," in Oleson and Brown, *Pursuit of Knowledge,* pp. 151–62; Hindle, *Pursuit,* pp. 357–58; American Academy of Arts and Sciences, Report of the Committee on the Business of Agriculture, 24 January 1786, Houghton Library, Harvard University, Cambridge, Mass.

tion of the MSPA obviously felt that something more was called for. On 7 March 1792 the society received its corporate charter and was off and running.[4]

In the composition of its members, this society dedicated to the promotion of agriculture was unabashedly mercantile. Let us look, for example, at the thirty-six trustees and officers who ran the MSPA in its first generation of existence, from 1792 to 1812.[5] Roughly one-third were merchants; another third, lawyer-statesmen; and the rest, a mix of physicians and ministers. All these men, however, not just those whose primary occupation was merchant, owed their basic allegiance to commerce, whether through a second profession, ties of kinship and marriage, patterns of investment, or tilt of profession. Aaron Dexter, M.D., for example, also acted as president of the Middlesex Canal Corporation. Merchant George Cabot sat in the U.S. Senate. Jonathan Mason, Jr., an attorney, grew up in a merchant's household. Richard Sullivan, also trained as a lawyer, was able to retire at an early age on the wealth of his father-in-law, MSPA trustee and merchant Thomas Russell. John Avery, Jr., secretary of state of the Commonwealth, added to his salary by investing in commercial ventures. The Reverend J. S. Buckminster preached to pews filled with Unitarians grown wealthy on maritime trade. The Lowells, father and son, practiced commercial law (fig. 13). And the MSPA trustees who sat in Congress—Senators Cabot, Gore, Mason, and Strong and Representatives Ames and Quincy—represented the interests and worldview of the Federalist mercantile elite.[6]

Even those with no obvious link to the commercial class participated in elite society through the complex network of Boston's high-toned cultural institutions. Foremost of these was Harvard College. Most of these men were Harvard graduates, and those who were not were mainly merchants, for whom an alternate route of education was entirely acceptable. A number were fellows of the Harvard Corporation or members of its faculty and administration. These men also associated with one another as fellow members of such learned societies as the American Academy of Arts and Sciences, the Massachusetts Historical Society, the Anthology Society, and

4. For the formation of the MSPA, see "Abstract of the Records, from 1792 to 1858," in *Transactions of the Massachusetts Society for Promoting Agriculture*, n.s., 1 (1858): 5–13; *Centennial Year (1792–1892) of the Massachusetts Society for Promoting Agriculture* (Salem, Mass.: n.p., n.d.), pp. 5–15.

5. For a list of trustees and officers, see *Centennial Year*, pp. 141–46.

6. For brief biographical sketches of the early MSPA trustees, see *Centennial Year*, pp. 8–14. On Sullivan, see Thomas C. Amory, *Memoir of the Hon. Richard Sullivan* (Cambridge: John Wilson and Son, 1885). On Buckminster, see Eliza Buckminster Lee, *Memoirs of Rev. Joseph Buckminster, D.D., and of His Son, Rev. Joseph Stevens Buckminster* (Boston: Wm. Crosby and H. P. Nichols, 1849).

13. *John Lowell (1743–1802)*. Lowell was a founding member and second president of the MSPA. Portrait attributed to John Johnston. (Courtesy Harvard University Portrait Collection. Gift of the Estate of Ralph Lowell, 1978.)

the Boston Athenaeum. These thirty-six doubtless shared a common identity—that of Boston's commercial elite.

The same profile extends to the general membership of the MSPA.⁷ The
list of eminent Bostonians who joined the agricultural society is lengthy
indeed. It included, not surprisingly, such gentleman farmers as Joseph
Barrell, encountered in the previous chapter, and E. Hasket Derby, better
known for his leading role in Asian commerce. Most members of the Essex
Junto who were not trustees of the MSPA joined as members: Stephen
Higginson, Jonathan Jackson, and Timothy Pickering. And of course
there were the merchants, men like David Sears, who within months of the
society's founding contributed a substantial sum to its coffers.⁸

The merchant's vision of the world thus dominated this society that set
out in 1792 to promote agriculture in the Commonwealth.⁹ Not six years
earlier, in a summer of discontent that culminated in Shays's Rebellion,
many of the state's farmers had put forth their own program for agricultural
promotion. Their plan, not surprisingly, aimed directly at the commercial

7. Lists of MSPA members were published periodically in MSPA publications. *Laws and
Regulations of the Massachusetts Society for Promoting Agriculture* (Boston: Isaiah Thomas
and Ebenezer T. Andrews, 1793)—hereafter *MSPA, Laws and Regulations, 1793*—pp. 16–
18; *Rules and Regulations of the Massachusetts Society for Promoting Agriculture* (Boston:
Thomas Fleet, Jr., 1796)—hereafter *MSPA, Rules and Regulations, 1796*—pp. 12–19;
*Papers on Agriculture, Consisting of Communications Made to the Massachusetts Society for
Promoting Agriculture, with Extracts from Various Publications; Recommended to the Attention
of Farmers, by the Trustees of the Society* (Boston: Young and Minns, 1799)—hereafter *MSPA
Papers, 1799*—pp. 97–102; *Papers on Agriculture, Consisting of Communications Made to the
Massachusetts Agricultural Society, with Extracts from Various Publications* (Boston: Young
and Minns, 1801)—hereafter *MSPA Papers, 1801*—pp. 87–95; *Papers on Agriculture,
Consisting of Communications Made to the Massachusetts Society for Promoting Agriculture*
(Boston: Young and Minns, 1803)—hereafter *MSPA Papers, 1803*—pp. 87–95; *Massachusetts Agricultural Repository and Journal* (hereafter *MSPA Journal*) 4 (January 1817): 305–
11. There was no effort to recruit working agriculturists into the society, and in fact, the rules
of the society essentially guaranteed their exclusion. To become a member, one could not
simply declare an interest and pay the dues. Instead, potential new members had to be
proposed by current MSPA members, their candidacy considered for a month, and only then
accepted or rejected by a vote of the society. "Abstract of the Records," p. 16.

8. For a complete list of donations, see *MSPA, Rules and Regulations, 1796*, p. 75.

9. Just how much this agricultural society was oriented to the world of commerce is
evidenced in the specifics of its operation. The first three meetings of the MSPA were held at the
council chamber of the State House; subsequent meetings were held either at the stockholders'
room of the Bank of the United States or at the Massachusetts Bank. The society's treasury
functioned like a well-run business. Receipts for donations were made out in duplicate, the
treasurer was bonded, and the accounts were subject to an annual audit. The donations
themselves reflect a certain business sophistication (as well as a distinctly Federalist bent) on
the part of the donors: United States stock, shares in the Bank of the United States, 6 percent
on four hundred British pounds. "Abstract of the Records," pp. 7, 11; *MSPA, Rules and
Regulations, 1796*, p. 75.

interests of the seaboard region. But the regulation of the legal profession, the closing of courts, the inflation of the money supply, and the imposition of a tariff on commerce were strategies unlikely to be adopted by a society of lawyers, judges, financiers, and merchants. The MSPA's program, emphasizing publication and the encouragement of empirical research, looked rather to the east—to British agricultural societies—than to the west— Daniel Shays's Hampshire County—for inspiration.

A cornerstone of the society's program was the acquisition and dissemination of information. Society members took it upon themselves to keep up with the latest agricultural intelligence, especially that emanating from Britain and the Continent.[10] To stay abreast of European developments was critical first, because, except through the medium of the MSPA, it could not be expected that practical farmers would ever be exposed to overseas intelligence and second, because Europe, especially Britain, was universally regarded by society members as far ahead of the United States in agricultural matters. To disseminate this vital information, the MSPA embarked on an ambitious program of publication, submitting original agricultural essays to Boston newspapers, reprinting foreign treatises under its own imprint, and, most important, issuing a regular series of transactions. Along this line, the MSPA in 1793 issued its *Laws and Regulations,* which included not only a prospectus of the new organization's concerns and activities but also, for example, an extract from the Bath Society's *Letters and Papers* on making butter, an English treatise on hemp, an article on maple sugar reprinted from the *American Museum,* and a communication on potato culture from the Reverend Cochran.[11] This first publication established the basic content mix of subsequent MSPA volumes: extracts from foreign and domestic periodicals and treatises, and communications, generally reporting results from "the field," addressed directly to the society.

As a second strategy, the society offered premiums. These were cash prizes awarded for achievements in specified categories, and as such they focused agricultural "research" on problems of special importance to Massachusetts. By offering money, the society may well have stimulated the exertions of practical farmers; such at least was its stated goal.[12] In the early years of the MSPA, a number of premium applicants and winners were men of humble station, anonymous characters with nary an "Hon." before or

10. Toward this end, the society established an agricultural library in 1797. "Abstract of the Records," p. 23.
11. *MSPA, Laws and Regulations, 1793,* pp. iii–iv, 13–15, 18–27, 40–42, 45–56.
12. *MSPA, Rules and Regulations, 1796,* pp. 3–4.

"Esq." after their names.[13] But the society trustees knew well that men who needed thirty dollars worth of encouragement could not be the only targets of MSPA premiums. Just how many practical farmers would have the resources—money, time, and education—to import sheep, to experiment at length with curing clover with salt, or to research and compose a treatise on the natural history of the cankerworm?[14] If we look at the men who did respond to the offer of these typical premiums, we have a clearer idea of just what kind of people were the objects of MSPA encouragement.

We find then such gentlemen as Col. David Humphreys of Connecticut, former minister to Spain, awarded the society's gold medal in 1802 for his importation of seventy merino ewes and twenty-five merino rams; merchants Samuel W. Pomeroy and E. Hersey Derby (son of E. Hasket), who in 1804 communicated results of clover-curing experiments conducted on their Waltham and South Salem estates; and scientist William Dandridge Peck, Harvard 1782, winner of the MSPA's first premium for his essay on cankerworms.[15] The lure of money was not what was inspiring these men, and the society recognized as much when in April 1793 it passed a resolution authorizing the award of a specially designed medal in place of cash to premium winners. "Many persons will engage in Agricultural experiments," read the resolution, "who would be more gratified by the most honorable testimony of their merit, than it is in the power of the Society to confer by pecuniary rewards."[16]

13. See, for example, Ezra Clap to the MSPA, 2 April 1793, Perez Bradford to Oliver Smith, 14 July 1794, and "Poor Farmer" to the President and Trustees of the MSPA, 10 March 1800, Massachusetts Society for Promoting Agriculture Papers (hereafter MSPA Papers), drawer A, folder VI, numbers 1, 3, Massachusetts Historical Society, Boston. Clap's communication is riddled with poor spelling and diction, as is that submitted by "Poor Farmer." This second communication took the form of a twenty-five-page pamphlet, with a stitched-on, rough burlap cover. Bradford begins his communication apologizing that "not being a Grammarian Naturalist nor Philosopher he [Bradford] cannot dress it [his communication] in that Polite Language which your Worthy Society deserve but in the plain and Common Stile of a farmer." More typical of the MSPA correspondents, of course, was "Philosophrune," who spelled his name in both English and Greek. "Philosophrune" to the MSPA, 10 September 1793, MSPA Papers, C–XLI–3–4.

14. MSPA, Rules and Regulations, 1796, p. 32; Papers on Agriculture; Consisting of Communications Made to the Massachusetts Society for Promoting Agriculture, with Extracts from Various Publications (Boston: Young and Minns, 1804)—hereafter MSPA Papers, 1804—p. 8; MSPA, Laws and Regulations, 1793, p. 13.

15. MSPA Papers, 1803, pp. 79–84; Papers on Agriculture; Consisting of Communications Made to the Massachusetts Society for Promoting Agriculture (Boston: Young and Minns, 1804), pp. 107–10 (this is not the same volume as MSPA Papers, 1804); William Dandridge Peck, "Natural History of the Cankerworm," in MSPA, Rules and Regulations, 1796, pp. 35–45; "Abstract of the Records," p. 20.

16. Report of a meeting of the Trustees, 26 April 1793, MSPA Papers, A–XXXII–21.

Stimulating the gentleman farmer to undertake agricultural research was the acknowledged strategy of the MSPA. At various times the society appealed to "those wealthy farmers, who can afford the risk" of experimental agriculture, to "wealthy and patriotick landholders," and to "wealthy experimental farmers."[17] By encouraging men of means to conduct costly or risky experiments, the MSPA hoped to excite a "spirit of emulation" whereby gentleman farmers would act as a kind of leaven in the agricultural populace, stimulating practical farmers to abandon their backward techniques for more successful ones pioneered by their well-to-do neighbors. The offer of premiums was only the primary way the MSPA hoped to set this process of emulation in motion. Also useful was the distribution of new seed types among society members, who would then be expected to try out these crops on their farms.[18] And the MSPA stimulated the exertions of Boston's gentleman farmers in a general way by providing a sense of common purpose and, more concretely, a forum for agricultural contributions. From the society's early days, some members—though a disappointing number considering how many gentleman farmers belonged to the MSPA—communicated their experimental results and observations.[19]

In its efforts to promote agriculture, the MSPA also decided to collaborate with Harvard College. In 1801 the society subscribed five hundred dollars to establish a professorship of natural history at Harvard; the professor was to oversee the operations of a botanical garden also to be established in Cambridge.[20] Four years later, William Dandridge Peck, a Har-

17. *MSPA Papers, 1799,* preface, p. 4; *Georgick Papers for 1809, Consisting of Letters and Extracts, Communicated to the Massachusetts Society for Promoting Agriculture* (Boston: Russell and Cutler, 1809)—hereafter *Georgick Papers, 1809*—preface, p. 5; *MSPA Journal* 3 (January 1815): 187.

18. Sometimes the society itself was responsible for ordering the seeds, but more often MSPA members or persons sympathetic to the cause of agricultural improvement donated them to the society for distribution. Thus gentleman farmers who belonged to the MSPA were able to test wheat from Virginia and Rio de Janeiro, courtesy of the society, and from Canada, Naples, and Siberia, courtesy of Thomas Austin Coffin of Quebec, Salem merchant Elias Hasket Derby, and Boston merchant Gorham Parsons, respectively. A related activity was the examination of new types of agricultural tools. During the first twenty years of the society's existence, members were able to inspect a model of Thomas Jefferson's moldboard plow, a machine for sowing seed, a newly patented device for shelling corn, a newly invented plow specially ordered from England, and a model of a double plow. MSPA to William Strickland, 8 October 1798, MSPA Papers, C–XLI–25; "Abstract of the Records," pp. 20, 24, 26, 27, 33, 51, 53.

19. See, for example, the contributions of Joseph Barrell, Timothy Pickering, James Winthrop, and Ward Nicholas Boylston in *MSPA Papers, 1803,* pp. 76–77; *Papers; Consisting of Communications Made to the Massachusetts Society for Promoting Agriculture* (Boston: Young and Minns, 1806)—hereafter *MSPA Papers, 1806*—pp. 9–19; "Abstract of the Records," pp. 14, 23, 32, 33.

20. *MSPA Papers, 1806,* preface; [John Lowell], "Account of the Establishment for

vard graduate but nonetheless self-taught botanist, was appointed to the academic post.[21] The garden itself gradually took shape over the next decade, thanks to an impressive sum of money pledged to the institution by an equally impressive list of subscribers, MSPA and legislative funds, Peck's plant collecting tour of Europe, the services of a specially imported English gardener, and the many donations of exotic plants from local country estate owners, European botanical gardens, and merchants traveling abroad (fig. 14).[22]

As much as Harvard College or the Boston Athenaeum or any of a number of similar Boston institutions, the MSPA was the domain of the Boston elite. Its membership list, numbering in the hundreds, comprised a good deal of the city's wealth, power, and learning. Its very activities—publication of learned treatises, promotion of expensive experiments, collaboration with Harvard on a botanical garden—effectively defined the MSPA as an upper-crust organization.

For all its elitist elements, however, the MSPA was not out to exclude practical farmers entirely. Quite the contrary; the trustees of the society repeatedly expressed the desire to hear from the common yeomen of Massachusetts on agricultural matters. Addressing "the Publick," the trustees called on farmers to undertake agricultural experiments and even more important to report their results, with any hints and observations, to the MSPA for publication. Without such communications, they acknowledged, "the Trustees are very conscious they can do but little good, notwithstanding their solicitude to be useful." To encourage submissions, the trustees volunteered their editing skills, on the theory that some farmers, lacking education and fearing ridicule, might hold back from sending in agricultural wisdom. "Every one may rely with confidence," reassured the trustees, that we "will never suffer an ingenuous mind to be wounded by committing to the publick any communications, without such corrections as shall not expose them to the sneers of the weak and uncandid."[23]

---

Natural History, in Cambridge, Massachusetts," *Monthly Anthology and Boston Review* (hereafter *MA*) 5 (November 1808): 595–98; "Abstract of the Records," pp. 28, 41.

21. Joseph Lovering, "Boston and Science," in Justin Winsor, ed., *The Memorial History of Boston, including Suffolk County, Massachusetts, 1630–1880*, 4 vols. (Boston: James R. Osgood, 1881), 4:518–19; "Memoir of William Peck," *Massachusetts Historical Society Collections*, 2d ser., 10 (1823): 161–70.

22. William Dandridge Peck to Dudley Tyng, 24 June 1808, MSPA Papers, C–XXX–16; [Lowell], "Account of the Establishment," pp. 596–97; John Lowell, Report of the Committee Appointed to Superintend the Garden, 24 September 1808, MSPA Papers, C–XXX–13; W. D. Peck, *A Catalogue of American and Foreign Plants, Cultivated in the Botanic Garden, Cambridge, Massachusetts* (Cambridge, Mass.: Hilliard and Metcalf, 1818).

23. MSPA, *Rules and Regulations, 1796*, pp. 4–5.

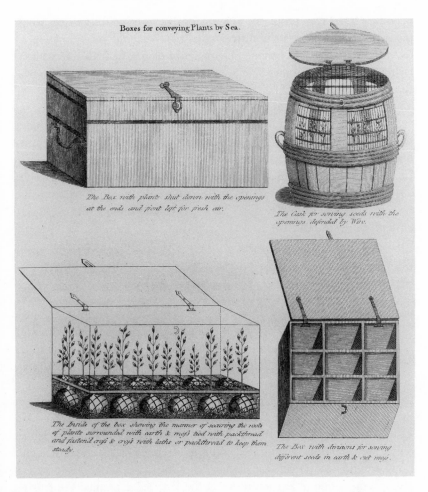

Boxes for conveying Plants by Sea.

*The Box with plants shut down with the openings at the ends and front left for fresh air.*

*The Cask for sowing seeds with the openings defended by Wire.*

*The Inside of the box shewing the manner of securing the roots of plants surrounded with earth & moss tied with packthread and fastend cross & cross with laths or packthread to keep them steady.*

*The Box with divisions for sowing different seeds in earth & out moss.*

14. *Boxes for Conveying Plants by Sea*. Reprinted from John Coakley Lettsom, *Natural History of the Tea-tree* (London, 1799). (Courtesy Yale University Library.)

Five years later the trustees expressed their "sensible regret" that the volume contained so little in the way of original communications. In light of their "repeated invitations" to ordinary farmers to submit agricultural communications, the trustees had "flattered themselves" that such communications would be forthcoming.[24] In 1809 the trustees renewed the offer to polish prose received from practical farmers and stressed that communications need *not* be scholarly. "Plain facts in plain language" (this in a volume entitled *Georgick Papers!*) is all they wanted. "It is by no means

24. *MSPA Papers, 1801*, preface, pp. 3–5.

necessary that a man profitably to write for this work"—the trustees would gladly correct any split infinitives received—"should be intimately acquainted with the structure and character of plants, or with the modes of farming in foreign countries, or with the ornaments of style, or with even the rules of grammar."[25]

In another attempt to ascertain the practices of practical farmers, the MSPA distributed twelve hundred copies of an agricultural survey around the Commonwealth.[26] "We do not . . . affect to disguise," wrote then president John Lowell, Sr., in the cover letter, that the usefulness of the society "is, and will be, very much circumscribed without the aid of the practical farmer."[27] Some replies were received, and on the strength of that initial response, a second questionnaire was circulated among Massachusetts farmers in 1800. But the society's luck did not persevere. In 1804 the trustees admitted to holding out for more responses before publishing the intelligence. "Will farmers, into whose hands they [the queries] are put," they pleaded, "favour them with their answers, that they may proceed to give the public the information received either entire or digested?" Not until 1807 did the society publish the responses to the circular, and even then it complained of having fewer replies than had been hoped.[28]

If the views of the practical farmer were considered so critical to the work of the MSPA, it was largely because society members made a point of disclaiming substantial agricultural knowledge, even though many of them, in their capacity as gentleman farmers, were not wholly ignorant on the topic. "We do not pretend to much knowledge," wrote President Lowell in 1800, "and that not the best, on the subject." The society claimed only to be a medium of communication, gathering agricultural intelligence from around the world, the nation, and the state and diffusing it via publication. "The object and duty of the Board," explained the trustees succinctly, "is to convey to practical farmers through the press, the agricultural information which they receive or learn from others."[29]

Contemporary opinion held such information collection and dissemina-

25. *Geogick Papers, 1809,* preface, p. 6.
26. The inspiration for this step may well have come from the Bath and West Society, which in 1780 had printed a list of questions sent to all the high sheriffs in England together with the sheriffs' replies. Hudson, *Bath and West,* pp. 19–20.
27. "Abstract of the Records," p. 25.
28. "Abstract of the Records," p. 26; *Inquiries by the Agricultural Society* (Boston: Young and Minns, 1800); *MSPA Papers, 1804,* preface, p. 5; *Papers; Consisting of Communications Made to the Massachusetts Society for Promoting Agriculture, and Extracts* (Boston: Adams and Rhoades, 1807)—hereafter *MSPA Papers, 1807*—pp. 4–5, 10–47.
29. John Lowell, prefatory letter, *Inquiries by the Agricultural Society,* n.p.; *MSPA Papers, 1804,* preface, p. 4.

tion as the basis of properly conducted science, so that in claiming to be no more than a medium of communication, the MSPA may have been implementing a research strategy. All scientific inquiry, ran the Baconian philosophy of science, should begin with the methodical collection of data. From this broad body of empirical knowledge, the truths of natural philosophy can be induced. Indeed, from the catalog of empirical phenomena, truth emerges almost spontaneously. When the MSPA set about composing its own catalog of information, then, the expectation had probably been that by merely compiling survey answers, the best mode of farming would become immediately and abundantly clear.[30]

But there was a good deal more to the disclaimers of expertise, the characterization of the MSPA as a mere clearinghouse of information than the proper practice of inductive science. By denying knowledge of and involvement with agriculture, MSPA members hoped to rule out personal advantage as a motive for promoting agriculture in Massachusetts. Indeed, they represented their sole qualification and reason for joining the MSPA as a kind of moral largesse. "The members of the Society," affirmed the *Rules and Regulations* of 1793, "have no other interest, than the benefit of the human species at large." They "expect no other advantage" than the satisfaction of helping their fellow members of what they termed "the great family."[31] It seems likely that in denying selfish gain as a motive for promoting agriculture, MSPA members wished to distinguish themselves from some of their British counterparts, for whom improvements in agriculture translated directly into higher rents. In fact, given that neither agriculture nor landholding constituted a major part of the incomes of MSPA members, if agricultural improvement were to benefit the society's members, it would have to be in some way other than simple monetary gain. Curiously enough, the expressions of disinterestedness were their own reward.

In the aftermath of the Revolution, as we have seen, public virtue replaced economic wealth and social prominence as the criterion for a legitimate ruling class. Clearly then, the demonstration of disinterested benevolence, the essence of public virtue, had political value in late eighteenth- and early nineteenth-century America. In an era which saw the Boston elite's authority challenged, as with Shays's Rebellion, or simply disregarded, as the growing strength of Jeffersonian republicanism in Massachusetts indicated, this political value could not be lightly dismissed. Wealthy and prominent Bostonians might continue to believe that it was

30. *MSPA Papers, 1807*, pp. 4–5.
31. *MSPA, Rules and Regulations, 1796*, p. iv.

their birthright to rule, that only such men as they had been bred to a high-minded stewardship of public affairs, but if they were still to win votes and command deference, they had best demonstrate their fitness as a ruling class as defined by the postrevolutionary criterion of virtue. What the MSPA provided, then, was not merely an opportunity for but a public stance of virtue.

This is not to say that MSPA membership was a matter of mere show (although, as we shall see, that charge was leveled against the agricultural society), only that it was a highly self-conscious act. The political symbolism and resulting value of the MSPA could hardly have escaped the society's members; MSPA membership *was* a matter of public image. But the whole notion of public image in this era was not freighted with suggestions of superficiality or insincerity. Public image was the ideal of one's public self. It was an ideal elite Bostonians sought to approximate in their public behavior, much as in their private behavior—a polite acquaintance with the classics, a polite interest in experimental farming—they strove to approximate an ideal image of the private man. Public image and self-image were one and the same. Thus what benefit MSPA membership offered—the public posture of virtue—was only what elite Bostonians regarded as appropriate and therefore natural to them in their capacities as public men. In their eyes, benefit was not selfishly contrived, only richly deserved.

Wealthy and prominent Bostonians made public demonstrations of disinterestedness in many ways, most notably through grandiose contributions to charity. But MSPA membership was an especially powerful expression of virtue because of the objects of that benevolence, agriculture and the yeoman farmer. Agriculture held a position of special importance and prestige in contemporary republican theory and political economy. The MSPA was careful to stress both. Agriculture, wrote one trustee, is "the most innocent, useful, and honourable of arts."[32] It was seen as both the moral basis of the Republic and the economic basis of the nation. This latter conviction was clearly embodied in the MSPA's official seal, which depicted a plow drawn by oxen, a stone wall and hedge, and sheep and cattle, along with the society's motto, "SOURCE OF WEALTH." To promote agriculture, then, was no ordinary act of benevolence. It was a public service of the highest order that carried with it the moral prestige and national importance of agriculture itself.

Besides agriculture, the other beneficiary of the MSPA was the farmer. And again, what could be more laden with moral significance? It would be

32. [William Emerson], Review of the MSPA's *Papers* [1807], *MA* 4 (October 1807): 570; "Abstract of the Records," p. 16.

hard to overstate the potential symbolic value of the MSPA's relation to the yeomanry. Here was the Boston elite aiding the farming populace of Massachusetts out of the most disinterested of motives; such stewardship was surely the sign of a legitimate ruling class. But the public virtue epitomized by such aid was itself associated with the yeoman class. There was thus an almost synergistic effect, whereby the moral content and hence the political value of MSPA membership increased.

And finally, inasmuch as MSPA members identified themselves with agricultural values, as farmers albeit theoretical ones, they tapped directly into the moral prestige of the yeoman farmer. Here was a case of virtue by association. Because "if the plough is deserving of high honours in any country on the globe, America is that country," wrote a reviewer of an MSPA publication of 1804, there is "every inducement" for Americans "to respect the citizen, who, if he cannot attend to the practice, endeavours to perfect the theory" of agriculture. "In this view," concluded the reviewer, "we commend the efforts of the *Massachusetts Society for Promoting Agriculture*."[33]

Hence the relation between the MSPA and practical farmers purposely functioned within narrowly defined limits. The practical farmer could neither be ignored nor treated as an equal working partner by the MSPA member if stewardship were to characterize their relationship. It was not just social snobbery that precluded efforts to recruit yeomen into the agricultural society. Such an arrangement would undermine the very raison d'être of the MSPA, the public stance of disinterestedness. What MSPA members wanted from the citizenry in return was recognition of their legitimacy as a ruling class and the deference that accompanied this recognition. Furthermore they wanted public gratitude. But, as the Federalist elite was only too quick to point out, such recognition and gratitude were rare among a people easily duped by flatterers and popularity seekers. Thankless public service would as likely be the fate of the Boston elite in their efforts to promote agriculture as in their efforts to rule the nation. So philosophized trustee Loammi Baldwin:

33. Review of the MSPA's *Papers on Agriculture* [1804], *MA* I (August 1804): 465. These comments can be compared with those of the Bath and West's Billingsley: "It seldom happens that a well-educated gentleman has a natural taste for agriculture. . . . The appearance, the manner, the habits of the farmer, are by no means attractive; nor do I think, independent of other incentives, one in ten of those who have put their hands to the plough, would have so done, had they not been induced by the fashionable prevalence of agricultural conversation at the tables of the great, and the cordial and honourable respect paid to those who shine most in topics of this nature" (John Billingsley, quoted in Hudson, *Bath and West*, pp. 51–52).

Agricultural occupations are of unquestionable importance to society, and immediately involve the general interest, the support, and happiness of a great proportion of labouring men. This science, in a high degree, requires the aid of rich, intelligent men, whose affluence and talents give them the power, and whose taste and judgment impel them to the pursuit. Such men, when they devote their talents to the subject, merit the highest praise, and it is with regret that they do not always meet their reward in . . . the gratitude of society.[34]

There are in fact strong indications that the Commonwealth's practical farmers regarded the MSPA with something other than a sense of enthusiasm and gratitude. For one, they voted with their feet: they refused to get involved. The many pleas of the MSPA trustees to submit agricultural communications fell on deaf ears. But the clearest picture of just what practical farmers disliked about the MSPA emerges from statements made by society officeholders themselves. As part of their continuing effort to woo practical farmers, MSPA officials repeated the criticisms of their organization in order to refute them. Thus, in the cover letter to the 1800 set of agricultural queries, President John Lowell attached a few rhetorical questions to the list. "But who are these Trustees?" he asked, "And why do they pretend to be the instructors of the Farmers of Our Country? Are they not a number of gentlemen, who live in or near the Metropolis, and who have little knowledge on the subject, except some theoretical notions derived from books?"[35] These questions, Lowell admitted, "have been frequently asked." In defending the MSPA, Lowell disclaimed any expertise, characterized the society as a neutral medium of communication, and stressed the disinterestedness of the trustees' motives. "The Trustees do not presume to dictate," he wrote. "They ask information, and are willing to distribute it; they love the pursuits they are encouraging, and will receive full compensation by the success of them."[36]

Of course, such statements did nothing to quiet criticism of the MSPA; the same charges surfaced again and again for decades. Fueling these charges was a hostility not easily diffused. This was the antipathy of people performing their labors day in and day out, year in and year out—work without glamor or riches—and then being corrected and criticized by men who had never milked a cow or swung a scythe in their lives. We can also

34. [Loammi Baldwin], Review of *Memoirs of the Philadelphia Society for Promoting Agriculture* [1808], *MA* 6 (February 1809): 108.
35. Lowell, prefatory letter, *Inquiries by the Agricultural Society*, n.p.
36. Ibid.

detect an antagonism toward MSPA members as upper-class "gentlemen" who assume the right to dictate to their social inferiors, leaders of that oppressive stronghold of commercial power, the "Metropolis" of Boston (fig. 15). The sentiments that lay behind Shays's Rebellion were hardly dead.

The criticisms of MSPA members as theoretical farmers oblivious to and ignorant of the practice of farming must have especially galled. A cornerstone of the members' worldview, as Federalists and as men of commerce (though the two can hardly be separated), was a distrust of theory and a hard-nosed reliance on the facts of experience. "In political affairs," wrote Fisher Ames, "there are no more self-conceited blunderers than the statesmen who affect to proceed, in all cases, without regard to circumstances, but solely according to speculative principles."[37] In Federalists' eyes, this kind of abstract approach was precisely the one taken by Jeffersonian republicans. The Virginian and his cohorts pushed aside the wisdom of the ages in favor of wildly visionary schemes. By contrast, the Federalists claimed to stand for tried-and-true principles and a sober-minded evaluation of the realities of human nature, society, and government.[38] How appalling the epithet "book farmer" must have appeared to an MSPA member like Ames, who disparagingly designated his political opponent as a "book politician"![39]

Members of the MSPA brought this outlook to their consideration of scientific endeavors. In general, men of this era adopted a strongly Baconian, utilitarian view of science. It was the practical usefulness of natural philosophy to humanity that justified its pursuit.[40] One factor that made agriculture so acceptable a field of scientific endeavor for the Boston Federalist was its obvious utility to the nation. And whatever the practical farmer might intimate, MSPA members insisted that their ultimate goal was useful knowledge, not abstract theory. Here they saw themselves in direct contrast to their ideological opponents. As part of their general critique of the Jeffersonians as impractical philosophes, Boston Federalists characterized their adversaries as pursuing scientific interests so chimerical as to be

37. Seth Ames, ed., *Works of Fisher Ames,* 2 vols. (Boston: Little, Brown, 1854), 2:334.
38. Linda K. Kerber, *Federalists in Dissent: Imagery and Ideology in Jeffersonian America* (Ithaca, N.Y.: Cornell University Press, 1970), pp. 1–22; James M. Banner, Jr., *To the Hartford Convention: The Federalists and the Origins of Party Politics in Massachusetts, 1789–1815* (New York: Alfred A. Knopf, 1969), pp. 128–29.
39. Ames, quoted in Banner, *Hartford Convention,* p. 129n.
40. Hindle, *Pursuit,* pp. 190–93, 353–55; John C. Greene, "Science, Learning, and Utility: Patterns of Organization in the Early American Republic," in Oleson and Brown, *Pursuit of Knowledge,* pp. 1–20.

View of the Seat of the Hon. MOSES GILL Esq. at Princeton in the County of Worcester. MASSA.

15. *Estate of Moses Gill.* Gill, a statesman and gentleman farmer, was one of the few MSPA trustees not from the Boston area. His estate was located in Worcester County. Reprinted from *Massachusetts Magazine* 4 (November 1792). (Courtesy Boston Athenaeum.)

ridiculous. Jefferson's interest in the bones of prehistoric animals, for example, was the object of many a Federalist satire.[41]

The charge of relying on "theoretical notions derived from books" must also have been aggravating to MSPA members as men of commerce. Merchants could not afford philosophical foolishness; they *had* to judge by results. If they were so foolhardy as to ignore the realities of trade in favor of some hypothetical account of commercial intercourse, they were liable to bankrupt themselves in a hurry. Surely the merchant in his countinghouse reckoning the bottom line on his balance sheets had as much claim to a practical mentality as the farmer attending to crop yields.

This almost temperamental abhorrence of theoretical notions even informed MSPA members' attitudes toward agricultural innovation. We may not be surprised to find these hard-headed conservatives expressing their intent to "set their faces against a wild spirit of innovation, as well in agriculture as in every social establishment." They were the first to admit

41. Kerber, *Federalists in Dissent,* pp. 67–94.

that "theory is good for nothing till sanctioned and confirmed by experience," and "that *farming by books* merely, is justly derided."[42] Yet as merchants the MSPA members had long recognized the wisdom and necessity of a calculated amount of innovation. The commercial world in the wake of independence from Britain bore a vastly different aspect from the prerevolutionary world, and to survive, Boston merchants were forced to experiment with new routes, products, and markets. Such innovation also sustained them through the changing commercial conditions engendered by the Anglo-French wars. Their own experience demonstrated to these merchants that unquestioning acceptance of tradition was ultimately *not* the most practical approach.[43]

The importance of innovation was not something elite Bostonians expected practical farmers to grasp spontaneously. Members of the MSPA continually represented Massachusetts farmers as hidebound traditionalists whose "blind adherence to the beaten track, . . . deems all disposition to improvement, disease."[44] Behind such condemnations lay popular stereotypes of the country dweller as a backward and ignorant bumpkin, and the farmer as a clownish dullard. This "clodhopper" image was both long-standing—the term dated back to the end of the seventeenth century—and persistent.[45] It lurked behind the MSPA warnings against a "bigoted attachment to injudicious customs" and the parallel argument that unless farmers followed the merchants' example in accepting and initiating change, agriculture in New England would only continue its precipitous decline.[46]

For all their disclaimers of agricultural expertise, MSPA members thus regarded themselves as uniquely qualified to improve agriculture because they *were* merchants and not farmers. In their estimation, who else but the

42. *MSPA Papers, 1799,* preface, p. 4; *MSPA Papers, 1804,* preface, p. 4.

43. Samuel Eliot Morison, *The Maritime History of Massachusetts, 1783–1860* (1921; reprint ed., Boston: Northeastern University Press, 1979), pp. 31–32, 38, 41–95, 160–212; Robert A. East, *Business Enterprise in the American Revolutionary Era* (New York: Columbia University Press, 1938), pp. 250–53; Frederic Cople Jaher, *The Urban Establishment: Upper Strata in Boston, New York, Charleston, Chicago, and Los Angeles* (Urbana: University of Illinois Press, 1982), p. 22.

44. *MSPA Papers, 1799,* preface, p. 4.

45. *Oxford English Dictionary,* c.v. "clodhopper." Ronald Story discusses the acceptance of this stereotype among the Boston elite in *The Forging of an Aristocracy: Harvard and the Boston Upper Class, 1800–1870* (Middletown, Conn.: Wesleyan University Press, 1980), p. 121. For an example of the continuing currency of the clodhopper image, see "[Review of] Colman's European Agriculture," *Christian Examiner* 46 (March 1849): 290, which condemns the tendency of "shallow-headed shopkeepers and silly merchants' clerks" to "have their jest at the clodhopper, when his blue frock brushes against their broadcloth" and the parallel tendency among "merchants of high ambition and extended operations . . . to look upon farming as a petty business."

46. *MSPA Papers, 1804,* preface, p. 4.

merchant with his broad outlook on the world, vast storehouse of experience, and familiarity with the workings of the world on the grand scale, was better able to see beyond the farmer's narrow understanding of his own circumstances? Who then could better recognize the farmer's errors or plot the path to agricultural improvement? And who else but the liberally educated man would be exposed to the latest developments in farming in other parts of the world or could appreciate the importance of science to agricultural improvement?[47]

We have seen how British landed merchants acted as models to their American counterparts. Here were men who united business mentality with refinement, thus avoiding both aristocratic decadence and nouveau boorishness. As gentleman farmers with country estates, elite Bostonians hoped to approximate the private characters of these British merchants. But just as the merchant's calling engendered such private virtues as thrift, sobriety, and industry, so also did it shape a man's public character. It was because the merchant by necessity acquired a broad and enlightened understanding of the world that he was especially fit for social and political leadership. Fisher Ames commended the Federalist "men of information and property" as worthy political leaders, though they be "stigmatized as aristocrats" by the people. Jonathan Jackson stipulated "converse with the world" as a vital qualification for public office. Theophilus Parsons, the Essex Junto's chief theoretician, characterized the natural leaders of society as men with "a thorough knowledge of the interests of their country, when considered abstractly, when compared with the neighboring States, and when with those more remote, and an acquaintance with its produce and manufacture, or its exports and imports."[48]

Thus it was not only disinterested benevolence that MSPA members wished to demonstrate; it was also mercantile wisdom. The vision of the commercial class as the appropriate, natural leaders of society was as central to the outlook of the MSPA as the impulse to appropriate some of the moral prestige of agriculture and the nation's agricultural class. Neither can be ignored. Members of the MSPA might identify themselves with agrarian

47. MSPA Papers, 1807, pp. 58–63.
48. Fisher Ames to William Tudor, 12 July 1789, quoted in "Memoir of Tudor," Massachusetts Historical Society Collections, 2d ser., 8 (1819): 318–19; [Jonathan Jackson], Thoughts upon the Political Situation of the United States of America . . . (Worcester, Mass.: Isaiah Thomas, 1788), p. 118; [Theophilus Parsons], Result of the Convention of Delegates Holden at Ipswich in the County of Essex (Newburyport, Mass.: John Mycall, 1778), pp. 18–20. It was also Parsons who advised aspiring public servants to "look after the politics of the country as you look after your ships, your banks, your mills, your business." Theophilus Parsons [Jr.], Memoir of Theophilus Parsons (Boston: Ticknor and Fields, 1859), pp. 120–21.

values by championing agriculture and the yeoman, but they knew themselves as men of commerce.

It is not surprising then that the MSPA looked to British merchants as
much as to the British gentry and aristocracy as men to venerate and
imitate. If Thomas Coke, earl of Leicester, was made an honorary member
of the society, so too was that spokesman for the minor gentry Arthur
Young and even more tellingly, so too was John Coakley Lettsom.[49] A
Quaker, learned physician, and philanthropist, Lettsom was an English-
man after a Boston merchant's own heart. When in 1767 he inherited a
West Indian plantation, he promptly emancipated his slaves, then went on
to make a pretty fortune through a lucrative London practice and marriage
to a woman of considerable means. When in 1793 he was made an honorary
member of the MSPA, Lettsom could be found on his suburban estate in
Camberwell, where he cultivated a botanical garden and busied himself in
agricultural improvement (fig. 16). He is known to have maintained an
agricultural correspondence with fellow physician and MSPA member Benjamin Waterhouse of Boston.[50]

When it came to establishing a civic institution, not surprisingly the
MSPA looked to that thriving center of British commerce, Liverpool. That
city's botanical garden was probably an important model for the one
founded by the MSPA, much as the clearest antecedent for the Boston
Athenaeum was the Liverpool Athenaeum.[51] When Joseph Buckminster,
soon to be an MSPA trustee, visited Liverpool's botanical garden in 1807, he
was delighted with what it represented in the cultural progress of the city.
Liverpool, wrote Buckminster in a letter printed in the *Monthly Anthology,*
had gone beyond the mere "focus of Guinea ships, and cent. per cent.
literati." It had "now reached that point of wealth at which societies, which

49. "List of Members of the Massachusetts Society for Promoting Agriculture," *MSPA Journal* 4 (January 1817): 311; "Abstract of the Records," p. 15; J. C. Lettsom to MSPA, 25 March 1794, MSPA Papers, A–XI–139.

50. Thomas Joseph Pettigrew, *Memoirs of the Life and Writings of the Late John Coakley Lettsom,* 3 vols. (London: Longman, Hurst, Rees, Orme, and Brown, 1817); *Dictionary of National Biography,* s.v. "Lettsom, John Coakley"; Benjamin Waterhouse to Dudley A. Tyng, 28 August 1806, MSPA Papers, C–XXX–9. In his letter accepting honorary membership, Lettsom praised the MSPA for its "spirit of enquiry after manly and rational pursuits. . . . pleasures that improve and dignify character." He also enclosed a ten-guinea contribution (J. C. Lettsom to MSPA, 25 March 1794, MSPA Papers, A–XI–139).

51. On the links between the Boston and Liverpool athenaeums, see Ronald Story, "Class and Culture in Boston: The Athenaeum, 1807–1860," *American Quarterly* 27 (May 1975): 184–86. See also John Codman to Catherine Amory Codman, 2 September 1800, Codman Family Manuscripts Collection, Society for the Preservation of New England Antiquities, Boston, Mass.

16. *Grove Hill, Seat of John Coakley Lettsom.* (Courtesy Yale Center for British Art, Paul Mellon Collection.)

have been hitherto merely mercenary and commercial, begin to turn their attention to learning and the fine arts, that is, when they perceive that something more than great riches is necessary to make a place worthy of being visited and interesting enough to be admired." Buckminster cited several "publick institutions" as evidence of this change: the city's public reading rooms, including the Athenaeum, and the botanical garden. Enclosed with the letter was the "charming address" written and delivered by none other than William Roscoe at the garden's opening. "It is worthy of being published in the *Anthology*," recommended Buckminster, "in order to promote the interests of the botanical institution at Cambridge."[52]

The members of the MSPA thus deemed it entirely correct that a society composed of mercantile men should take the lead in promoting Massachusetts agriculture. But they were less than successful. Their transactions never seemed to contain enough original communications; premiums went abegging without winners; and the operation did not enjoy the support of the farming populace. After a full generation of unsatisfactory

52. J. S. Buckminster, "Literary Institutions in Liverpool," *MA* 4 (November 1807): 597, 599; Henry Roscoe, *The Life of William Roscoe,* 2 vols. (Boston: Russell, Odiorne, 1833), 1:186–92.

return for their efforts, the trustees were ready to admit as much and, by way of vindicating themselves and inspiring cause for hope, to explain the disappointing results. "If the efforts of the society have been heretofore more feeble than could have been wished," they wrote, "or than the ardour of their own hopes and those of their friends had led them to expect, should it not be admitted as a sufficient apology, that the institution has been hitherto in its infancy, that it necessarily required much time to introduce it to general attention, to inspire confidence in its utility, and to draw forth the latest knowledge and talent of the country upon this interesting branch of human industry." A slow start such as that experienced by the MSPA was inevitable and in no way boded ill for the ultimate success of the society. "While the seed was in the ground, or just starting from its bed," continued the trustees, "it would have been preposterous and unreasonable to expect a harvest. Time and cultivation and labour were requisite to prepare it for a valuable and productive crop."[53]

Following the War of 1812, the MSPA did in fact experience a resurgence, whether measured by frequency of publication, size of membership, or sheer level and scope of activities. When this resurgence occurred, however, it was not engendered by what in the trustees' analysis was lacking in the society's infancy, namely, the faith and interest of the general population. What the MSPA did have that was new was a dedicated cadre of men who devoted themselves to experimental agriculture as both private *and* public men. That they did so is largely because the state of agriculture in Massachusetts became a matter of social and political urgency in this period. At issue was no longer the mere promotion of agriculture as a form of self-characterization but the complete reform of agriculture as a social and political necessity. It was not, as the trustees might hope, the passage of time that would revitalize the MSPA. It was the changing times.

---

53. *MSPA Journal* 4 (January 1816–July 1817), preface to the volume, pp. i, ii.

# PART TWO

## Between Generations

# Introduction

OR the Boston elite, the War of 1812 came as an act of ultimate
folly, ultimate gall, and ultimate humiliation. It was folly because, in
their view, if the United States should be fighting any nation, it
should be France and not the last outpost of European civilization, Great
Britain. It was gall because it was only the final in a series of policy
decisions made by the Jefferson and Madison administrations—the Louisiana Purchase and subsequent statehood of Louisiana, commercial embargo, and nonintercourse—that went against the wishes and interests of
Massachusetts Federalists. It was humiliation because it dramatized the
Federalists' decline in national power and influence since the turn of the
century. The Federalist elite interpreted this disastrous series of events as
part of a massive conspiracy. The South, having already established its
power base with the Constitution's three-fifths clause,[1] allied with the
growing West in order to humble New England. It did so by supporting
territorial expansion, the institution of slavery, and by doing all in its
increasing power to destroy commerce.[2]

After 1815, Massachusetts Federalism lost any pretensions to national

1. Had it been repealed, the three-fifths clause would actually have increased slave state
power in Congress—assuming, of course, that slaves would have been counted as full human
beings for the purposes of congressional representation. Boston Federalists hoped for the
opposite, that is, that repeal would mean the total exclusion of the slave population from the
formula for representation. James M. Banner, Jr., *To the Hartford Convention: The Federalists
and the Origins of Party Politics in Massachusetts, 1789–1815* (New York: Alfred A. Knopf,
1969), pp. 101–4.

2. Banner, *Hartford Convention*, pp. 84–89, 99–109; Linda K. Kerber, *Federalists in
Dissent: Imagery and Ideology in Jeffersonian America* (Ithaca, N.Y.: Cornell University
Press, 1970), pp. 23–66.

political power. Until 1823, when its candidate for governor, Harrison Gray Otis, lost to the opposition, it remained a regional power, but one looking nostalgically back to its days of glory.[3] Perhaps it was just as well. The elite's traditional sense of duty to assume political power had long been on the wane. Members of the old generation, men like George Cabot, complained that younger men shunned their civic duty in their drive for wealth.[4] What replaced the old guard was a new generation of Federalists with a similar political ideology but distinctly Jeffersonian political tactics. If statesmen like Cabot had *stood* for office, politicians like Harrison Gray Otis *ran* for office.[5]

Ironically, for all their opposition to the war, for all the loss of political influence the war represented and the economic setbacks it engendered,[6] the War of 1812 infused the Boston elite with a new vitality and power. Specifically what it gave them was a new source of wealth—textile manufacturing. Bostonians had been involved in textile mills since 1789, when George Cabot established the Beverly Cotton Manufactory. This enterprise did not last; the competition from British imports was too stiff.[7] Under conditions of embargo and war, however, there was no competition. In contrast to the earlier mill in Beverly, the Boston Manufacturing Company, chartered in 1813 by Patrick Tracy Jackson and Francis Cabot Lowell, was a success. Both these men had impeccable mercantile credentials. Jackson, son of Jonathan Jackson of the Essex Junto, began his business career in the India trade. Lowell, brother-in-law of his business partner, nephew of George Cabot, son of old judge John, and half-brother of the Federalist pamphleteer of the same name, also began as a merchant. Their textile company opened a new era of Boston business enterprise, one that culminated in dozens of successful mills in Lowell and Lawrence, Massachusetts, southern New Hampshire, and southern Maine.[8]

3. Banner, *Hartford Convention,* p. 349.
4. Ibid., pp. 66–70.
5. This shift is the major theme of David Hackett Fischer, *The Revolution of American Conservatism: The Federalist Party in the Era of Jeffersonian Democracy* (New York: Harper and Row, 1965).
6. Frederic Cople Jaher, *The Urban Establishment: Upper Strata in Boston, New York, Charleston, Chicago, and Los Angeles* (Urbana: University of Illinois Press, 1982), p. 45; Samuel Eliot Morison, *The Maritime History of Massachusetts, 1783–1860* (1921; reprint ed., Boston: Northeastern University Press, 1979), pp. 187–91, 205–7.
7. Hannah Josephson, *The Golden Threads: New England's Mill Girls and Magnates* (New York: Duell, Sloan and Pearce, 1949), pp. 13–14.
8. On the textile industry, see Josephson, *Golden Threads;* Caroline Ware, *The Early New England Cotton Manufacture* (Boston: Houghton Mifflin, 1931); Paul M. McGouldrick, *New England Textiles in the Nineteenth Century: Profits and Investment* (Cambridge: Harvard

This was no easy transition. Within a few years of the founding of the mills, the Boston elite was divided into mercantile and manufacturing camps. This division took many forms. It was social, as the "old" commercial families snubbed such self-made, newly wealthy manufacturers as Nathan Appleton and the Lawrence brothers, Amos and Abbott. It was cultural, as Lowells, Cabots, and Higginsons took offense at newly appointed arrivistes in the Harvard administration for what they regarded as boorish materialism. It was political, as advocates of free trade squared off against those favoring a tariff on imported textiles. And it was economic, as some individuals steadfastly refused to invest in manufacturing enterprises while others scurried to turn their mercantile fortunes into industrial ones. The advent of the industrial age challenged the unity of the Boston elite to an extent that is hard to underestimate.[9]

By the end of the 1820s, however, these tensions had largely resolved themselves, and from the turmoil of a decade emerged a newly consolidated, even stronger elite. Manufacturing had succeeded in establishing itself as the new Boston enterprise. The Appletons and Lawrences married into established Boston families and became good catches in their own right. Harvard's old families came to accept a new style of Harvard administration, and the college became a training ground in business values and business mentality. In 1830 protectionist Nathan Appleton defeated diehard free trader Henry Lee for a seat in Congress. And hardly an elite Boston family did not have its fortunes tied up in some manner with the textile industry. Even the Massachusetts Hospital Life Insurance Company, a huge financial institution charged with investing and perpetuating the wealth of Boston's most prominent families, became a major source of capital for the textile industry as early as 1826.[10]

University Press, 1968); and Frances W. Gregory, *Nathan Appleton: Merchant and Entrepreneur, 1779–1861* (Charlottesville: University Press of Virginia, 1975).

9. Jaher, *Urban Establishment*, pp. 47–48; Ronald Story, *The Forging of an Aristocracy: Harvard and the Boston Upper Class, 1800–1870* (Middletown, Conn.: Wesleyan University Press, 1980), pp. 41–52. For evidence of mercantile hostility toward manufacturing in general and the tariff in particular, see "State of Agriculture in Italy," *North American Review* 11 (July 1820): 51–56, and "Report of the Committee of Merchants and Others of Boston, on the Tariff," ibid. 12 (January 1821): 60–88.

10. Jaher, *Urban Establishment*, p. 49; Story, *Forging of an Aristocracy*, pp. 52–56; Gerald T. White, *A History of the Massachusetts Hospital Life Insurance Company* (Cambridge: Harvard University Press, 1955), pp. 41–54. For many years, this funding of textile enterprises was actually illegal, since it took the form of accepting out-of-state or company stock as collateral for loans, a practice prohibited by the MHLIC charter. Even when in 1839 an amendment to the company's statute of incorporation legalized this practice, loans to manufacturers still occasionally violated other rules.

A consolidated elite meant a closed one. By 1830 it was no longer possible to penetrate Boston's innermost social circles the way the Appletons and Lawrences had done just a few years earlier, that is, by merely accumulating wealth. Only a few individuals, such as Edward Everett, Henry Wadsworth Longfellow, and Louis Agassiz (who married the daughters of Peter Chardon Brooks, Nathan Appleton, and the granddaughter of Thomas Handasyd Perkins, respectively), squeezed into the elite by virtue of their cultural or political accomplishments. The reverse was equally true; the already rich maintained a near monopoly on acquisition of further wealth.[11] And a consolidated elite meant an inward-looking one, much less concerned with its national position or its public responsibilities to other social classes. For that brief generation of turmoil, however, that interregnum lasting from about 1810 to 1830, the Boston elite continued to look outward if only because it experienced difficulty defining it own boundaries. Just how far did its power extend? And what would be the new balance among the elements in the social and economic equation—agriculture, commerce, and manufacturing? In this context of change and adjustment to change, rural pursuits took on an altered meaning for merchants in metamorphosis.

11. Edward Pessen estimates that 94 percent of the wealthiest men in Boston in 1833 descended from rich and/or eminent families. The lumping of wealth with social standing is troublesome here, because in the early nineteenth century, a number of Unitarian ministers and miscellaneous literati, often associated with Harvard, were allowed into the elite as "cultural ornaments," although they had little money and humble family origins. Nevertheless, inasmuch as these men were part of the elite, marrying merchants' daughters, for example, the point that elite Bostonians of the antebellum era were not self-made men is well taken. (*Riches, Class, and Power before the Civil War* [Lexington, Mass.: D. C. Heath, 1973], pp. 85–86).

# THREE

# The Agricultural Society Revitalized

I T was in the midst of his rage against the Madison administration's policies of "Perpetual War," "Pretended Negotiations for Peace," and "the Establishment of an Immense Standing Army of Guards and Spies, under the Name of a Local Volunteer Force,"[1] that John Lowell contemplated the impact of the MSPA on Massachusetts agriculture. Here too he had to admit the failure of Boston's best men to determine the shape and course of their society. "It has occurred to me as a subject of regret," he wrote his fellow trustees in January 1813, ". . . that the efforts of this society have appeared to produce so little effect upon the general agriculture of this State." According to Lowell, no one could blame "the enlightened portion of the community" for lack of interest or energy. After all, that stratum had long been the mainstay of both the MSPA and local agricultural societies. "And yet perhaps," he concluded wistfully, "it is doubtfull, at the present day, whether any benefit proportioned to the length of time in which these institutions have existed, the extent of their means, the intelligence & patriotism of their members, has hitherto resulted."[2] We have

1. [John Lowell], *Perpetual War, the Policy of Mr. Madison. Being a Candid Examination of His Late Message to Congress, So Far as Respects the Following Topicks. . . . viz. the Pretended Negotiations for Peace. . . . the Important and Interesting Subject of a Conscript Militia. . . . and the Establishment of an Immense Standing Army of Guards and Spies, under the Name of a Local Volunteer Force, by a New-England Farmer* (Boston: Chester Stebbins, 1812).

2. John Lowell to MSPA, 20 January 1813, Massachusetts Society for Promoting Agriculture Papers (hereafter MSPA Papers), drawer D, folder V, number 4, Massachusetts Historical Society (hereafter MHS), Boston.

labored diligently for a generation, the corresponding secretary meant to say, and what have we to show for it?

It was thus at the time of his most intense political activity that John Lowell undertook the additional task of revitalizing the MSPA. In his battle against the Jefferson and Madison administrations, the New-England Farmer, as Lowell styled himself in print, could point to no concrete successes. In his battle to breathe new life into the moribund agricultural society, Lowell achieved some true victories.

In February 1813, one month after Lowell's despondent letter to the board, the MSPA set about stirring up interest in agriculture by encouraging the formation of local agricultural societies. Heretofore, some local societies had been established, but not in the numbers the state society had envisioned.[3] Accordingly, the society sent out a circular letter to Commonwealth towns, urging the formation of local groups and requesting agricultural intelligence from them. At the end of the letter appeared a signature designed to carry some weight: "John Adams, President."[4] (Of the MSPA, of course.)

In light of the society's private acknowledgment of its failings, the circular letter was less than candid. It represented the MSPA's board of trustees, for example, as "composed almost wholly of gentlemen who are practical farmers," not, in the parlance of the day, an accurate statement. It also stated that, as "the Trustees are happy to observe," the society's publications had "been of essential advantage to the community," again hardly a unanimous verdict, not even within the ranks of the society. The MSPA was ready to admit, however, that the cause of agriculture would have been more advanced had "the Society been favoured with more frequent communications from intelligent farmers."[5]

Over the next few months, many local agricultural societies were established,[6] and some intelligence, scattered responses to yet another set of

3. *Centennial Year (1792–1892) of the Massachusetts Society for Promoting Agriculture* (Salem, Mass.: n.p., n.d.), p. 7n.
4. John Adams, President [of the MSPA] to the Inhabitants of the Town of ———, February 1813, MSPA Papers, C-VII-31. As incentive for cooperation, the MSPA promised free copies of its publications to participating towns, suggested that members might receive new seeds for crop trials, and hinted that worthy farmers communicating with the state society might find themselves winners of cash premiums.
5. Ibid.
6. Andrew Nichols [corresponding secretary, Danvers Agricultural Society] to R. Sullivan [recording secretary, MSPA], 16 July 1813, and Paul Davis [Holden town clerk] to R. Sullivan, 30 August 1813, MSPA Papers, C–IX–5, C–X–15; *Massachusetts Agricultural Repository and Journal* (hereafter *MSPA Journal*) 3 (November 1813): 55–68, 80; 3 (May 1814): 115–28; 3 (January 1815): 259–71; 3 (June 1815): 338–49; 4 (January 1816): 45–

agricultural queries, trickled in. No flood of information from farmers around the state ensued, however, and never would it. The MSPA seemed incapable of establishing a true following from among the Commonwealth's yeomanry. It was far more successful at broadening its base among the metropolitan elite.

Not long after it attempted to form farmers around the state into local agricultural societies, the MSPA launched a membership drive of its own. The society elected prominent citizens to MSPA membership, apparently unbeknownst to them, informing the new members of their nomination and election only after the fact. "To endeavour to give a new vigour to the Society," read the form letter to the members-elect, "to attempt to combine the talents & exertions of respectable gentlemen in various parts of the State they [the MSPA] have recently extended the limits of their body & have elected a few members in every part of the State of which, you, Sir, are one."[7] More than "a few" new members were involved. In January 1817, the MSPA had 365 members. By July 1818, it had added another 114; by July 1820, an additional 128; and by June 1822, another 123, exactly doubling the membership in a mere five years.[8]

At the same time, the MSPA sought to expand its network by electing many new honorary members. Most of these were agricultural reformers and experimental farmers from other regions of the nation, but several were men of great importance and prestige in foreign agricultural circles.[9] In 1817 Sir Benjamin Hobhouse, son of a Bristol merchant, by profession a lawyer and statesman, was elected by virtue of his position as president of the Bath and West Society.[10] Also elected that year was the even more renowned Sir Joseph Banks, KCB, a wealthy baronet with a strong interest in natural history (fig. 17). He had been the naturalist on Cook's first voyage, president of the Royal Society, director of Kew Gardens, and the most important patron of the Horticultural Society of London.[11] Banks

---

53; "Abstract of the Records, from 1792 to 1858," in *Transactions of the Massachusetts Society for Promoting Agriculture,* n.s., 1 (1858): 59.

7. John Lowell [corresponding secretary, MSPA], Circular letter to newly elected members, 29 January 1816, MSPA Papers, C–VII–5.

8. Membership figures compiled from membership lists published in the following issues of the *MSPA Journal:* 4 (January 1817): 305–10; 5 (July 1818): 216–19; 6 (July 1820): 107–11; and 7 (June 1822): 195–210.

9. For lists of honorary members elected, see ibid. 4 (January 1817): 311; 4 (July 1817): 408; 5 (July 1818): 219; 6 (July 1820): 111; 6 (July 1821): 410; and 7 (June 1822): 210–11.

10. *Dictionary of National Biography* (hereafter *DNB*), s.v. "Hobhouse, Sir Benjamin." For Hobhouse's gracious response to the MSPA, see *MSPA Journal* 5 (January 1818): 81–83.

11. Harold R. Fletcher, *The Story of the Royal Horticultural Society, 1804–1968* (London: Oxford University Press, 1969), pp. 9, 27–29; *DNB,* s.v., "Banks, Sir Joseph."

17. *Sir Joseph Banks*. Engraving by N. Schiavonetti, after Thomas Philips, 1812. (Courtesy Yale Center for British Art, Paul Mellon Collection.)

responded to his election with sentiments that must have been music to the ears of Boston's gentlemen. "Allow me Sir," he wrote to John Lowell, "to assure you that I am very sensible of the value of the good opinion of the gentlemen who comprise the Society who have been induced by a well directed patriotism to associate together & to give their gratuitous services in Promoting the genl interest of their Country."[12] Four or five years later, the MSPA elected a friend of Sir Joseph, Thomas Andrew Knight. Knight was a scientific cattle breeder, the president of the Horticultural Society of London, and the owner and manager of a ten-thousand-acre estate, Downton Castle, in Herefordshire (fig. 18).[13]

It was no secret that election to honorary membership implied either gratitude for past services rendered to the society or an obligation to be of some aid in the future. Hobhouse's membership, for example, followed his gift of eight volumes of the Bath and West transactions to the MSPA, in turn a response to the MSPA's gift of *its* publications to the English society.[14] Banks came in handy when he assisted MSPA trustee Samuel G. Perkins in purchasing books for the society's library.[15] Thomas Andrew Knight proved the most useful of all. Both before and after his election to the MSPA, Knight sent fruit trees and cuttings to John Lowell, an honorary member of Knight's Horticultural Society of London, to be distributed to other horticulturists in Massachusetts.[16]

Even more spectacular than the increase in MSPA membership was the increase in the society's activity. Probably the first evidence of this stepped-up level of enterprise was the publication, beginning in November 1813, of what quickly became a semiannual periodical.[17] The driving force behind the *Massachusetts Agricultural Repository and Journal* was its editor, John Lowell. It was said that Lowell composed no less than half of the material in

12. Sir Joseph Banks to John Lowell, 24 August 1818, Autograph File, Houghton Library, Harvard University, Cambridge, Mass.

13. Fletcher, *Royal Horticultural Society,* pp. 45, 63–64, 131–32; *DNB,* s.v. "Knight, Thomas Andrew."

14. Benjamin Hobhouse, President, to John Lowell, Corresponding Secretary, 19 December 1815, *MSPA Journal* 4 (June 1816): 157–59.

15. S. G. Perkins to John Lowell, 27 June 1815, MSPA Papers, D–I–7.

16. John Lowell, "Some Notice of Thomas Andrew Knight, Esq. President of the Horticultural Society of London. His Experiments and Present to This Society," *MSPA Journal* 7 (June 1823): 331–42; "Another Present from Mr. Knight to the Horticulturists," ibid. 8 (June 1825): 344–46; John Lowell, "New Presents of Fruits to the Citizens of the United States, by Tho. A. Knight, Esq.," ibid. 10 (June 1828): 205–8.

17. After 1826, its functions increasingly assumed by a growing number of independent agricultural newspapers, the journal appeared more fitfully, ceasing publication altogether in 1832. Lowell to Pickering, 3 July 1826, Timothy Pickering Papers, reel 32, frame 213, MHS; "Introductory Remarks," *MSPA Journal* 10 (April 1832): 330.

DOWNTON CASTLE,
*HEREFORDSHIRE.*

18. *Downton Castle, Seat of Thomas Andrew Knight.* Reprinted from J. P. Neale, *Views of the Seats of Noblemen and Gentlemen, in England, Wales, Scotland, and Ireland,* 2d ser. (London, 1826). (Courtesy Yale University Library.)

the journal during the years when he was MSPA secretary, that is until 1823 and again from 1828 to 1830.[18]

In his capacity as chairman of the committee appointed to superintend the garden, Lowell was also largely responsible for bringing the botanical garden into fruition. By 1811, the garden was so far along in its establishment—plants cultivated, gardener in charge, greenhouse erected—that Lowell recommended that the committee be dissolved.[19] Donations of exotic plants continued to pour into the garden from friends around the world and from suburban Boston greenhouses. As a result, as Professor Peck was forced to admit in the preface to his 1818 catalog of the garden, though "the collection is enriched with many very curious plants, . . . the number of native plants is comparatively small."[20]

This was probably not quite what the state legislature had intended

18. "Abstract of the Records," p. 55; Lowell to H. A. S. Dearborn, 20 May 1823, C. E. French Papers, MHS; F. W. P. Greenwood, *A Sermon on the Death of John Lowell, LL.D., Delivered in King's Chapel, Boston, March 22, 1840* (Boston: Charles C. Little and James Brown, 1840), p. 22.

19. John Lowell, "Report of the Committee for Superintending the Botanic Garden," 27 July 1811, MSPA Papers, C–XXX–29.

20. W. D. Peck, *A Catalogue of American and Foreign Plants, Cultivated in the Botanic Garden, Cambridge, Massachusetts* (Cambridge: Hilliard and Metcalf, 1818), p. iii.

when in 1814 it authorized the first of a series of annual grants to the garden. "I beg you to recollect," John Lowell had written at that time to the speaker of the Massachusetts house of representatives, "that this is not a private application for the benefit of Individuals or any particular Corporation but the solemn & deliberate recommendation of a publick society . . . [devoted] to the advancement of the best & most important Interests of the State, the advancement of agriculture & science."[21] In aiding the garden, the legislature stipulated that just such utilitarian purposes be emphasized. It wanted the garden to concentrate on indigenous plants, culinary vegetables, pasture grasses, and only such rare plants as might prove to be of economic value.[22] Lowell was soon forced to admit "that the garden does not in any considerable degree promote these objects." We cannot deny, wrote Lowell, that we are "in the unpleasant & embarassing predicament of receiving from the Publick Treasury, an aid for objects which if the true state of the case was known might not perhaps be given."[23]

Lowell's committee recommended that native trees, shrubs, and plants be collected for the garden.[24] Under the curatorship of Thomas Nuttall, who succeeded Peck as head of the garden in 1823, some collecting trips were made in New England,[25] but the garden never attained the utilitarian cast envisioned by the legislature and the legislature's petitioners. Instead it became, in addition to a teaching aid for Harvard students, a sort of nursery and florist for Boston's elite. Merchants and Harvard faculty members patronized the botanical garden to buy plants for their gardens and flowers for their tables.[26] The garden, then, accepting donations from and selling to Boston's elite, functioned as a medium for the exchange of botanical specimens among the city's select.

The MSPA, as distinct from the botanical garden, also functioned as a clearinghouse for new seeds, cuttings, and plants. During this period, donations and acquisitions increased dramatically. "There is scarcely a citizen of intelligence in this State who is abroad, or placed in circum-

21. Lowell to Hon. Mr. Bigelow, Speaker of the House, 9 February 1809, MSPA Papers, C–VII–15.
22. John Lowell, "Report on the best mode of appropriating the money that may be granted by the State Legislature," 26 March 1814, MSPA Papers, C–XXX–34; Lowell, "Report of the committee on the condition of the Botanick Garden," n.d., MSPA Papers, C–XXX–8.
23. Lowell, "Report of the committee on the condition of the Botanick Garden."
24. Ibid.
25. On Nuttall, see Jeannette E. Graustein, *Thomas Nuttall, Naturalist: Explorations in America, 1808–1841* (Cambridge: Harvard University Press, 1967).
26. See the accounts of income taken in by the botanical garden from sales in MSPA Papers, C–XXXI–52, 75, 90, 91, 97, 142.

stances favorable to the acquisition of seeds or plants, which he thinks may be important," read the MSPA's journal in 1821, "who remains forgetful of the interests of his native state."[27] In came onion seeds from Fayal, cauliflower from Italy, bulbs from the Cape of Good Hope, and wheat from Poland.[28] The MSPA also acquired agricultural implements, some in response to premium announcements, others by special order of the society (fig. 19).[29] In 1817, when the MSPA placed an order for an Alderney bull and two Alderney cows to be sent from France,[30] it embarked on a new program of acquisition. It had been in the seed and tool line for years, but livestock importation on its own account was something altogether new. This novel line of undertaking was really the logical culmination of the MSPA's years of efforts to improve animal breeds in Massachusetts through premiums, special awards, publications, and general encouragement of stock importers and breeders.

In its first set of premiums the MSPA hoped to encourage the rearing of productive livestock, but in 1801 the society first endorsed what quickly became the favored strategy for improving animal breeds—importation. In that year, it offered a $30 premium for the introduction of a superior ram or ewe into the Commonwealth—$50 if from abroad.[31] Two years later, Col. David Humphreys of Connecticut informed the MSPA of his importation of merino sheep (fig. 20), native to Spain, celebrated for their high quality wool, and he was promptly awarded the society's gold medal for his accom-

27. "Agricultural Intelligence," *MSPA Journal* 6 (January 1821): 307.

28. Ibid., pp. 307–8; "Agricultural Intelligence," ibid. 5 (July 1819): 389. Local members known for their extensive agricultural operations and active in the MSPA seem to have been favored when it came to seed and plant distribution. Thus, for example, twenty-two men received samples of Spanish wheat from the MSPA in 1819; almost all of these, small-town men of only local prominence, received just one or two quarts of the wheat. By far the largest amounts of wheat, sixteen and twenty quarts, respectively, were distributed to the wealthy landed merchant of Cambridge Andrew Craigie and the wealthy landed merchant of Brighton Samuel W. Pomeroy. "List of the Gentlemen to Whom the Spanish Wheat was Distributed, April 1819," MSPA Papers, D–VII–29.

29. "Abstract of the Records," pp. 58–59, 60, 63, 64, 65, 66; "List of Implements Belonging to the Massachusetts Society for Promoting Agriculture, Now in Their Hall at Brighton," *MSPA Journal* 5 (July 1819): 392–93.

30. The manner in which the cattle were selected well illustrates the purpose of honorary members. John Lowell, as corresponding secretary of the MSPA, "without any previous acquaintance with the persons he addressed," requested the Agricultural Society of Caen to select the animals for him. Shortly thereafter, the secretary of the French society, a Monsieur Lair, addressed a gracious letter to Lowell assuring him of the society's cooperation in the matter. Within a year, Lair was made an honorary member of the MSPA. "Agricultural Intelligence," *MSPA Journal* 5 (January 1818): 78–81; ibid. 5 (July 1818): 219.

31. "Abstract of the Records," p. 30.

19. *Hotchkiss' Improved Patent Straw Cutter.* After examining a model of this implement, the MSPA purchased Hotchkiss's patent in 1815 and subsequently hired a man to manufacture and distribute the straw cutters to state agricultural societies. Reprinted from *Memoirs of the Philadelphia Society for Promoting Agriculture* 4 (Philadelphia, 1818). (Courtesy Yale University Library.)

plishment.[32] By 1809, the MSPA was offering a good deal of money for merino importation. Captain Cornelius Coolidge, for example, pocketed a cool $250 for his ovine cargo.[33] Thus the MSPA played its part in what John Lowell later called "the merino contagion."[34] The epidemic had a strong ideological content in these years of embargo and war; encouragement of a domestic supply of wool was regarded as a blow against America's cursed dependence on British manufactures and for the creation of a proud, in-

32. Humphreys, "Some Account of the Spanish Sheep," *Papers on Agriculture, Consisting of Communications Made to the Massachusetts Society for Promoting Agriculture* (Boston: Young and Minns, 1803), pp. 79–84.

33. *Georgick Papers for 1809, Consisting of Letters and Extracts, Communicated to the Massachusetts Society for Promoting Agriculture* (Boston: Russell and Cutler, 1809)—hereafter *Georgick Papers, 1809*)—p. 8; *Papers for 1810, Communicated to the Massachusetts Society for Promoting Agriculture* (Boston: Russell and Cutler, 1810), p. 5; "Abstract of the Records," pp. 47, 51.

34. John Lowell, "Some Remarks upon Merino Sheep, Shewing That They Ought Not To Be Abandoned in Despair . . . ," *MSPA Journal* 5 (July 1818): 167. For further evidence of the merino contagion in Boston, see, for example, *Monthly Anthology and Boston Review* 7 (December 1809): 410–14. On the craze elsewhere, see Carroll W. Pursell, Jr., "E. I. duPont and the Merino Mania in Delaware, 1805–1815," *Agricultural History* 36 (April 1962): 91–100.

20. *Merino Ram.* Reprinted from L. A. Morrell, *The American Shepherd: Being a History of the Sheep, with Their Breeds, Management, and Diseases* (New York, 1846). (Courtesy Yale University Library.)

dependent network of home manufactures. Merino breeders were thus praised as "wealthy and patriotick landholders," who "give promise of serving at once the agriculture and the manufactures of the nation."[35]

During the War of 1812, with commerce severely interrupted, the merino mania only worsened. Wrote Mary Lee to her husband, Henry, a merchant stranded in India by war: "The embarassments attending any mercantile transactions are now so great and so perplexing that I sometimes think . . . that we had better go upon a farm when you return and raise Merino sheep." A few months later, she was more skeptical. "J[ohn] Bromfield and Frank [Lee]," she wrote of two merchants, "have been on a jaunt to Rhode Island and have returned Merino-mad: all the gentlemen are talking of raising sheep as the most profitable business now to be done."

35. John Lowell, "An Address Delivered before the Massachusetts Agricultural Society at the Brighton Cattle Show, October 13, 1818," *MSPA Journal* 5 (January 1819): 231; *Monthly Anthology and Boston Review* 6 (January 1809): 67–70; *Georgick Papers, 1809,* preface, p. 5.

Mary Lee did not "rely much" on that judgment, fearing "they may not do so well as they think they shall."[36]

She was correct. By the end of the war, the bubble had burst. "Indeed it was impossible it could be otherwise," commented Lowell with, as "one of the very few men of property and leisure who escaped the merino contagion," some degree of smugness. "If the merino had yielded what the Argonauts went in search of, it would have left many of the patients who laboured under that desperate disease exceedingly feeble, and purse-sick. What animal of that size could possibly repay the prize of one thousand and even three thousand given for a single male, and two hundred dollars for a single female . . . ?"[37]

Almost without pause, Boston's gentlemen moved onto something else, this time the importation of other livestock animals, especially British cattle. As mentioned earlier, the MSPA imported cattle on its own account as early as 1817, but it soon found itself the beneficiary of the general enthusiasm for imported stock among Boston's elite. In 1818 the MSPA received its first gift of an imported animal, a bull improbably named Fill Pail, donated by merchant Israel Thorndike. Before long, all manner of cattle, sheep, and horses were presented to the society.[38] The tour de force came in 1825, when Admiral Sir Isaac Coffin, an expatriate Loyalist from Nantucket, presented the society with a pedigreed English mare and stallion clearly bred for the coach and *not* the plow. Included with the gift came another export, an English groom.[39]

The society's major effort in the field of livestock improvement and its

36. Mary Lee to Henry Lee, 21 May, 21 August 1813, in Frances Rollins Morse, *Henry and Mary Lee: Letters and Journals, with Other Family Letters, 1802–1860* (Boston: privately printed, 1926), pp. 184, 198.

37. Lowell, "Some Remarks upon Merino Sheep," pp. 167–68.

38. Donors included John Coffin, D. L. Pickman, Thomas Handasyd Perkins, Francis Peabody, and Admiral Sir Isaac Coffin. Pedigreed cattle from the last were placed at the farms of prominent MSPA members and their stud services offered for a small fee. From these Herefords and shorthorns were descended some of the most celebrated cattle of the era. "Abstract of the Records," pp. 66, 70–71, 78–80; T. H. Perkins to the Corresponding Secretary, "Long Woolled [*sic*] Sheep of the Netherlands," *MSPA Journal* 8 (June 1824): 200–201; "Agricultural Intelligence," ibid. (January 1825): 284; E. H. Derby, "Pedigree of the Bull Admiral," *New England Farmer* (hereafter *NEF*) 11 (1 August 1832): 19; George F. Lemmer, "The Spread of Improved Cattle through the Eastern United States to 1850," *Agricultural History* 21 (April 1947): 82, 87.

39. "Abstract of the Records," p. 88; Bill of Lading, Earles & Carter of Liverpool to J. Lowell, pres. MSPA, 11 June 1825, MSPA Papers, A–V–4, 5. Oliver Wendell Holmes recalled this Yorkshire groom as "a stocky little fellow, in velvet breeches, who made that mysterious hissing noise, traditionary in English stables, when he rubbed down the silken-skinned racers" ("The Professor at the Breakfast-Table," *Atlantic Monthly* 3 [March 1859]: 351).

21. *Road Scene in Brighton. Driving to Market.* Both before and after it hosted agricultural fairs, Brighton was the traditional site for livestock sale and slaughter in Boston. The building at the left is the Cattle Fair Hotel. Reprinted from John Warner Barber, *Historical Collections of Every Town in Massachusetts with Geographical Descriptions* (Worcester, 1839). (Courtesy Massachusetts Historical Society.)

most important innovation in the postwar period was undoubtedly its sponsorship of an annual cattle show in the town of Brighton (fig. 21). The MSPA's first cattle show, held in October 1816, was a relatively modest affair. Premiums totaling $290 were offered for various categories of live-stock. Three trustees and "two gentlemen well skilled in such subjects" comprised the judging committee. The entire affair took place over the course of one Tuesday: a meeting of the board of trustees, remarks by President Aaron Dexter and Secretary John Lowell followed by an address by Dexter, inspection of the animals, a dinner at Hasting's Tavern for the board and "a numerous company of distinguished and respectable cit-izens," and finally a public announcement of the premium winners.[40] The MSPA pronounced the show an almost unqualified success. "In one point, that of *fat* cattle, it was rather meagre," conceded the MSPA's journal. "In all other respects we should have been well satisfied to have placed it down at Smithfield [fig. 22] or Lewes, or Bath, or at Mr. Coke's sheep shearing, at Holkham."[41]

40. "Abstract of the Records," pp. 61–63.
41. "Account of the Cattle Show at Brighton, in October, 1816," *MSPA Journal* 4 (January 1817): 300. The writer was referring to the celebrated livestock markets and shows of England.

22. *A Bird Eye View of Smithfield Market.* By the early nineteenth century, Smithfield, London's traditional commercial meat market, hosted highbrow livestock exhibitions sponsored by the elite Smithfield Society. Aquatint by J. Bluck, after A. Pugin and T. Rowlandson, 1811. (Courtesy Yale Center for British Art, Paul Mellon Collection.)

Over the years the Brighton fairs became far more ambitious and elaborate. In the show's second year, premiums were given not only for superior livestock but also for crop experiments, agricultural tools and machines, success in a plowing match, and domestic manufactures. The cash value of the premiums more than quadrupled over the previous year, to almost thirteen hundred dollars, of which the state legislature, as part of a new arrangement, paid five hundred.[42] In subsequent years, new premium categories were added, soon encompassing dairy products, grain and vegetable crops, forest trees and hedges, honey, cider, and wine, all manner of textile products, and Britannia metalware, artificial flowers, and straw bonnets. Within single categories, the number of premiums offered increased, as did the number of entrants.[43]

42. "Cattle Show and Exhibition of Manufactures, at Brighton, on the Second Tuesday of October, 1817," *MSPA Journal* 4 (January 1817): 302–4; "Account of the Cattle Show and Exhibition of Agricultural Products and Manufactures at Brighton, . . . on the 14th and 15th Days of October, 1817 . . . ," ibid. 5 (January 1818): 5–6.

43. "Premiums Awarded by the Trustees of the MSPA . . . at the Cattle Show at

Just who won the premiums? In spite of accusations that the MSPA unofficially reserved awards for gentleman farmers,[44] many a common man walked away with a Brighton prize. In fact, over the years, the trend was definitely away from gentleman farmer to practical farmer winners. Premiums awarded to elite agriculturists were concentrated mainly in the livestock categories, especially where imported livestock was specified, and even here gentleman farmers were liberally sprinkled but not dominant. In the category of manufactures, the winners were of a totally different sort. Some were manufacturing companies, but most of the winners of the numerous five- and ten-dollar premiums for such items as gloves and bonnets were women—and *not* the wives of Boston's gentleman farmers.[45]

Within a few years of its establishment, the Brighton show had thus developed into a major affair. By any measure—value, number, variety, and scope of premiums, number and diversity of competitors—the show became more ambitious with each passing year. Not surprisingly, then, the show became more ambitious in its arrangements as well.[46] For one, by the second show, it was a two-day event, with an auction of livestock and goods scheduled for the second day.[47] By 1818 the MSPA had acquired a lot in Brighton and a long list of subscribers to an exhibition pavilion. A permanent, fenced fairground shortly took shape.[48] Every October thousands of people and hundreds of carriages now descended on the town. So crowded did Brighton become that it was said that one visitor, on discovering that every hotel bed was taken, offered two dollars for the overnight use of a sofa, only to be told that "the Judge has engaged it, and the sheriff sleeps under it."[49] At the fairgrounds themselves, hucksters worked the crowds. There

Brighton Oct 15 1828," MSPA Papers, C–XXXIV–11; "Abstract of the Records," p. 73; "Premiums Awarded at the Brighton Cattle Show 13 & 14 Oct 1818," MSPA Papers, C–XXXIV–2; Brighton premiums for 1820, MSPA Papers, C–XXXIV–4, 5.

44. John Lowell, "Address of the Hon. John Lowell, President of the Massachusetts Agricultural Society, . . . delivered . . . on the 17th [October 1827]," *MSPA Journal* 10 (June 1828): 103.

45. The above conclusions are based on the following premium winner lists: "Account of Premiums Paid for the Exhibitions of 13 & 14 Oct 1817 at Brighton," MSPA Papers, C–XXXIV–1; "Premiums Awarded . . . 1818"; Brighton premiums for 1819, MSPA Papers, C–XXXIV–3; Brighton premiums for 1820; Brighton Premiums for 1824, 1826, MSPA Papers, C–XXXIV–6, 7, 8; "Premiums Awarded . . . 1828."

46. For a firsthand description of the 1819 Brighton fair, see William Bentley, *The Diary of William Bentley, D.D.*, 4 vols. (1907; reprint ed., Gloucester, Mass.: Peter Smith, 1962), 4:622.

47. John Lowell, "Mr. Lowell's Report," *MSPA Journal* 9 (January 1826): 2.

48. "Abstract of the Records," p. 66; Call for and list of subscribers to the Brighton pavilion, 24 June 1818, MSPA Papers, C–XXXV–3; *Centennial Year*, pp. 65–67.

49. "Cattle Shows and Conventions, and Other Matters," *New England Magazine* 3 (November 1832): 411.

were now plowing matches, processions complete with fife, drum, clarinet, and cymbal accompaniment, and prayers and addresses.[50] And the formal dinners, complete with celebratory, often self-congratulatory toasts,[51] were also elaborate affairs. The bill of fare for one of these included boiled and roasted leg of mutton, roast beef, beef "a la mode," roast pig, ham, boiled and roasted chicken, boiled and roasted turkey, goose, duck, oyster sauce, cranberry sauces and jellies, pies, puddings, tarts, custards, melons, apples, pears, grapes, and peaches. To wash it all down, the dinner's organizers arranged for fifty-five bottles of Madeira for every hundred guests.[52] On another occasion, the MSPA was lucky enough to have the wine furnished free of charge. It seems that John B. Dabney, U.S. consul general in the Azores, had acknowledged his election to the MSPA by sending a quarter pipe of his best wine—what amounted to between 120 and 130 bottles worth—to be consumed at the next Brighton dinner.[53] Surely a good time was had by all.

The MSPA was convinced of its success. It felt certain that the Brighton show had stimulated a spirit of emulation, engendered a dramatic improvement in the quality of Massachusetts livestock, and spread knowledge and appreciation of agriculture.[54] But the fairs stirred up their share of controversy and resentment as well. Not everyone approved of all the MSPA did in Brighton.

In its early days, stated John Lowell in his cattle show address of 1827, the Brighton fair "was improperly viewed as the exhibition of the more opulent farmers, in which a plain cultivator stood a very humble chance."[55] Many a practical farmer did win MSPA premiums, but suspicion that the fair was somehow rigged nevertheless ran high. In 1818 the MSPA felt obliged to defend itself. "It may be of use," read the preface to that year's *Journal,* "and produce confidence in the decisions of the Trustees, to state, that in every branch in which any one of the Trustees was a competitor, there were two judges of great skill and irreproachable character chosen out of the board, and not one Trustee was permitted to sit even as a member, much

50. "Brighton Cattle Show," *American Farmer* 4 (18 October 1822): 250; "Rules and Regulations of the Cattle Show in Brighton, October 14, 1835," MSPA Papers, C–XXXIV–38; *Centennial Year,* pp. 62, 67.

51. For a sampling of toasts, see *Salem Gazette,* 13 October 1822, p. 1.

52. "Bill of fare for the dinner on the 18th of October instant (1833) at the cattle show & for the Massts Society for Promoting Agriculture," MSPA Papers, C–XXXIV–33.

53. John B. Dabney to John Lowell, 13 July 1819, MSPA Papers, A–XI–38.

54. See, for example, *MSPA Journal* 5 (January 1818–July 1819), preface to the volume, pp. i–ii, and John Lowell, Report of the committee on domestic animals, ibid. 6 (January 1821): 219–220.

55. "Address of the Hon. John Lowell . . . [1827]," p. 103.

100 ·  BETWEEN GENERATIONS

less to give a vote on any Committee appointed to decide on any class of articles, in which such Trustee was a competitor." As evidence of impartiality, the MSPA noted that as many trustees lost out on premiums as nontrustees, in proportion to their numbers.[56] In 1823 the MSPA went so far as to publish a list of the cash value of Brighton premiums broken down by town in order to "prove to our country friends, that although our *funds* are derived wholly from subscriptions in Boston and its immediate vicinity, yet a very trifling part of the premiums are awarded near our 'Head Quarters' but are diffused very generally through the state."[57]

The MSPA also wished to counter a specific allegation raised against the trustees—namely, that they had purchased prizewinning cattle before the show in order to carry off the premiums themselves. The trustees had bought the livestock in question, it was explained, but only out of the most laudable of motives. Evidently the previous owner was unwilling to drive the cattle all the way from Springfield to the fair at his own risk. And yet, in light of the fame of these oxen, the MSPA trustees desired that they somehow be exhibited, thereby handing Massachusetts the credit it deserved as a pasture state. Accordingly, "some generous publick-spirited gentlemen, out of the board, and a few within it, subscribed a sum to purchase the cattle in order that they might be exhibited at Brighton, and," it was added almost poignantly, "at a certain, inevitable, expected loss." So disinterested were these gentlemen that they insisted that the original owner accept the premium. "There has been, as was expected, a loss," the writer (probably John Lowell) concluded, "but the remuneration consists in having shewn to thousands of spectators, the finest animals *probably* at *that moment* in the world, the products of the rich pastures of Massachusetts."[58]

That final statement contained no small amount of calculation, for the characterization of homegrown oxen as the finest in the world touched on yet another sensitive issue. Just how to improve the livestock of Massachusetts was, as John Lowell freely admitted, "a subject of some delicacy and difficulty."[59] Was the answer careful breeding of native stock, or was it necessary to import animals from Europe? Proponents of native stock pointed to the celebrated Oakes cow of Danvers—four hundred pounds of butter a year and every inch American (fig. 23). Small wonder she took

56. *MSPA Journal* 5 (January 1818–July 1819), preface to the volume, p. iii. See also John Lowell, "Report of the Committee on Fat Oxen, Bulls, and Bull Calves," *American Farmer* 5 (7 November 1822): 257.
57. *NEF* 2 (15 November 1823): 126.
58. *MSPA Journal* 5 (January 1818–July 1819), preface to the volume, pp. iii–iv.
59. Lowell, "Mr. Lowell's Report," p. 12.

23. *Oakes's Prize Cow*. Portrait by Alvan Fisher. Reprinted from the *Massachusetts Agricultural Repository and Journal* 4 (January 1817). (Courtesy Yale University Library.)

twenty dollars for the best milk cow at the 1816 show.[60] Proponents of the latter view, by contrast, pointed to the numerous imported cattle, also judged as superior animals. "No man who ever saw Denton, Mr. Williams's bull," wrote Lowell of a celebrated imported Shorthorn, "—Fill Pail, Mr. Thorndike's, presented by him to the Agricultural Society—Coelebs, sent to our country by Mr. Coolidge—or Holderness, imported by Mr. Parsons, could entertain a doubt, that they were superior to any animals of the same description which we had ever seen." Native stock had their place, too, of course. The best of them were to be crossed with the foreign breeds.[61]

Not every gentleman farmer favored stock importation. Timothy Pickering, for example, saw nothing wrong with working with native breeds only.[62] But most of Boston's elite agriculturists seem to have agreed with Lowell on the importation issue, and furthermore, the controversy over

60. E. Hersey Derby, "Letter Respecting the Danvers Prize Cow," *MSPA Journal* 4 (January 1817): 254–55; "Abstract of the Records," p. 63.

61. 1822 Brighton committee report, "Abstract of the Records," pp. 77–78; Lowell, "Mr. Lowell's Report," pp. 10–13; Lemmer, "Spread of Improved Cattle," p. 82.

62. Timothy Pickering, "On Improving the Native Breed of New England Cattle," *NEF* 3 (15, 22, 29 April, 6 May 1825): 297–99, 305–6, 316–17, 321–22.

stock improvement seems to have run parallel to the one over rigged premiums. Indeed, it may well have boiled down to the same resentments and set of issues.

Of the premiums offered for livestock at the Brighton show, several were reserved for imported stock, and these premiums invariably carried with them the highest cash values. In 1819, for example, awards for imported cattle ranged from seventy-five to one hundred dollars; other livestock premiums were worth only ten to fifty dollars.[63] It would have been the rare yeoman indeed with the money and resources to import animals or even to purchase those imported by others. Gentleman farmers, then, received these premiums in disproportionate numbers. Even premiums without any such specification were often awarded to the progeny of imported animals crossed with native. Farmers complained that there was no sense in improving their native breeds when the crosses invariably beat them out for premiums. To this complaint, wrote John Lowell on behalf of the Brighton cattle committee, "we reply that though this is partially true, it is not entirely so, and what would the farmer have us to do on such an occasion? If, in fact, the full blooded or half blooded descendant of imported stock is superior, shall we refuse to admit it *so* to be? This would be indeed sacrificing the best interests of our country in relation to this object, as well as violating our solemn pledges, to gratify an improper national prejudice."[64]

Practical farmers probably had their own idea of just who was guilty of "an improper national prejudice." The whole question of foreign versus native stirred up feelings that had little to do with cattle, sheep, and pigs. Not long before, Boston's Federalist elite—a good portion of which sat on the Brighton committees—had been accused of dismissing native culture as inferior and slavishly admiring all that was British. That just such men should hail the Ayrshires while denigrating native breeds was tiresomely predictable. Not all the imported livestock were *British* breeds, of course, but that detail may have gotten lost in the emotion. The MSPA's encouragement of livestock importation, somewhat analagous to its concentration on exotic plants at the botanical garden, may have appeared not only snobbish but downright unpatriotic.

If all was not sweetness and light at the Brighton shows, they still represented a great success for the MSPA. For the first time the society was able to involve substantial numbers of practical farmers in its activities.

63. Brighton premiums for 1819, MSPA Papers, C–XXXIV–3.
64. John Lowell, "Report of the committee on all the larger horned cattle," 9 October 1822, *MSPA Journal* 7 (January 1823): 239.

And yet by as early as 1824, the eventual end of the shows was foretold. In that year fewer entered for premiums than in previous years. The problem was competition from livestock shows sponsored by the growing number of county agricultural societies. In 1827 the Brighton show was cut short to a single day. By 1830 the trustees were beginning to consider the idea of shows only every other year, or even every three, four, or *five* years. And in fact the Brighton show was held only sporadically in the next few years, closing for good in 1837. By 1844 the society had sold its Brighton property.[65]

In the decade following the War of 1812, the MSPA did pull itself out of the doldrums. The society could point to some real successes: a greatly increased membership, a regularly and frequently published journal, a cattle show that drew large crowds. Two things, however, did not change. One was the MSPA leaders' acknowledgment that practical farmers regarded their organization as useless and MSPA members as insincere and self-serving. The other was these same leaders' insistence on the utility of their enterprise and on disinterested benevolence as their only motive.

In what way, asked the practical farmers of Massachusetts, are your society, your efforts, your exhibitions of real use to us? "Are they not institutions of mere show, and parade," they accused, "calculated to place in a prominent view the immediate actors in them, as men professing a regard to the publick good, without affording any substantial benefit to the important art which you profess to encourage?"[66] In reply, the MSPA humbly admitted its failings while proudly pointing to the ways in which it had encouraged the improvement of agriculture. Above all, it reiterated its innocent and praiseworthy motives. The trustees "offer the best pledge of their devotion to the common cause of agriculture," read the society's journal of 1816–17. Their enthusiasm had no base motive; they felt "no other zeal than what would naturally arise in the breasts of men anxious to fulfil honourably a public trust."[67]

But the basic suspicion of the MSPA as little more than a public relations scheme, an elitist sham, lingered and underlay many of the specific complaints raised against the society. Farmers were leery, for example, of a state society whose trustees were all from the Boston area. "This is true," admitted the MSPA, "and how could it be otherwise? Of what value would a

65. "Abstract of the Records," pp. 87, 92–93, 98, 102; John Lowell to William Prescott, 7 February 1833, MSPA Papers, C–XXXIV–28; "Report of a Committee as to the Expediency of a Cattle Show, 3 August 1834," MSPA Papers, C–XXXV–49; *Centennial Year,* p. 67.

66. Lowell, "Address . . . 1818," p. 224. In his speech, Lowell raised "questions, which may be often secretly asked, though not avowed" (p. 225).

67. *MSPA Journal* 4 (January 1816–July 1817), preface to the volume, p. viii.

body of Trustees be, whose members lived at fifty or hundred and fifty miles asunder?" It would be impossible to convene, as was then the case, on a monthly basis. We have tried our best to reach all parts of the state, continued the defense, by urging the establishment of local societies. "If they are not extensive, and so active as we could wish, and as we most earnestly hope they will be, it is not our fault."[68]

Farmers also wondered what all those Boston high-livers were doing with all that MSPA money, and where it came from in the first place. Were they somehow putting up the cash for salaries or, worse yet, for expensive entertainments? Again, the MSPA was forced to respond to what must have been a humiliating accusation.

> Our funds, which are almost entirely the produce of private munificence of gentlemen in the capital, are exclusively devoted to the publick.
>
> Not one cent is employed in paying an officer, or in the expenses of the society at their meetings.
>
> The whole expense is borne by the members, and their whole efforts are directed by the great object of the institution.[69]

But obviously, these annoying charges kept reappearing. In 1823 John Lowell felt obliged to say the same thing all over again. "It will be found," he wrote, "that this whole [MSPA] fund was principally raised by donations from *opulent* men." It has increased over the years "by the disinterested conduct of the trustees who have never expended one cent for their own advantage or entertainment, but have husbanded the funds as if they were their own."[70]

In defending their society, MSPA members seemed both hurt and bewildered, as if they could not understand why practical farmers would not be grateful for all the MSPA was doing for them, much as they could not understand, in their capacities as Federalist leaders, why the Massachusetts population at large no longer recognized them as their natural leaders. In both roles, they regarded themselves as martyrs to the fickleness and foolishness of the common man, the unappreciated benefactors of the Commonwealth.[71] Their image of the world made no room for social conflict; as

68. Ibid., pp. vi–vii.
69. Ibid., p. vii.
70. John Lowell, "Editorial Remarks, by John Lowell, One of the Editors," *MSPA Journal* 7 (June 1823): 315.
71. For an example of this sense of ingratitude, see John Lowell to Timothy Pickering, 6 February 1816, Pickering Papers, 31:27, in which Lowell feels he can hope only for the "silent approbations of the wise and good"; Lowell to Caleb Cushing, 10 October 1823, Caleb

long as each group accepted its proper role in society, there could only be harmony among the classes, a complete solidarity of interest.[72] The proper role for members of the elite, of course, was that of disinterested benevolence and for those below them in the social scale, that of grateful deference. When practical farmers reacted to MSPA generosity with hostility, the society's members could only regard them as cruelly ungrateful.

Practical farmers were correct in pointing out just how important it was to MSPA members to assume a public stance of benevolence, or as Lowell paraphrased their taunts, "to place [themselves] in a prominent view . . . as men professing a regard to the public good."[73] The society seemed to avail itself of every possible opportunity to reaffirm its essential disinterestedness and patriotic beneficence. Even the distressing allegations that MSPA members were self-serving and insincere came in handy in this respect, since they provided a chance to praise wealthy members for their public-spirited donations, to recapitulate the patriotic efforts of the society, and, perhaps just as important, to assume a stance of wounded honor. The public expression of benevolence, as we saw in the previous chapter, was tremendously significant to the MSPA. Yet ironically it was in this period immediately after the War of 1812 that the private face of Boston's elite most nearly corresponded with the public face, at least in the matter of agricultural improvement. For a brief time, fifteen or so years, the state of Massachusetts farming became a vital concern to Boston's mercantile elite as both public *and* private men. Let us travel, then, from the bustle of the Brighton cattle show to the private world of the country estate.

Cushing Papers, Library of Congress, Washington, D.C.; and Lowell to John Skinner, 16 May 1824, Houghton Library.

72. James M. Banner, Jr., *To the Hartford Convention: The Federalists and the Origins of Party Politics in Massachusetts, 1789–1815* (New York: Alfred A. Knopf, 1970), pp. 10–12, 27–29, 53–54.

73. See note 66, above.

# *F O U R*

# Agricultural Reform and the Aging of New England

*I*N 1797 Harrison Gray Otis, the Federalist lawyer and statesman known for his dandyish habits and opulent style of living, rejected the idea of buying a "box in the country for a summer residence." In 1808–9, however, he purchased a twelve-acre estate in suburban Waltham, which he named Oakley (fig. 24). "It seems you have bought a villa," wrote John Rutledge, a former congressional colleague from South Carolina, to Otis in June 1809, "& are going to indulge in a little rural felicity. This I presume is the *Ton* at Boston, & Mrs. Otis & the President[1] are at the head of the fashionables. Getting this country seat was, I presume, quite 'en regle.'"[2]

Rutledge presumed correctly. In the 1790s the kind of estate living enjoyed by the likes of Ames and Cabot, Gore and Adams, Lyman and Barrell was a well-accepted choice for the wealthy and prominent, but it was not yet the dominant fashion. By the second decade of the nineteenth century, however, some form of rural pursuits seemed almost de rigueur for the elite. One Bostonian after another purchased a rural residence. Probably the most popular location for a country seat was the little town of Brookline, which quickly became, according to one Bostonian, a neighborhood of "tasteful pleasure-grounds . . . occupied by a cluster of refined and cultured families."[3] But not only Brookline felt the effects of the new

1. Otis was then president of the Massachusetts Senate.
2. Otis to Sally Foster Otis, quoted in Samuel Eliot Morison, *Harrison Gray Otis, 1765–1848: The Urbane Federalist* (Boston: Houghton Mifflin, 1969), p. 82; John Rutledge to Harrison Gray Otis, 6 June 1809, quoted in ibid., p. 200. Morison notes Otis's Waltham purchase on pp. 197, 200.
3. Thomas C. Amory, *Memoir of the Hon. Richard Sullivan* (Cambridge, Mass.: John Wilson and Son, 1885), p. 16. On Brookline's development as an elite community, see John

24. *Oakley, Seat of Harrison Gray Otis.* Sketch by J. R. Watson, 1816. (Courtesy Society for the Preservation of New England Antiquities.)

fashion for rural living. Elite Bostonians purchased summer estates or transformed ancestral farms in Braintree, Brighton, Cambridge, Charlestown, Dorchester, Medford, Roxbury, Waltham, and Watertown. Most of these men indulged in some sort of agricultural pastime, even if just the cultivation of orchards. Not all were sincerely interested in rural pursuits. On purchasing Oakley, Harrison Gray Otis found himself with property to landscape and a farm to run, neither task for which he had any great inclination. When in the summer of 1809 Otis requested his friend Rutledge to send him some seeds and plants for the Waltham garden, Rutledge could only shake his head at the Yankee's ignorance. "You are in the very horn book of Botany & Gardening," he wrote, "in supposing that Plants can be removed at this Season." By 1815 Otis was forced to turn to John Lowell for advice on renting and running his farm, and in 1825 he sold the estate for good.[4]

But for many, perhaps most, of Boston's new country dwellers, rural living and rural occupations represented a sincere commitment. Wrote one elite Bostonian of this era: "The principal merchants and other wealthy inhabitants of Boston had summer residences in the beautiful country

Gould Curtis, *History of the Town of Brookline Massachusetts* (Boston: Houghton Mifflin, 1933); Samuel Aspinwall Goddard, *Recollections of Brookline, Being an Account of the Houses, the Families, and the Roads, in Brookline, in the Years 1800 to 1810* (Birmingham, Eng.: E. C. Osborne, 1873); and Theodore F. Jones and Charles F. White, *Land Ownership in Brookline from the First Settlement* (Brookline, Mass.: Riverdale Press, 1923), esp. maps 5–8.
4. John Rutledge to Harrison Gray Otis, 6 June 1809, quoted in Morison, *Otis*, p. 200; John Lowell to Harrison Gray Otis, 20 September 1815, Harrison Gray Otis Papers, Massachusetts Historical Society (hereafter MHS), Boston; Morison, *Otis*, p. 201.

round the city. They realized how much could be accomplished by scientific study and experiment towards improving the breed of horses and cattle for the general benefit, and they were constantly zealous in introducing new flowers, fruits and vegetables, trees and shrubs."[5]

In the second and third decades of the nineteenth century, an increasing number of the mercantile elite thus saw fit to concern themselves with cow manure and peach tree blight. No doubt gentleman farming continued to fulfill the same function it had for an earlier generation of gentleman farmers, that of establishing a private identity. John Lowell, for example, wrote with great admiration, perhaps even envy, of George Lee, a wealthy English banker. "You must understand," he stressed to his son in 1817, "that he is a man of £250,000 who lives in the country on a great landed estate but who is so looked up to in this business, that nothing is done without him."[6] Not a bad model for the men of Boston's commercial elite.

But self-characterization was only part of the reason elite Bostonians of the post–1812 generation became gentleman farmers. For them, experimental farming was not just a private act but also a civic responsibility, for by the end of the war, agriculture, and specifically the allegedly backward state of agriculture in New England, had acquired political and social ramifications that a responsible elite could not ignore. Thus in this generation, we see not merely agricultural promotion, as the very name of the MSPA would call for, or even agricultural improvement, as the doctrine of disinterested benevolence would prescribe. Instead we see agricultural *reform*.

But first, to the reformers themselves.

John Lowell inherited the life of a gentleman farmer (fig. 25). His father was a founder and president of the MSPA and in 1785 purchased the Roxbury farm his son would inherit.[7] But Lowell's legacy was also thoroughly mercantile. He followed his father into commercial law, and from his admission to the bar in 1790 to his early retirement from practice in

---

5. Amory, *Sullivan,* p. 10. Amory was probably incorrect in including horses as among the concerns of this generation of agricultural reformers. Only after about 1830 did elite Bostonians take an interest in breeding horses.

6. John Lowell to John Amory Lowell, 11 August 1817, quoted in Ferris Greenslet, *The Lowells and Their Seven Worlds* (Boston: Houghton Mifflin, 1946), pp. 178–79.

7. See "Schedule of Property in the hands of J. Lowell—division of J. Lowell's estate (Judge) July 11 1803," Francis Cabot Lowell Papers (hereafter FCL Papers), box 3, folder 12, MHS.

25. *John Lowell (1769–1840)*. Portrait by Gilbert Stuart, c. 1824. (Courtesy Harvard University Portrait Collection. Gift of the Estate of Ralph Lowell, 1978.)

1803, Lowell made a substantial living—nine thousand dollars a year—representing the interests of Boston merchants.[8]

Just why he abruptly ended his legal career is uncertain. Lowell's minister attributed the retirement to the torment the lawyer experienced when a client Lowell believed innocent was found guilty of murder and executed. At one point in his life, Lowell pointed to his father's death and the "melancholy state of mind" it engendered as the cause of his premature retirement. But just one month later, Lowell wrote that he left the law because he had been "worn out by professional exertions."[9] For whatever reason, it seems likely that some sort of emotional collapse put Lowell on a vessel for England in October 1803. On shipboard, Lowell reported being "somewhat nervous." After a month in England, he wrote his brother: "We are all well except myself. I still have many of my old feelings about me occasionally but I hope I shall wear them away."[10]

Lowell spent three years traveling through England, France, Switzerland, and especially Italy, tracing the Grand Tour incumbent on Britain's true and would-be aristocrats. Lowell's approach to Europe had much in common with that of his British counterparts. For one, he treated the Grand Tour as something of a grand shopping spree, purchasing everything from galvanic batteries to statues to books to marble mantelpieces.[11] Lowell also took pains to see the recognized sights, the cultural resources and antiquities of the Continent, and he responded to them in a highly stylized manner, that is, in terms of precisely defined aesthetic categories—the Beautiful, the Picturesque, and the Sublime. Lowell's descriptions of Europe could have been transcribed verbatim from any Grand Tour diary.[12]

With one exception. When he described the bustle of a busy harbor Lowell broke from literary conventions and demonstrated a genuine, spontaneous aesthetic response. Here his voice rang true. "The sail up the

8. Greenslet, *Lowells,* pp. 88–89; John Lowell to Caleb Cushing, 3 October 1823, Caleb Cushing Papers, Library of Congress, Washington, D.C.

9. F. W. P. Greenwood, *A Sermon on the Death of John Lowell, LL.D., Delivered in King's Chapel, Boston, March 22, 1840* (Boston: Charles C. Little and James Brown, 1840), pp. 11–13; Greenslet, *Lowells,* pp. 95–111; John Lowell to Caleb Cushing, 3 October, 19 November 1823, Cushing Papers.

10. "Observations by J. Lowell Esq. on his passage to Europe 1803," 17 October 1803, FCL Papers, 3:14; John Lowell to Francis Cabot Lowell, 14 December 1803, FCL Papers, 3:14.

11. John Lowell to Francis Cabot Lowell, 16 March 1804, 16 January, 21 February, 15 May, 25 September 1805, FCL Papers, 4:3, 9, 10, 14, 5:3.

12. See, for example, John Lowell to Rebecca Lowell, 17 December 1804, FCL Papers, 4:8; [John Lowell], letter of 1 December 1804, *Monthly Anthology and Boston Review* 5 (May 1808): 243–47.

Thames is beautifull beyond description," he wrote his brother in March 1804. He described the ships packed nine deep along the banks, the many vessels plying the waterway, and those crowding the West India Docks (fig. 26). For Lowell the beauty of these docks lay in the commercial greatness they both represented and made possible. He rhapsodized over the "Immensity of this operation," the "scenery of the Ships lying so quietly & yet so conveniently afloat at the very door of the Stores," and the stores themselves, "strong and beautifull in their architecture," holding an "immense & inconceivable quantity of valuable goods." Until you have seen it, wrote the enthralled Bostonian, you can "have no conception of the beauty & grandeur of this Commercial River."[13]

Six months later, this time in Bordeaux, Lowell once more succumbed to the commercial sublime. "The circumstance which contributes most to the beauty of Bordeaux," he wrote his mother, "is the view of the Ships at anchor and passing up & down the river. As you walk along the finest Street in the town you see the hundreds of large vessells either at anchor, or in motion, & I know of no object more beautifull than this."[14]

The man had the soul of a merchant, yet when he returned to the United States in 1806, he did not return to the practice of commercial law. Already in 1805 he had envisioned a new kind of life for himself. "A little commerce," he wrote his brother from Paris, "a little agriculture, much gardening, and a devotion to science, are the objects which I have fondly, perhaps vainly, sketched out as future occupations." Back on his "little fèrme ornèe [*sic*], the solace of my fathers latter days, & the best consolation of my own," Lowell found "what nothing else could give, quiet & health."[15]

On Bromley Vale, as he named the estate, Lowell experimented with such novel crops as sea kale and sweet potatoes,[16] but he was most active as a horticulturist. Through his many contacts all over the world, Lowell received seeds, scions, and cuttings.[17] One of a few American honorary

13. John Lowell to Francis Cabot Lowell, 29 March 1804, FCL Papers, 4:3.
14. John Lowell to Rebecca Lowell, 22 September 1804, FCL Papers, 4:6.
15. Lowell, quoted in Greenwood, *Sermon,* p. 32; John Lowell to Joseph Story, 9 July 1827, Miscellaneous Manuscripts, MHS.
16. John Lowell, "On the Use and Culture of Sea Kale," *Massachusetts Agricultural Repository and Journal* (hereafter *MSPA Journal*) 3 (January 1815): 246–48; John Lowell, "The Carolina Potato, or Sweet Potato," ibid. 7 (June 1823): 381–83.
17. See, for example, John Lowell to Francis Cabot Lowell, 22 March 1816, FCL Papers, 8:11, in which he reports the arrival from Le Havre of six bundles of fruit trees he had ordered seven years earlier, before "our amiable system of Embargoes, & war," and John Lowell to John Skinner, 16 May 1824, Houghton Library, Harvard University, Cambridge, Mass., in which he sends a noted agricultural editor some melon seed received from Spain. "I know

26. *West India Docks*. Aquatint by J. Bluck, after A. Pugin and T. Rowlandson, 1810. (Courtesy Yale Center for British Art, Gift of Chauncey Brewster Tinker.)

members of the Horticultural Society of London, Lowell initiated a correspondence with that society's president, Thomas Andrew Knight, and was soon the grateful recipient of several boxes of fruit trees from England. These took root at Bromley Vale, and Lowell's orchards soon parented the gardens of other gentleman farmers.[18] As Boston's resident expert, Lowell received and responded generously to the many requests for horticultural materials and advice that came his way.[19]

Of the fourteen acres he owned in Roxbury, just one was cultivated as a

nothing of them," he wrote Skinner, "except that they were packed & sent at great expence, via New York & that Spain is preeminently the country for melons, which with her other natural productions, are about the only good things she can at present boast."

18. John Lowell, "Some Notice of Thomas Andrew Knight, Esq. President of the Horticultural Society of London. His Experiments and Present to This Society," *MSPA Journal* 7 (June 1823): 331–42; "Another Present from Mr. Knight to the Horticulturists," ibid. 8 (June 1825): 344–46; John Lowell, "New Presents of Fruits to the Citizens of the United States, by Tho. A. Knight, Esq.," ibid. 10 (June 1828): 205–8.

19. See, for example, John Lowell to George Carter, 8 July 1826, Miscellaneous Manuscripts, MHS, in which Lowell responds to the Virginian's request for sea kale seeds; John

garden, in addition to a greenhouse. He employed a year-round gardener, a farm laborer seven months of the year, and an extra hand to help out with the month's worth of planting and haying. "It is impossible that there can exist more steady and laborious men than mine," he boasted to Harrison Gray Otis in 1815. "They work on average 14 hours per day & they are the quickest men I ever saw." His labor costs totaled six hundred fifty dollars per year.[20]

As was the usual Boston practice, Lowell spent the coldest months of the year at his city residence, but from spring through autumn he was always in his garden at Bromley Vale, and even in winter he frequently visited his greenhouse. "Nothing but a tempest or a fit of illness could keep him away,"[21] wrote Lowell's minister, F. W. P. Greenwood. "To see him, and hear him converse, in his farm or his garden, one would suppose that all his occupation was farming and gardening. He would discuss the qualities of a fruit-tree or an exotic plant with the same earnestness, and the same copiousness, and the same ready and various learning, that he would have given to a question of politics, a point of law, or a case of divinity."[22]

Yet we must not forget that Lowell led a double life. Lowell must be remembered as the man who composed both "Raw Potatoes Bad for Milch Cows" and *Mr. Madison's War*.[23] Lowell was both the gentleman farmer par excellence and a strident defender of the interests of the Boston mercantile elite. Even as he championed the yeomanry of Massachusetts, Lowell— whether blasting the Jeffersonian policies of embargo and war, upholding the rights of Unitarian pewholders, or protecting the Harvard College Fellows—demonstrated his allegiance to the commercial elite.[24] In this

Lowell to Henry A. S. Dearborn, 2 April 1829, Houghton Library, in which Lowell forwards the names of eminent European horticulturists at Dearborn's request; and William Ellery Channing to John Lowell, 1 May 1832, Autograph File, Houghton Library, in which the celebrated Unitarian divine requests information on the best types of fruit trees and the nurseries at which they can be obtained. Channing felt at liberty to make the request in light of Lowell's known "disposition to afford every aid in this particular to your friends."

20. Lowell to Otis, 20 September 1815; John Lowell, "On the Change, or Supposed Change in the Character of Fruits," *MSPA Journal* 9 (July 1826): 132–33; *Magazine of Horticulture, Botany, and All Useful Discoveries, and Improvements in Rural Affairs* 3 (January 1837): 27–28.

21. Greenwood, *Sermon*, p. 33.

22. Ibid., p. 22.

23. John Lowell, "Raw Potatoes Bad for Milch Cows," *MSPA Journal* 10 (June 1828): 154–56; [John Lowell], *Mr. Madison's War. A Dispassionate Inquiry into the Reasons Alleged by Mr. Madison for Declaring an Offensive and Ruinous War against Great-Britain. . . . By a New-England Farmer* (Boston: Russell and Cutler, 1812).

24. For Lowell's views on the Unitarian controversy, see [John Lowell], *An Inquiry into the Right to Change the Ecclesiastical Constitution of the Congregational Churches of Massachusetts* (Boston: Wells and Lilly, 1816). On the issue of the Harvard Fellows, see Lowell,

manner, Lowell typified the gentleman farmers of his generation. These were all men who, though passionately devoted to mangel-wurzel and Alderney cattle, were unmistakably mercantile in their allegiance, politics, values, and very outlook on life.

Probably second only to Lowell in commitment to the agricultural society was Josiah Quincy (fig. 27). Quincy served as an MSPA trustee from 1805 to 1826, in addition to publishing numerous communications in the society's journal and sitting on many Brighton committees over the years.[25] Quincy had been elected to Congress in 1804, and there until his resignation at the outbreak of the War of 1812 he was one of the most outspoken New England Federalists. He represented his mercantile constituency with vigor, speaking out against what he saw as threats to the New England way of life—Virginia and the slave system in general, the growing West, and war with Britain.[26] But from his resignation until his election as mayor of Boston in 1823, Quincy had nothing to do. He might have returned to his original occupation, law, but preferred instead to take up the life of a gentleman farmer on his ancestral acres.[27]

Quincy had spent summers on his 170-acre Braintree farm even before he resigned from Congress.[28] In 1811 he confessed to being "wholly occupied with thoughts of agriculture" and to finding in it both intellectual stimulation and adequate occupation. "Rosebugs and caterpillars and slugworms," he wrote his "agricultural patron" Timothy Pickering, "give me amply scope for the exercise of my philosophy as well as industry."[29] It was only in 1814, however, that Quincy took up farming in earnest, assuming management of the dairy farm from his tenant, the "faithful and intelligent"

---

*Remarks on a Pamphlet Printed by the Professors and Tutors of Harvard University, Touching Their Right to the Exclusive Government of That Seminary* (Boston: Wells and Lilly, 1824).

25. For Quincy as for other gentleman farmers discussed in this chapter, information on service as an MSPA trustee and/or official and on Brighton committees has been gleaned from the following sources: "Abstract of the Records, from 1792 to 1858," in *Transactions of the Massachusetts Society for Promoting Agriculture*, n.s., 1 (1858), pp. 5–153; *Centennial Year (1792–1892) of the Massachusetts Society for Promoting Agriculture* (Salem, Mass.: n.p., n.d.); *MSPA Journal* 4–10 (1816–32). See also Edmund Quincy, *Life of Josiah Quincy of Massachusetts* (Boston: Ticknor and Fields, 1868), pp. 265–66.

26. Robert A. McCaughey, *Josiah Quincy, 1772–1864: The Last Federalist* (Cambridge: Harvard University Press, 1974), pp. 20–76.

27. Ibid., pp. 77–113. On the Quincy homestead, see Elizabeth Redmond, "Colonel Josiah Quincy House, Wollaston, Massachusetts," *Antiques* 129 (March 1986): 632–34.

28. Quincy, *Josiah Quincy*, pp. 107, 137, 194, 205, 261; Josiah Quincy, "On the American Hedge Thorn," *MSPA Journal* 3 (November 1813): 27; Quincy to Timothy Pickering, 20 June 1811, Quincy Papers, reel 36, frames 584, 585–56, MHS.

29. Josiah Quincy to Timothy Pickering, 20 June 1811, Quincy Papers, 36:584, 585.

27. *Josiah Quincy.* Portrait by Gilbert Stuart, c. 1824. (Courtesy Museum of Fine Arts, Boston. Gift of Eliza Susan Quincy.)

Alpheus Cary of Braintree, to conduct experiments with various types of cattle feed and feeding techniques.[30]

Like Lowell and Quincy, Richard Sullivan was a Harvard graduate and a successful lawyer who ended up as a full-time gentleman farmer. Sullivan was able to quit his profession when in 1804 he married Sarah Russell, the daughter of the fabulously wealthy merchant (and the MSPA's first president) Thomas Russell. Since his wife had inherited a large fortune, Sullivan was, in the words of his biographer, "quite willing to leave the honors and opportunities of professional life to those that needed them more, content to perform his share of the world's work without compensation."[31] The first such global responsibility he assumed was a three-year sojourn in Europe, similar to Lowell's Grand Tour.[32]

On the Sullivans' return to Boston in 1808, the family moved into a town house, but in about 1810, Sullivan purchased an eleven-acre estate in fashionable Brookline. In his funeral eulogy of 1861, Sullivan was praised as "among the first of those, who, nearly half a century ago, gave an impulse to rural tastes and pursuits."[33] He busied himself with farming and gardening, devoting special attention to hothouse plants. Sullivan served the society faithfully as its recording secretary (1811–22), corresponding secretary (1823–27, 1830–35), trustee (1828–29), and perpetual chairman of the Brighton committee on manufactures.[34]

Peter Chardon Brooks also attempted early retirement to a suburban estate. By age thirty-six, in 1803, Brooks had accumulated such a fortune in the business of marine insurance that he was able to trade the life of a merchant for that of a gentleman farmer on the paternal farm in Medford. He increased the size of the farm by purchasing contiguous acreage, planted thousands of trees, superintended agricultural operations, and in 1804 replaced the modest cottage in which he had been raised with a substantial residence appropriate to a man of his wealth and standing.[35]

30. McCaughey, *Quincy*, p. 86; Quincy, "American Hedge Thorn," p. 27; Quincy, "Remarks on Soiling," *MSPA Journal* 6 (July 1820): 113–25.

31. Amory, *Sullivan*, p. 11.

32. For biographical details on Sullivan, see Amory, *Sullivan*, and S. K. Lothrop, *Firmness and Gentleness United in the Christian Character: A Sermon Preached in the Brattle-Square Church, Dec. 15 1861, the Sunday Succeeding the Death of Hon. Richard Sullivan* (Boston: John Wilson and Son, 1862).

33. Lothrop, *Sullivan*, p. 17.

34. Goddard, *Brookline*, p. 10; Jones and White, *Brookline*, p. 32 and map 6; Amory, *Sullivan*, p. 16.

35. Edward Everett, "Peter Chardon Brooks," in Freeman Hunt, ed., *Lives of American Merchants*, 2 vols. (New York: Office of Hunt's Merchants' Magazine, 1856; Derby and Jackson, 1858), 1:161–62; Scott Paradise, "Some Memories of an Old House," *Medford*

Brooks was not long content with this life of gentlemanly retirement and rural occupation. By 1806 he was back in the business world as president of the New England Marine Insurance Company, accumulating an ever-larger fortune, and in the political world as a Federalist state senator. Brooks did not abandon his agricultural interests, however. His service to the MSPA as trustee and vice president extended from 1809 to 1845, and when he retired a second time, it was once again to the Medford estate. There he carried on diverse farming operations, though his greatest interest was in stock importation and breeding.[36] "He found in these rural pursuits," wrote Edward Everett in a memoir, "not merely rational amusement, but great benefit to his health, and at the same time afforded to the neighborhood an example of well-conducted husbandry."[37]

Most gentleman farmers, however, were not retired from the world of affairs. Gorham Parsons remained active as a merchant in Boston even as he oversaw agricultural operations on his estate in Brighton, Oakland. In the early part of the century, an English traveler described Oakland as a *"ferme ornée"* that, though not identical to the most famous British example of that style, Leasowes, was nevertheless of the same general character.[38] Nevertheless, this was a working farm, run day to day by a year-round foreman and a combination dairy maid-laundress-seamstress-cook.[39] Here Parsons experimented with grain and root crops, cultivated apple and pear orchards, and bred the highest quality cattle, sheep, swine, and even cashmere goats from imported livestock. It was this last field of endeavor that was Parson's forte. His Alderney bull, Holderness, was the talk of the Brighton shows, and it, along with Parsons's other prize cattle and his merino sheep, won several premiums. In all his agricultural undertakings, Parsons hoped to benefit his fellow farmers, gentleman and otherwise, as well. He contributed the results of his farming operations and experiments to the MSPA journal, held a public demonstration of a new plow, and made available the stud services of his famous Alderney to the farmers of Essex county. And he devoted a good deal of time to the MSPA, as a trustee from

---

*Historical Register* 31 (March 1928): 9–14; *Dictionary of American Biography* (hereafter *DAB*), s.v. "Brooks, Peter Chardon."

36. Everett, "Brooks," pp. 164–72, 177; *DAB*, "Brooks"; Brooks to Richard Sullivan, 26 November 1814, Massachusetts Society for Promoting Agriculture Papers (hereafter MSPA Papers), drawer D, folder I, number 6, MHS; Brooks to B. Guild, 10 April 1840, MSPA Papers, C–XXIII–30; Brooks to MSPA, 25 August 1845, MSPA Papers, A–XI–21.

37. Everett, "Brooks," p. 161.

38. Edward Augustus Kendall, *Travels through the Northern Parts of the United States, in the Years 1807 and 1808,* 3 vols. (New York: I. Riley, 1809), 3:10.

39. Parsons to B. Guild, 1 March 1831, MSPA Papers, D–I–43.

1811 to 1822, and then, until 1833, as recording secretary, and as a member of various cattle show committees.[40]

By 1835, however, illness had severely restricted Parsons's ability to continue as a gentleman farmer. "Notwithstanding I retain all my attachment to Agriculture," he wrote to Benjamin Guild, the MSPA's assistant recording secretary, "I am oblig'd to feel and have felt for more than a year past, that the greatest pleasure which attaches to the business I am depriv'd of, that is personal attention." This, he explained further, "is a deprivation occasion'd by so much pain and long suffering that I sometimes feel quite discourag'd." At this point Parsons seriously considered selling his Brighton farm, as he had already done the previous fall with a second property, Fatherland Farm in Byfield. Though a "sincere friend to temperance," Parsons felt desperate enough to try opium. "I get no sleep" without it, he wrote Guild, " . . . and sometimes experience a sort of struggle between pain and torpor." He died in 1844.[41]

Also in Brighton, also an active merchant, and also an avid gentleman farmer and MSPA official was Samuel W. Pomeroy. Kendall, the English traveler who praised Parsons's estate, regarded Pomeroy's as finer than that of his Brighton neighbor and even those of Christopher Gore and Theodore Lyman.[42] Pomeroy pursued varied agricultural activities and concerns. He experimented with curing clover with salt, cultivating flax, and breeding livestock. He won Brighton premiums for a milk cow and a sow, standard accomplishments for Boston's gentleman farmers, but also for currant wine.[43]

40. On Parsons's agricultural activities, see Parsons, "Experiments of Raising Wheat, Barley, &c., with Remarks," *MSPA Journal* 3 (January 1815): 271–73; Parsons, "On the Comparative Advantage of Raising Carrots on Ridges and in Beds," ibid. 3 (January 1815): 273; Parsons, "Product in Meat, Tallow, and Wool, of a Merino Wether," ibid. 4 (June 1816): 160–61; Parsons, "Field Culture of Wheat, Rye, Corn, &c.," ibid. 4 (January 1817): 267–70; Parsons to Aaron Dexter, 7 May 1817, "Result of an Experiment with Johnson's Apparatus," ibid. 4 (July 1817): 315–16; *American Farmer* 2 (19 January 1820): 341; Parsons to B. Guild, 4 January 1825, 1 March 1831, MSPA Papers, C–XXXV–26, D–I–43; "Account of Premiums Paid for the Exhibitions of 13 & 14 Oct 1817 at Brighton," MSPA Papers, C–XXXIV–1; "Premiums Awarded at the Brighton Cattle Show 13 & 14 Oct 1818," MSPA Papers, C–XXXIV–2; Brighton premiums for 1819, MSPA Papers, C–XXXIV–3; Parsons to Timothy Pickering, 31 October, 8 November 1825, 23 August 1826, 26 August 1828, Timothy Pickering Papers, reel 45, frames 335, 338, 353, 354, and reel 23, frame 386, MHS. See also the many references to agricultural operations scattered throughout Parsons's correspondence with his nephew Winthrop Sargent in the Parsons-Sargent Papers, MHS, especially in the years 1825–28.

41. Parsons to B. Guild, 7 February 1835, MSPA Papers, C–XXXV–45.

42. Kendall, *Travels,* 3:10–11.

43. *Papers on Agriculture; Consisting of Communications Made to the Massachusetts Society for Promoting Agriculture* (Boston: Young and Minns, 1804) (hereafter *MSPA Papers,*

Probably because of the traditional commercial rivalry between Boston and Salem—and the consequent political split that rivalry engendered—gentleman farmers from Salem's merchant families played a less active role in the MSPA than might be expected. But there were exceptions. In Salem was the 110-acre farm and garden of Ezekiel Hersey Derby (fig. 28), son of the famous East India merchant Elias Hasket Derby, from whom he had inherited an interest in agricultural and horticultural experimentation. (See the entry on Derby in the Appendix.) Farming was a lifelong pursuit for the younger Derby. In 1850 a writer for an agricultural periodical "found him still active, personally superintending his extensive farming operations, and earnestly awake to every practical improvement."[44] At that date he had been a member and sometime trustee of the MSPA for over fifty-seven years.[45]

These men were only a few of the many gentleman farmers of the generation active after the War of 1812. Most were merchants, the rest, the type of Boston lawyer-statesman whose allegiance belonged to the mercantile elite. As men of the commercial elite, however, gentleman farmers were open to the hostility and suspicion of the state's agricultural population. Practical farmers ridiculed them, stigmatizing them as "theoretical" or "book" farmers, "making manure, and breeding cattle in their libraries."[46] In response, gentleman farmers sought to establish the direct usefulness of both commerce and commercial men to agriculture. Just as only commerce can bring polish—fine manners, appreciation of the arts, progress in the sciences—to a virtuous but crude agrarian society, so too is commerce the key to bringing agriculture out of a primitive state. If we look at those European countries with the most advanced agriculture, noted Richard Sullivan, we will find that it was "commerce which nurtured it, and finally gave to it all its refinement."[47]

---

*Communications, 1804*), pp. 107–10; Pomeroy, "Essays on Flax Husbandry," *MSPA Journal* 6 (July 1821): 309–31; Pomeroy, "On Dairy Stock," ibid. 6 (January 1820): 87–90; "Premiums Awarded . . . 1818"; Brighton premiums for 1824, 1826, MSPA Papers, C–XXXIV, 6–7, 8.

44. "Notes on Massachusetts Farming," *The Cultivator,* n.s., 7 (January 1850): 40.

45. *MSPA Papers, Communications, 1804,* p. 110; *New England Farmer* 1 (10 August 1822): 15; Derby to Timothy Pickering, 24 March 1825, Pickering Papers, 45:320; John Welles, "Report of the Committee on Live Hedges," 30 January 1833, MSPA Papers, D–XI–62; "Notes on Massachusetts Farming," p. 40; Nina Fletcher Little, "Cornè, McIntire, and the Hersey Derby Farm," *Antiques* 101 (January 1972): 226–29.

46. "Editorial Remarks, by John Lowell, One of the Editors," *MSPA Journal* 7 (June 1823): 313.

47. Richard Sullivan, "An Address Delivered before the Massachusetts Agricultural Society at the Brighton Cattle Show, October 17, 1820," *MSPA Journal* 6 (January 1821): 212.

28. *The Farm of Ezekiel Hersey Derby.* Oil painting by Michel Felice Cornè, c. 1800. (Private collection.)

A corollary of this view was that gentleman farmers could take credit for most of the improvements made in the field of agriculture. Lowell drew up a list: the introduction of new types of crops, the improvement of horse, cattle, and sheep breeds, progress in the design of farm implements, and innovations in farm management.[48] An issue from 1817 of the MSPA's journal applauded the efforts of gentleman farmers: "Some illustrious instances there are of men, in the community, who while extensively engaged in commerce, and still in the meridian of life, have directed an ample portion of their fortunes into the channels of agriculture, and have afforded, in many things, a valuable example to the plain farmer, and a noble and important patronage to this class."[49]

48. John Lowell, "An Address Delivered before the Massachusetts Agricultural Society at the Brighton Cattle Show, October 13, 1818," *MSPA Journal* 5 (January 1819): 227–35; "Editorial Remarks, by John Lowell," pp. 316–19.

49. Prefatory remarks, "Sketch of the Character of William West, a Distinguished Farmer of Pennsylvania," *MSPA Journal* 4 (July 1817): 385–86.

There was even the suggestion that merchants were of greatest help to the farmer not through any direct aid to agriculture but by the respectability they lent to the husbandman's occupation through their mere association with agricultural societies and gentleman farming. "The diffusion of knowledge, and the reward of successful enterprize, are not the chief benefits of this Association," stated Oliver Fiske of the MSPA. "The personal respectability and influence of its founders, and the members who now compose it, have raised this degraded calling to its legitimate standing." One writer to the *New England Farmer,* who represented himself as a common yeoman, expressed his gratitude to gentleman farmers for "placing themselves, as it were, among us," thereby "making the calling of the farmer so respectable." (We may wonder whether this was truly a practical farmer who deferentially added "Bless you, Sir!")[50]

Nevertheless, though commerce and commercial men might be defended and even praised, the essentially agricultural nature of the Republic could not be questioned. Hence we see the same men who championed commerce as a positive force in society even giving it credit for agricultural progress, insisting that merchants were, in the words of John Lowell, *"mere brokers of agriculture."* "A single shower of rain," continued Lowell poetically, ". . . is of more actual value and profit to a nation than the gains of all its exterior commerce for a year."[51] Furthermore, though men of commerce might be individually worthy, they did not come by their moral sturdiness as farmers did, merely by virtue of their membership in a particular class. The yeoman retained his position as pillar of the Republic.[52] If the argument that commerce advances a nation forward into refinement suggested change over time, the argument that commerce was a mere subsidiary to agriculture left the vision of a static agricultural society essentially intact. Room had been made for merchants, but agriculture as the economic and moral basis of the Republic still determined the basic character of the nation. At least on the abstract level on which they discussed the nature of their own society, then, Boston's agricultural reformers

50. Oliver Fiske, Address to the Worcester Agricultural Society, in *New England Farmer* 2 (6 December 1823): 146; ibid. 8 (20 November 1829): 137–38. See also Gardner B. Perry, Address to the Essex Agricultural Society, in *Genesee Farmer* 3 (13 July 1833): 223.

51. Lowell, "Address," pp. 222, 223. See also Josiah Quincy, "An Address Delivered before the Massachusetts Agricultural Society, at the Brighton Cattle Show, October 12th, 1819," *MSPA Journal* 6 (January 1820): 2, and Sullivan, "Address," pp. 210–11.

52. For an overview of this rhetoric as it characterized agricultural reform in the northeastern states, see Donald B. Marti, "In Praise of Farming: An Aspect of the Movement for Agricultural Improvement in the Northeast, 1815–1840," *New York History* 51 (July 1970): 351–75.

did not develop an unambiguously dynamic vision of social and economic change. But if we look further to the program of reform they put forth with increasing vigor after the War of 1812, the picture changes.

Having established the yeomanry as the economic foundation and moral strength of Massachusetts, Josiah Quincy continued: "I am thus distinct, in declaring my sentiment concerning the importance and value of this class of men . . . because being about to hint concerning errors and defects in our agriculture, I am anxious that such a course of remark should not be attributed to any want of honour, or respect, for the farming interest." Quincy then proceeded to "hint" that the farmer is "ignorant of the A B C of his art," "careless and deficient," and "wasteful, absurd, and impoverishing." He took farmers to task for everything from allowing pigs to roam the parlor to letting manure wash away in the rain.[53] One after another, Boston's agricultural reformers criticized farmers for their lack of skill, knowledge, and enterprise. The merchant, mechanic, and navigator all improve their knowledge and their fortunes, noted "A Middlesex Farmer" in 1818. "And shall the farmer alone be stationary?" he asked. "Shall agriculture, the surest foundation of the wealth and happiness of nations, be so degraded—be the only calling *in our country,* that does not improve our wealth and knowledge as a people?"[54] Reformers agreed that the United States was far behind Europe, especially Great Britain, in its agriculture, and that the northern states were the most backward of all.[55]

Agricultural reformers may well have gotten a measure of satisfaction in so roundly condemning Massachusetts farmers; as gentleman farmers, they had taken their share of abuse from the yeomanry. And these diatribes certainly partook of the traditional image of the farmer as ignorant clodhopper. But these attacks represented far more than sour grapes and elitist stereotyping. They must be placed against a background of rural depopulation in the Commonwealth. Squeezed by population pressures, forced to work ever smaller, more marginal, and more costly plots of land, Massachusetts farmers left in droves for the rich lands of the great, empty West. The result: Massachusetts grew only slowly, losing ground to other rapidly

53. Quincy, "Address," pp. 2, 5, 6.
54. "A Middlesex Farmer," "On Reclaiming Low or Meadow Land," *MSPA Journal* 5 (July 1818): 127.
55. H. A. S. Dearborn to John Lowell, 25 January 1817, *MSPA Journal* 4 (January 1817): 290; [John Lowell], "Analysis or Examination of the present state of Agriculture in Massachusetts, so far as the same can be ascertained by the answers of several highly respectable Gentlemen, in various parts of the State," ibid., pp. 283–84; Lowell, "Some Notice of Thomas Andrew Knight," p. 332; Sullivan, "Address," pp. 204–5; [William Tudor], "General Humphreys' Discourse on the Agriculture of Connecticut," *North American Review* (hereafter *NAR*) 4 (November 1816): 98–99.

growing states in population rank. In 1790 the number of people living in Massachusetts, even excluding the District of Maine, was still greater than the number living in New York; thirty years later, with its upstate agricultural region booming, New York had more than two and a half times the population of its Yankee neighbor.[56] Our state has "been a hive swarming for the benefit of other regions," complained John Lowell in 1819. "Other states have been replenished by its vigour, while our own has augmented in a ratio so small, compared with the wonderful increase of other states, that it can be considered now, for half a century, scarcely more than stationary."[57] In criticizing Massachusetts farmers as backward, Boston's agricultural reformers sought to prove that emigration was unnecessary. There was nothing inherently unprofitable about farming in New England, they insisted. If only farmers farmed the right way, they could make a good living right at home. "Were the modern improvements . . . allowed to spread themselves over the face of our country, and to fertilize our fields," stated Richard Sullivan at the Brighton cattle show of 1820, "much of the emigration would cease."[58]

It is instructive to note that elite Bostonians were not the only agricultural reformers concerned with the phenomena of agricultural decline and emigration to the West. In 1810, for example, John Taylor of Caroline took up the same issues in his *Arator,* though predictably his analysis was almost a mirror image of that offered by his Boston counterparts. "The effects of yoking agriculture to armies, navies, paper frauds, treasury frauds, and protecting duty frauds," he wrote in true Country party rhetoric, " . . . are visibly an increase of emigration, a decrease in the fertility of land, sales of landed estates, a decay and impoverishment both in mind and fortune of the landed gentry, and an exchange of that honest, virtuous, patriotic and bold class of men, for an order of stock-jobbers in loans, banks, manufactories, contracts, rivers, roads, houses, ships, lotteries, and an infinite number of inferior tricks to get money, calculated to instil opposite principles." Boston

56. On the consequences of population pressures for New England society, see, for example, Kenneth Lockridge, "Land, Population and the Evolution of New England Society, 1630–1790," *Past and Present* 39 (April 1968): 62–80, and Hal S. Barron, *Those Who Stayed Behind: Rural Society in Nineteenth-Century New England* (Cambridge: Cambridge University Press, 1984). On Massachusetts's declining rank in population, see James M. Banner, Jr., *To the Hartford Convention: The Federalists and the Origins of Party Politics in Massachusetts* (New York: Alfred A. Knopf, 1969), pp. 4–15. The Massachusetts and New York population figures are from the U.S. Bureau of the Census, *A Century of Population Growth from the First Census of the United States to the Twelfth, 1790–1900* (Washington, D.C.: Government Printing Office, 1909), p. 57.

57. [John Lowell], "Remarks on the Agriculture of Massachusetts," *MSPA Journal* 5 (July 1819): 318. This article is attributed to Lowell in "Abstract of the Records," p. 70.

58. Sullivan, "Address," p. 216.

reformers, of course, looked to the leadership of just such "inferior trick-sters" (themselves in fact!) to solve the problems of agricultural decline and rural depopulation.[59]

Further north, the Philadelphia Society for Promoting Agriculture, an organization similar in social profile, goals, and strategies to the MSPA, also addressed these problems, but here again with a critical difference. Simply stated, Philadelphians betrayed nowhere near the anxiety displayed by Bostonians over rural depopulation. Although they admitted occasional concern over "unnecessary emigration" and hoped to forestall it with improved agricultural techniques applied to worn-out land, they also expressed tremendous optimism for America on the basis of their nation's amazing geographic expansion. So confident did they seem to be that westward settlement was ultimately beneficial—to them, one must add—they actually offered a premium for the best "mode of clearing and cultivating new settlements, in an unseated, and theretofore uninhabited part of this state, *or one in its neighbourhood* (emphasis added)."[60] Unlike Boston, Philadelphia processed and exported huge amounts of grain from its hinterland; evidently, in the context of a state and national program of internal improvements, its merchants looked forward to dealing with ever-more distant suppliers. But, as we shall see, if a premium encouraging out-of-state migration would have been unthinkable to the MSPA, it was not only because agriculture in Massachusetts did not serve the same economic function for Boston's merchants as it did for those in Philadelphia. Another issue was at work.

If the yeoman was the guarantor of public virtue, Boston's agricultural reformers had every right to be concerned over his emigration; every farmer who crossed the state line represented that much virtue lost to the Commonwealth. But these were men used to assuming the moral superiority of New England and to attributing that superiority at least as much to the region's mercantile class as to its farming population.[61] As the Federal-

59. *Arator, Being a Series of Agricultural Essays, Practical and Political,* 6th ed. (Petersburg, Va.: Whitworth and Yancey, 1818), pp. 31–32. *Arator* was originally published as a series of newspaper essays in 1810.

60. *Memoirs of the Philadelphia Society for Promoting Agriculture* 1 (Philadelphia: Jane Aitken, 1808), p. xlii; ibid. 4 (Philadelphia: Benjamin Warner, 1818), pp. i–iii; Richard Peters, "A Discourse on Agriculture," in ibid., pp. xxi–xxiii. Closer in spirit to agricultural reformers in Massachusetts were those in Connecticut, as described in Richard J. Purcell, *Connecticut in Transition: 1775–1818* (1918; Middletown, Conn.: Wesleyan University Press, 1963), pp. 91–112.

61. Banner, *Hartford Convention,* pp. 84–89; Linda K. Kerber, *Federalists in Dissent: Imagery and Ideology in Jeffersonian America* (Ithaca, N.Y.: Cornell University Press, 1970), pp. 23–66.

ist agricultural reformers saw it, the problem was hardly that Massachusetts was losing its superior moral position but that it was losing what was surely a rightful extension, a logical concomitant of that superiority, namely, the right to enforce its moral will on the rest of the nation. The election of 1800, the embargo of 1807, the War of 1812—all were humiliating proofs of the Commonwealth's inability to shape national policy. If these same Federalists fretted over emigration, then, it was because their state's declining rank in population meant a declining rank in the size of its congressional delegation and hence in the extent of its political power and the prestige it represented and engendered.[62] Such men would hardly contemplate, as their Philadelphia counterparts did, actually rewarding farmers for leaving the state.

The agricultural reformers' program of improvement in a sense looked to the past. An improved agriculture would insure a healthy population increase, thereby regaining for Massachusetts the standing it had once enjoyed. But far more striking about the reform program is the degree to which it acknowledged the massive social and economic changes New England was then undergoing. Its basic message to the farmer was: "Massachusetts is changing. You must change with it."

The reform program consisted largely of British agricultural practices and innovations, including new crop rotations, deep plowing, marshland reclamation, systematic livestock breeding, the use of manure, gypsum, lime, and plaster to improve the soil, the substitution of barnyard feeding for pasture grazing, the cultivation of root crops for animal feed, and, in general, habits of neatness, precision, and attention to detail.[63] All recommendations were based on the strategy of realizing the maximum output from the least amount of land—that is, they were the latest word in intensive agriculture. The enthusiasm for British farming methods stemmed less from anglophilia than from a perception that British agricultural practices would be appropriate to Massachusetts simply because New England was coming to resemble Old England. Like the nation for which it was named, New England was long settled and crowded. Land was scarce and the population pressed for subsistence.

"Wherever there is a crowded population," explained Richard Sullivan, "the husbandman may be compelled to seek his subsistence within the limit

---

62. Banner, *Hartford Convention*, pp. 99–121.

63. This agricultural improvement program is reflected in almost every page of the MSPA's journal, in premiums offered, British treatises reprinted, communications presented, books reviewed, and in editorial comment. For a succinct and representative statement of the program, see Sullivan, "Address," p. 208.

of a few acres." With improved methods of agriculture, however, the constraint posed by land scarcity should pose no problem. Sullivan estimated that a mere five acres "under faithful management" could provide a living to a farm family.[64] John Lowell was more generous. He allowed thirty to forty acres as sufficient, in contrast to the usual one-hundred acre estimate, whereas William Tudor stated that farmers own four to five times the amount of land they can cultivate to advantage.[65] To Josiah Quincy the link between excessively large farms and the farmer's economic plight was obvious. "The great secret of European success, in agriculture, is stated to be, 'much labour on, comparatively, little land,'" he wrote. "Now the whole tenor of Massachusetts husbandry, from the first settlement of the country, has been little labour, on much land. Is it wonderful then, that success should be little, or nothing, when conduct is in direct violation of the principle, on which success depends?"[66]

On his own farm in Braintree, Quincy hoped to demonstrate the solution that intensive agriculture offered the Massachusetts farmer (fig. 29). He experimented with three interrelated innovations: soiling cattle, using root crops as livestock feed, and cultivating hedges. Contemporary practice in Massachusetts was to let cattle feed themselves by grazing in a pasture. It was incumbent on the farmer, then, to separate arable land from pasture with either rail fences or stone walls. As Quincy saw it, grazing cattle involved unnecessary labor and, even more critically, required too much land. He recommended that farmers feed their cows in barnyard stalls, a practice known as soiling, with root crops from the field or hay from the meadow. Then they would not need to expend labor on interior fences or walls, and—here was the main point—they would need much less land to maintain the same number of cows. Whereas a fifty-acre farm could sustain fifteen pasture-fed cattle, estimated Quincy, a mere seventeen acres would suffice for twenty soiled cattle.[67]

In practice, however, Quincy's innovations were less successful. As his son Edmund wrote, "his agricultural experience, like that of most gentle-

64. Ibid., p. 203.
65. [Lowell], "Remarks on the Agriculture of Massachusetts," pp. 220–26; [Tudor], "Agriculture," p. 102.
66. Quincy, "Address," p. 13.
67. Josiah Quincy, "On the American Hedge Thorn," *MSPA Journal* 3 (November 1813): 27–30; Quincy, "On Cutting Carrot Tops," ibid. 3 (January 1815): 181–82; Quincy, "On Soiling," ibid. 4 (January 1816): 20–22; Quincy, "Field Culture of Carrots," ibid., pp. 24–25; Quincy, "On the Field Culture of Vegetables, as Food for Cattle in Winter," ibid. 4 (January 1817): 211–17; Quincy, "Remarks on Soiling," ibid. 6 (July 1820): 113–25; Charles Arthur Hammond, "'Where the Arts and the Virtues Unite': Country Life near Boston, 1637–1864" (Ph.D. diss., Boston University, 1982), pp. 184–92.

29. *Josiah Quincy's Seat in Braintree.* Watercolor by Eliza Susan Quincy, 1822. (Courtesy Massachusetts Historical Society.)

man farmers, was rather profitable to others than to himself." His daughter Eliza Susan was more direct in her assessment. "My father on settling his accounts the first of January found that his expenses were exceeding his income," she wrote in her diary of 1820, adding that "his farming experiments were the cause of this difficulty."[68] If Quincy with his 170 acres could not turn a profit, how was he to convince Massachusetts farmers to be content with a farm a mere tenth the size? The situation only grew worse when in 1829 Quincy leased his farm and moved to Cambridge to assume the presidency of Harvard. The tenant, it would seem, did not go in for soiling. Cattle wandered freely on the Braintree farm, browsing contentedly on Quincy's prize English hawthorn hedges.[69]

More importantly, however, Quincy's improvements, adopted wholesale from British agricultural reformers, made little sense in New England. Stone walls were a practical response to the rocky Massachusetts soil. Since

68. Quincy, *Josiah Quincy,* p. 365; Journal of Eliza Quincy, quoted in McCaughey, *Quincy,* p. 87.
69. Quincy, *Josiah Quincy,* p. 366.

much of the land in the state was not arable, growing turnips, carrots, or mangel-wurzel for cattle feed was not always feasible, and the alternative, growing hay, entailed the labor of manuring and harvesting. In either case, the farmer was forced to undertake the additional work of bringing feed into the barnyard.[70]

Quincy himself recognized that his system was not always practical. He acknowledged that soiling made no sense for "the greater number" of Massachusetts farms, since these were good for nothing *but* pasture. "But," he continued, "to that class, whose farms are small, and who are stimulated by that correct ambition of possessing a little land highly cultivated, rather than a great deal miserably managed," soiling was clearly advantageous.[71]

John Lowell had his reservations as well. Perhaps English hawthorn worked well for Quincy, he wrote (probably out of politeness), but by and large it is better than useless in New England; worms love it. Better to go with buckthorn hedges, and even then, only where the ground is not stony. As for soiling, Lowell approved the practice for highly populated areas where land was valuable but not for the usual rocky-pastured farm of Massachusetts.[72]

Lowell tended to be more practical and realistic in assessing agricultural innovations than any of his fellow gentleman farmers. He criticized his colleagues' superficial knowledge of agriculture. Remarking on the disenchantment with merino sheep, he wrote: "The merino, like every other sheep, requires some skill, some previous acquaintance with its nature and proper treatment, for which neither the comptinghouse nor the workshop are the proper places of education." He agreed with Timothy Pickering's assessment of a newly touted hedge type as unsuitable to New England soils and climate. Just another "of the many cases in which zeal outstrips knowledge, and judgment," he wrote. And for the same reason Lowell protested the wholesale acceptance of foreign agricultural treatises and experiments as applicable to Massachusetts. "Have we not," he asked his fellow MSPA trustees, "pursued an erroneous system in copying from English publications, the course of their agriculture without accompanying them with remarks which could adapt them to the state of our own country?"[73]

70. Hammond, "Country Life near Boston," p. 188.
71. Quincy, "On Soiling," p. 20.
72. "J. L.," "Remarks on the Manner, in Which This Journal is Conducted, and the Rules by Which the Committee Entrusted with the Publication, Are Governed," *MSPA Journal* 7 (June 1822): 118–19; John Lowell, "Live Hedges for New England," ibid. 10 (April 1832): 411–12.
73. John Lowell, "Some Remarks upon Merino Sheep, Shewing That They Ought Not

British farming techniques, then, were fine in their place of origin, but applied to New England only where it resembled Old England. But that was just the point; more and more New England *was* coming to resemble Britain. It was urban. It was crowded. Reviewing a French treatise on soiling in 1815, a writer for the MSPA *Journal*—in all likelihood, Lowell—acknowledged that in labor-poor, land-rich America, pasture feeding might automatically make more sense than barnyard feeding. But, he continued, some parts of Massachusetts are already so improved as to make the issue relevant now. He singled out regions of the state near major towns and Essex, Hampshire, and Worcester counties as areas where soiling might be a viable option.[74]

Similar conditions applied to the practice of what Quincy termed "horticultural neatness,"[75] that is, a level of attention to detail and painstaking care appropriate to a one-acre garden and now recommended for a forty-acre farm. The standard wisdom on such an approach to farming was that it made sense in overcrowded Europe, where labor was cheap, but that it was not applicable to the United States. Traveling in Flanders in 1795, Thomas Handasyd Perkins, merchant and amateur horticulturist, commented on the labor-intensive agriculture of that region. "Not a stone is to be seen," he wrote in his diary. "They have all been picked up, centuries since." And, he added, "the population of America must be very much increased before we can have our grounds in such order as here."[76] By the 1820s, however, New England at least seemed to have achieved the correct population density. "An improved state of agriculture," wrote John Lowell in 1826, "such as we are constantly striving to encourage, such indeed as these old-settled States of the north seem to require, if they would wish to keep their excellent population at home, is nothing less than a system of enlarged horticulture—it is the application of gardening to field cultivation." What was specifically required were "habits of care and neatness" developed in the garden and transferred to the farm. To the objection that "we cannot afford the time; it will be too expensive," Lowell scoffed: "What? cannot our farmers afford as much time as the common labourers of other countries who

---

To Be Abandoned in Despair . . . ," ibid. 5 (July 1818): 168; Lowell to Timothy Pickering, 19 March 1821, Pickering Papers, 31:341; Lowell to the MSPA, 20 January 1813, MSPA Papers, D–I–4.

74. "On the Relative Advantages of Feeding Cattle in the Stable or Farm Yard, or Sending Them to Pastures," *MSPA Journal* 3 (June 1815): 318–19.

75. Quincy, "Address," p. 10.

76. Journal of Thomas Handasyd Perkins, 15 May 1795, in Thomas G. Cary, *Memoir of Thomas Handasyd Perkins; Containing Extracts from His Diary and Letters* (Boston: Little, Brown, 1856), p. 136.

work from sunrise to sunset for from thirty to forty cents per day?"[77] The New World was not so different from the Old World after all.

The message that Massachusetts agriculture must adapt to conditions reminiscent of the Old World rang even more clearly in the calls for farmers to change their crops. It could hardly be expected that grain farming in New England could compete with grain farming in the rich soils of the newly settled West. Even more critical, there were new urban and industrial populations to feed in Massachusetts. There are now fourteen towns in Massachusetts numbering a total of one hundred thousand people, estimated John Lowell in 1823. These people will require fruits and vegetables and it will take a population of at least fifty thousand to meet their demands.[78]

The onset of manufacturing was changing the face of Massachusetts and therefore of its agriculture. Writing in 1818, Josiah Quincy foresaw the flow of capital from commerce to manufacturing. Eventually, he explained, manufacturing capital would benefit agriculture because mills mean mill towns and therefore mill workers to feed.[79] With the passage of a protective tariff on foreign textiles in 1816, the flow of capital from commerce to industry and the shift of Massachusetts from an agricultural to a manufacturing state seemed inevitable. "The new interests created by the policy of the national government, are so great and extensive," commented John Lowell in 1826, "that we must be a manufacturing people." The farmer must adapt, continued Lowell, by becoming a gardener. "Villages, towns, and even cities will arise, in places, where agriculture would never have flourished without such an excitement. The sandy and unfertile banks of the Merrimack; the sterile plains of the Seekonk, must be made to furnish the vegetables and fruits necessary to the support and comfort of many thousands of persons employed in manufactories."[80]

The message that Boston's agricultural reformers wished to convey was clear. The society and economy of your state have become anglicized, they

77. [John Lowell], "Review" (J. C. Loudon, *An Encyclopaedia of Gardening*), *MSPA Journal* 9 (January 1826): 55; "Editorial Remarks, by John Lowell," p. 231. The attribution of the Loudon review is based on the following factors: first, that Lowell, as editor of the MSPA's journal, provided much, if not most, of the material in the journal not specifically attributed to other authors; second, that he, more than any other individual in the Boston elite community, kept abreast of British horticultural progress; and, finally, that the themes and wording of this article are identical to those in another article entitled "On Horticulture" (ibid. 7 [June 1822]: 136–39), signed "A Farmer," headed "Roxbury," and referring to the author's editorial capacity vis-à-vis the journal.

78. "Editorial Remarks, by John Lowell," p. 320.

79. [Josiah Quincy], "Agriculture," *NAR* 8 (December 1818): 136–37.

80. [Lowell], "Review," pp. 55–56.

told the yeomen, so you must anglicize your agriculture. Massachusetts is densely populated and land is scarce, so you must practice intensive agriculture. It has become urban and industrial, so you must become truck farmers, providing the cities and mill towns with fruits and vegetables. But agricultural reformers did not stop there. If farmers were to remain in Massachusetts, they must anglicize not only their farming but also their expectations, that is, they must be satisfied with less. They must close their eyes to the vision of unlimited bounty and mobility in the New World.

A critical aspect of this message, as we have seen, was the call for smaller farms. The promise of boundless land held out by America must be forgotten, for New England was new no longer. Instead the farmer must be content with a mere thirty (Lowell), seventeen (Quincy), even five (Sullivan) acres. And the lowering of expectations applied to more than just land. Even as Boston merchants and industrialists constructed expensive town houses and adorned their suburban estates with fabulous greenhouses, Massachusetts yeomen were urged to keep their dwellings simple and cheap. John Lowell steered farmers away from building "showy houses" toward ameliorating their diets and improving "the neatness and comfort of their furniture." Josiah Quincy, too, advised farmers to invest their capital in farm operations and not in large, elegant farmhouses. "When will man learn," he exclaimed, "that his true dignity, as well as happiness, consists in proportion! In the proportion . . . of conduct to the condition of life, in which a kind Providence has placed him."[81] In other words, the farmer must know his place. Knowing one's place meant staying in one's place—literally. The farmer was not to seek his fortune in western farmlands, and he was not to be "repining at his lot" in comparison to that of a merchant, manufacturer, or professional. It was a "vulgar pride" that convinced the farmer's son that manual labor was degrading and that motivated him, "a young man with no qualifications but a little bad Latin picked up at a miserable village school," to try his luck at the law. He should instead stay on the farm, content with the security of an agricultural life.[82] Here was something of the Old World peasant, born into his station, forever fixed to the land.

Ultimately, lowering expectations meant abandoning the goal of wealth altogether, whether in the form of a big farm, a fancy house, a share of Canton cargo, or stock in a textile mill. "What is essential to a farmer's

81. John Lowell, "Some Remarks on the Necessity and Importance of Improving the Manufacture of Cyder," *MSPA Journal* 4 (June 1816): 172; Quincy, "Address," pp. 10–11.

82. Quincy, "Address," p. 15; "Considerations Connected with a Survey of the Agriculture and Manufactures of Massachusetts," *MSPA Journal* 5 (July 1819): 374; "State of Agriculture in Italy," *NAR* 11 (July 1820): 51.

prosperity?" inquired the Reverend Henry Colman, a Unitarian minister and agricultural writer, at the Brighton Cattle Show in 1821.

> I do not intend therefore merely his getting rich. . . . That farmer is prosperous, who is able . . . to provide for the ordinary wants of himself and his family; to give his children a suitable education and establishment, in that situation in life, in which they are likely to be placed; to keep himself free from the curse of debt and mortgage; to maintain the character and assert the rights of the independent freeholder; to contribute something every year to the improvement of his estate, and . . . to provide against a season, when the accidents of life or the infirmities of old age may render it necessary to repose from his labours and cares. This is all the prosperity which a reasonable farmer ought to expect or wish.[83]

A very modest prosperity indeed.

Lowering one's sights did offer compensations, however. By staying put, the Massachusetts farmer did not have to face the horror that was the West. "If you follow them in imagination, into the wilderness," stated Richard Sullivan of the westward emigrants, "you will see that its morbid dampness and the numerous privations and hardships, to which they are unavoidably exposed, soon finish the work of destruction, which a miserable agriculture had begun."[84] (fig. 30.) Of even greater importance than the torments of the West were the blessings of New England. There was no substitute for the values of New England civilization and the institutions these values had spawned over two hundred years. "We are convinced," wrote John Lowell in 1826, "that by remaining at *home,* much more and greater personal comfort will be secured to the individual—much greater opportunities afforded for literary, moral and religious instruction."[85] Where in the barbarous West would the New Englander find a lyceum, a temperance club, a proper church?

Resisting the lure of commerce and manufacturing also had its compensations. If farmers might never accumulate the riches of a China merchant or a textile magnate, neither would they face the possibility of economic ruin. Only "consider how independent is agriculture of the hazards and reverses to which commerce and manufactures are exposed," stated Rich-

83. Henry Colman, "An Address Delivered before the Massachusetts Agricultural Society at the Brighton Cattle Show, 17th Oct., 1821," ibid. 7 (January 1822): 2. On Colman, See Donald B. Marti, "The Reverend Henry Colman's Agricultural Ministry," *Agricultural History* 51 (July 1977): 524–39.
84. Sullivan, "Address," pp. 215–16.
85. John Lowell, "Mr. Lowell's Report," *MSPA Journal* 9 (January 1826): 4.

## WESTERN EMIGRATION.

### JOURNAL

OF

DOCTOR JEREMIAH SMIPLETON's

## TOUR TO OHIO.

CONTAINING
An account of the numerous difficulties, Hair-breadth
Escapes, Mortifications and Privations, which the
DOCTOR and his family experienced on their
Journey from Maine, to the ' Land of Pro-
mise,' and during a residence of three years
in that highly extolled country.

BY H. TRUMBULL.

*Nulli Fides Frontis.*

BOSTON--PRINTED BY S. SEWALL.

30. *The Horrors of the West Exposed.* Cover illustration from H. Trumbull, *Western Emigration: Journal of Doctor Jeremiah Simpleton's Tour to Ohio. . . .* (Boston, 1819). (Courtesy American Antiquarian Society.)

ard Sullivan. "It is true," he conceded, that "the face of a country may be swept by hostile armies, but it is only the harvest of a season which can fall within their destructive grasp." The farmer can always plant—and earn— again, but "the wealth of the merchant may perish irretrievably by the conflagration of a city, or be sunk in the ocean."[86]

Agricultural reformers, then, insisted that the husbandman and his agricultural enterprise should be spared the disrespect they apparently suffered when compared with the merchant and *his* business undertakings. Such lack of regard proceeded not only from the image of the farmer as

86. Sullivan, "Address," p. 211.

clodhopper but also from a common perception that farming was economically unviable, and just that sort of perception had farmers running for the state line. "We are willing to hear, with too much acquiescence, the scoffs against the occupation of the husbandman,"[87] argued a writer for the MSPA *Journal* in 1819. "As the character of the staples of Massachusetts is humble, . . . we sometimes hear agriculture spoken of, as a pursuit, in terms of derision. But we know no part of the world in which the great body of the people have it in their power to live more independently and happily, than in this Commonwealth. And if the hazards of foreign trade are taken into view, there is no class of men, who hold their earnings in so great security as the farmers, or who have it so certainly in their power to better their condition by regular and progressive steps."[88] Because he can make a decent living at agriculture, the farmer is no fool to be ridiculed. Here was "a full answer to those who call into question" what were invariably linked together, "the profitableness and dignity of agricultural pursuits."[89]

The ultimate compensation, of course, was the "deference" accorded the yeoman as the moral and economic pillar of the Republic. Here was the trade-off. In return for a decidedly middling social and economic status, farmers would be granted an exalted moral status. Regarded in this light, the statements that farmers "are the chief strength, support, and column of our political society" and agriculture "the support and stay of all other arts" and that both are seriously and unfairly undervalued[90] emerge as a good deal more than rhetorical flourishes or ritual restatements of accepted moral and economic philosophy. They take on something of the character of payment, or, what is another term for the same thing, compensation.

The message of Boston's agricultural reformers is remarkable in two respects: first, as it ran counter to the "spirit of the times," and second, as it represents a true confrontation with modernization. The two of course are interrelated. In an age of millennial hope and boundless aspiration, the agricultural reformer stressed the limits the yeoman must place on his expectations. In an age of restless mobility, the farmer was told to stay put. In an age in which Americans still hoped to step out of time, reformers made it clear that America had not escaped the fate of other nations, that New England at least was aging. If this message was austere, it was because its ultimate goal was to force farmers to face the realities of irreversible change in Massachusetts—agricultural decline, land scarcity, population

87. "Considerations Connected with a Survey of . . . Massachusetts," p. 368.
88. Ibid., p. 374.
89. Prefatory remarks, "Sketch of the Character of William West," p. 385.
90. Quincy, "Address," p. 2; Lowell, "Address," p. 222.

pressure, emigration, competition from the West, urbanization, industrial-ization—in other words, modernization.

Yeoman farmers were not the only ones confronting rapid social and economic changes in Massachusetts. So were the agricultural reformers, and for them, no less than for the yeomen, adjustment to and acceptance of change was not easy. They were schooled in a political philosophy and a theory of history that emphasized the maintenance of a yeoman class and an agricultural society; both were disappearing from Massachusetts. As we have seen, Boston's merchant class had long made room for commerce in their personal philosophies, but manufacturing was something else al-together. Most of Boston's agricultural reformers were men whose wealth and allegiance were solidly based in maritime commerce. For them, the advent of the textile industry after the War of 1812 was problematic.

To the end of his long life—he lived from 1772 to 1864—Josiah Quincy refused to invest in manufacturing or to support a protective tariff on manufactured goods. In his view, industrialization was a source of political and social danger. Richard Sullivan, in his agricultural address of 1820, railed against the tariff, claiming that its end result was not only "to compel the farmer to abandon the pursuits of husbandry, for the spindle and shuttle," but also "to convert a merchant into a manufacturer, at the plea-sure of Congress." Lowell also came out strongly against the tariff in that same year. In his view it was "a disgrace to our nation, thus systematically to cultivate unfriendly feelings towards Great Britain, who is, after all, our best customer, & our most reasonable one."[91]

In the summer of 1820, Samuel W. Pomeroy, the Boston merchant and Brighton gentleman farmer, suggested to Timothy Pickering that perhaps it was time for the agricultural societies to take a stand against the tariff in particular and manufacturing interests in general. "Does it not behoove the friends to Agriculture," he asked Pickering, then president of the Essex Agricultural Society, "to endeavor to arrest the progress of this manufactur-ing mania, before it prostrates with [*sic*] the commerce of the Country?" Connecticut has been making efforts in this direction, Pomeroy com-mented, and "yet the most lowliest apathy appears to pervade the commer-cial cities, particularly in Massachusetts. . . . would it be advisable for the *State* or *County* Agrl Societies to take any measures . . . ?"[92]

By that autumn, such a movement was afoot. In September, John Lowell wrote and the MSPA trustees unanimously endorsed a circular letter

91. McCaughey, *Quincy,* p. 82; Sullivan, "Address," p. 213; Lowell to Timothy Picker-ing, 24 September 1820, Pickering Papers, 31:331.

92. Pomeroy to Timothy Pickering, 7 June 1820, Pickering Papers, 45:290.

to the state's agricultural societies, calling for action against the tariff on behalf of the Commonwealth's agricultural interests. As far as we know, only the Essex Agricultural Society, under Pickering, responded to the letter. In other words, it would seem that the two agricultural societies most dominated by commercial interests (Boston and Salem) were the ones to oppose the artificial encouragement of manufactures. The Essex society enthusiastically endorsed the MSPA letter and adopted a letter drafted by Pickering.[93] Pickering's letter condemned the tariff as sacrificing the interests of the many, namely the state's agricultural population, to those of a few manufacturers. Should the tariff go into effect, the result would be not only decreased imports of manufactured goods but also decreased exports of American farm products. Pickering condemned the manufacturers themselves, who, under temporary circumstances of embargo and war, had flourished and now expected government to prolong conditions favorable to industry artificially. How foolishly had they rushed into manufacturing enterprises in the embargo and war years! "Such speculators were not without a warning of the consequences of their precipitation," wrote Pickering, "but absorbed in their golden dreams, they were deaf to the voice of disinterested Prudence. They are now only in the condition of other improvident adventurers, distressed by incidents from which human affairs can never be exempt, laws for whose relief, no one would ever contemplate the imposing of a tax on the community, such as would be, in effect, the result of gratifying the manufacturers by the adoption of the proposed tariff."[94]

As for Lowell, he could not long maintain an uncompromising position against manufactures. After all, one of those "improvident adventurers" had been his half-brother Francis Cabot Lowell. Lowell himself had invested some of his mercantile wealth in the textile enterprises established by Francis and his associates. "It will not be supposed," wrote Lowell in 1826, "that I am unfriendly to manufactures, in which the fortunes of those most dear to me, and a large portion of my own are engaged." Yet he did continue to oppose the tariff as fostering "an unnatural and morbid extension" of manufactures, in effect, aging New England before its time.[95]

93. John Lowell to Timothy Pickering, 24 September 1820, Pickering Papers, 31:332; Vote of the Essex Agricultural Society, Board of Trustees, 5 October 1820, Pickering Papers, 45:240; Pickering to Lowell, 20 October 1820, MSPA Papers, C–III–6; Pickering to Lowell, 21 October 1820, Pickering Papers, 16:228–29; Lowell to Pickering, 25 October 1820, Pickering Papers, 31:334.

94. Timothy Pickering [president, Essex Agricultural Society] to John Lowell [corresponding secretary, MSPA], 20 October 1820, MSPA Papers, C–III–6.

95. Lowell, "Mr. Lowell's Report," p. 10. See also Sullivan, "Address," pp. 213–15. On the association of the government protection of manufactures with the premature decay of

Lowell was uncomfortable with the changes for which he and his kind were responsible, yet he meant to acknowledge them as irreversible. "It is of little moment now to consider," he wrote, "whether it was, or was not wise, to divert the capital of this country from commerce to manufactures. It *has been done,* and every wise man will admit, whatever may be his views of the tariff policy, that it is *irrevocably* done."[96] Although Lowell recognized what was coming, what was in fact already *here,* he could not see himself as part of the future, and lived only uncomfortably in the present. "I happen to have lived," he wrote in 1823, " . . . in a *middle* generation, between the revolutionary patriots, & the *modern* man."[97] John Lowell was a man caught between generations.

It was probably Lowell who, in his capacity as editor of the MSPA *Journal,* chose to close the January 1816 issue of that periodical with an excerpt from Thomas Malthus's *Essay on the Principle of Population.* [98] The excerpt was printed without commentary; indeed, as the final item in the issue, it acted as something of a commentary on what had preceded.[99] No explanation was really needed, for Malthus's ideas were sure to address the concerns of the journal's readership. "If the population of a country outrun its means of raising or acquiring subsistence," wrote Malthus, "it must unavoidably be checked by scarcity or emigration." The latter, of course, was uppermost in the minds of Boston's agricultural reformers. Malthus then drew the critical links among "the strength of countries," their "numbers and population," and "the degree of improvement and most perfect cultivation of the soil." He concluded that "it is therefore both the interest and the duty of those who have the power, to use every means of promoting such improvement." Lest there be any question as to who these men of power might be, Malthus specified "those who by their situation are exempt from bodily labour," that is, "those who are at the head of society."[100] Boston's gentleman farmers, acknowledging Old World social and economic conditions as relevant to New England in the fortieth year of the Republic, recognized this interest and duty as their own.

---

society, see Drew R. McCoy, *The Elusive Republic: Political Economy in Jeffersonian America* (New York: W. W. Norton, 1980), pp. 42–46.

96. [Lowell], "Review," p. 55.

97. Lowell to Caleb Cushing, 31 October 1823, Cushing Papers.

98. "Remarks from 'Malthus on Population,'" *MSPA Journal* 4 (January 1816): 95. For the place of Malthus's ideas in American political economy, see McCoy, *Elusive Republic,* pp. 190–95.

99. The excerpt was the final substantive item in the issue. It was followed by what became standard for the closing pages, the official announcement of the Brighton cattle show and its list of premiums.

100. "Malthus," p. 95.

# PART THREE

# The Consolidated Elite

# Introduction

SOMETIME around 1830 a newly consolidated elite came into its
own. Never before had this class—now a mix of merchants, financiers, manufacturers, railroad men, professionals, and literati—
enjoyed such power. Its hold on the regional economy was near absolute;
its hold on cultural affairs no less so; and if Boston's Whigs could not afford
to ignore an often unpredictable electorate, neither did they suffer the
interests of the elite to be passed over in the halls of Congress, the state
house, and the mayor's office.[1]

This elite was now closed, and not only in the sense that entrance into it
was effectively a thing of the past. Gradually the elite ceased to look
outward; it became closed in the sense of self-preoccupied. Its concerns
shifted subtly from political and social leadership to individual and class
self-justification. What guaranteed that the wealthy merchant or manufacturer was more than an especially lucky materialist? And what, in nominally egalitarian America, formed the basis for upper-class authority? In
coping with these nagging questions, the Boston elite found itself up
against its own entrepreneurial ethos, long proudly maintained but now
distinctly problematic.

One cornerstone of this ethos was the high value placed on such entrepreneurial traits as frugality, industry, sobriety, and personal simplicity.
These were likely to make a man rich, of course, but they were also valued

---

1. For an overview of this generation of the Boston elite, see Frederic Cople Jaher, *The
Urban Establishment: Upper Strata in Boston, New York, Charleston, Chicago, and Los Angeles*
(Urbana: University of Illinois Press, 1982), pp. 44–87.

as ends in themselves, properly republican and a refreshing contrast to the decadence that characterized many members of Old World elites. Also basic to the Boston ethos was the conviction that accumulation of wealth alone did not justify high social status. One must have riches, but more important one must rise above them, valuing them only for the good they can do in this world.[2] These ideas undoubtedly constituted the creed of the Boston elite, but to what degree wealthy Bostonians actually succeeded in transcending their wealth is another question. In the post–1830 generation, that potential inconsistency seemed to trouble the elite as never before.

Within elite circles, the reputation of the merchant and industrialist was curiously double.[3] On one hand, men of business represented all that was forward-looking, liberal, and virtuous; on the other, they were portrayed as men of narrow minds, closed hearts, and tight fists. In the mercantile propaganda of the antebellum era, the merchant and the industrialist were praised for their overriding interest in the public good. Thus Nathan Appleton commended Abbott Lawrence for investing in railroads not for the sake of profit but for the sake of national progress. The benevolence of Samuel Appleton, wrote Ephraim Peabody, "showed that men might accumulate money, and yet value it for its true uses." Edward Everett praised Peter Chardon Brooks for exhibiting "no taste for luxurious personal indulgences" but instead spending his money on benevolent institutions and public-spirited causes.[4]

Yet some insisted on documenting a less virtuous side of the mercantile character. They portrayed the merchant as grasping and rapacious, narrow-

2. On the ethos of the Boston elite, see Paul Goodman, "Ethics and Enterprise: The Values of the Boston Elite, 1800–1860," *American Quarterly* 18 (Fall 1966): 437–51, and Jaher, *Urban Establishment*, pp. 29–44, 57–67, 75–87. For the role of Unitarian moral philosophy in this ethos, see Daniel Walker Howe, *The Unitarian Conscience: Harvard Moral Philosophy, 1805–1861* (Cambridge: Harvard University Press, 1970), pp. 137–44, 226–34. The most useful sources are contemporary diaries, memorial sermons, merchant biographies, and addresses before mercantile groups. For an exquisite profile of the prototypical Boston merchant and his ethos, see Octavius Brooks Frothingham's account of Peter Chardon Brooks in his *Boston Unitarianism, 1820–1850* (New York: G. P. Putnam's Sons, 1890), pp. 93–128.

3. The term *merchant* was used to refer to both the man of commerce and the man of industry.

4. Nathan Appleton, *Memoir of the Hon. Abbott Lawrence* (Boston: J. H. Eastburn, 1856), p. 18; Ephraim Peabody, "Samuel Appleton," in Freeman Hunt, ed., *Lives of American Merchants,* 2 vols. (New York: Office of Hunt's Merchants' Magazine, 1856; Derby and Jackson, 1858), 1:441; Edward Everett, "Peter Chardon Brooks," excerpted in Freeman Hunt, ed., *Worth and Wealth: A Collection of Maxims, Morals and Miscellanies for Merchants and Men of Business* (New York: Stringer and Townsend, 1856), p. 50.

minded and boorish.[5] In response, businessmen articulated a defense. The "selfish principle" may be the basis of the merchant's profession, replied Nathan Appleton, but it did not follow that the merchant himself was selfish. As for the insinuation that Boston wealth might have been acquired by unscrupulous means, nothing could be more insulting. "Mercantile honor is as delicate and fragile as that of a woman," declared Appleton. "It will not bear the slightest stain."[6] Furthermore, in Appleton's opinion, no occupation liberalized the mind more than that of merchant. Others agreed. "Before he disdains companionship with the man of business," wrote George R. Russell, himself an East India merchant, the man of books should think about who was endowing the libraries. He should recall "the merchant Solomon" and note that Solomon's wisdom was not "impaired by his trade to Ophir, or his gentility doubted in consequence of his maritime expeditions."[7]

Yet one wonders to what extent the attack on businessmen as narrow materialists was merely external and to what extent it took the form of an internal battle. It would be unwarranted to read all or even most defenses of the businessman's character as the defensive reactions of troubled consciences—Nathan Appleton, at least, sounds like a man who slept well—but evidence of inner turmoil does exist. Textile millionaire Amos Lawrence, for example, found inner peace elusive. The stumbling block was clearly identified as the feverish pursuit of wealth. Wrote Lawrence in his diary of 1826: "I now find myself so engrossed in its [business's] cares, as to occupy my thoughts, waking or sleeping, to a degree entirely disproportionate to its importance. The quiet and comfort of home are broken in upon by the anxiety arising from the losses and mischances of a business so extensive as ours; and, above all, that communion which ought ever to be kept free between man and his Maker is interrupted by the incessant calls of the multifarious pursuits of our establishment."[8]

Similarly, in entry after entry in a diary spanning forty years, William Appleton examined his soul and found it hideously preoccupied with

5. See, for example, Theodore Parker and Henry Ward Beecher, excerpted in Hunt, *Worth and Wealth,* pp. 236, 382–83.

6. Appleton, *Memoir,* pp. 4–6. See also Nathan Appleton to Ezra Gannett, 24 January 1828, Appleton Family Papers, Massachusetts Historical Society, Boston.

7. Appleton, *Memoir,* p. 5; Russell, "Introductory Essay," in Hunt, *American Merchants,* 1:x, xxxviii.

8. William R. Lawrence, ed., *Extracts from the Diary and Correspondence of the Late Amos Lawrence, With a Brief Account of Some Incidents in His Life* (Boston: John Wilson and Son, 1855), p. 49.

things of this world. "I feel that I am quite eaten up with business," he wrote in 1822. "While in Church, my mind . . . was flying from City to City, from Ship to Ship, and from Speculation to Speculation." In 1836 he complained of an "unaccountable desire for business success" and feared it would be his ruin. He attempted to concentrate on spiritual matters, but, once in "the vortex of business," his mind could not be freed. Appleton agonized over taking communion for the first time; suffered dyspepsia; contemplated giving money to missions. Yet he had to admit to himself that, even as he knew himself to be in error, he continued to be engrossed in worldly concerns.[9]

Even if all Boston merchants and industrialists were not as torn by their consciences as was William Appleton, it is safe to say that they all had to come to terms with a demanding social ethos. Somehow, each individual had to prove a transcendent virtue. It was a difficult task.

Then, too, the mercantile value system created problems for the elite as a class. These values were consistent with what may be loosely termed the egalitarian "spirit of the age," that is, the faith in the equality of opportunity and the perfectibility of all men. Indeed, in some measure they constituted the gospel of success by which any Jacksonian Common Man hoped to rise. What business values were not so easily compatible with was any sort of aristocratic pretension, any longing or reverence for closed caste and inherited status. Yet as the elite sought to prove itself above a sordid preoccupation with business, and as the consolidation of the elite precluded any means of entry into the elite *but* birth, aristocratic values gained an increasing foothold in Boston high society.

The signs of this gradual identification with Old World notions of aristocracy are many. We might regard the introduction of the term *Boston Brahmin* on the eve of the Civil War as just such a straw in the wind.[10] So too was Nathan Appleton's acquisition of a family coat-of-arms.[11] We detect also subtle shifts away from the attitudes of the older commercial elite. Mercantile traits continued to be valued, for example, but such polite virtues as refined manners or an appreciation of the arts were newly held up for admiration. The sense of civic duty experienced by men of John Lowell's generation gradually gave way to something closer to noblesse oblige. Nor can we ignore the growing group of Brahmin intellectuals— Thomas Gold Appleton, Francis Parkman, Richard Henry Dana, Jr.—

9. Susan M. Loring, ed., *Selections from the Diaries of William Appleton, 1786–1862* (Boston: privately printed, 1922), pp. 36, 46, 49, 52, 61, 64, 72–73, 82, 91.

10. The term is most often associated with Oliver Wendell Holmes's discussion of "the Brahmin Caste of New England" in his novel *Elsie Venner* (1861).

11. Jaher, *Urban Establishment,* p. 81.

who unabashedly preferred the fixed social hierarchy and static social order of the Old World to the lack of inherited distinction and reverence for the past in America, conditions they regarded as engendering a decidedly philistine society.[12]

It was not the first time the commercial spirit had been attacked in Boston. "In-house" critics of business values had long existed. Back in the days of the *Monthly Anthology,* contributors to that journal had blasted the materialistic tendencies of Boston's mercantile class. ("Everything smells of the shop," wrote one disgusted Anthologist in 1806, no doubt holding his nose.)[13] Whatever shortcomings might appear in reality, however, there had been no true theoretical objections to members of the merchant class as the rightful and worthy leaders of society. In fact, as we have seen, in those earlier generations, a commercial ruling class was self-confidently regarded as the ideal medium between a decadent British-style aristocracy and the ignorant and irresponsible masses. What was needed now, in an age in which the masses no longer deferred to their betters and every American joined in the scramble for wealth, was a step beyond and above the entrepreneurial outlook. Aristocracy looked better and better. Inasmuch as the Boston elite continued to participate in American society, however, if only as elected officials, these sorts of leanings could not be openly acknowledged, at least not in so blatant a form. What, then, in a nation that rejected inherited distinctions and celebrated the ability of each to transcend all limits, gave the Boston elite its legitimacy and authority as a privileged class?

In many ways, the years 1830 to 1860 saw the heyday of the Boston elite. They enjoyed economic, social, cultural, and political power as never before. Yet if one consequence of class consolidation was increased strength, another was a growing tendency to self-preoccupation, self-examination, and hence a need for self-definition and self-justification. In this generation, as in those that preceded it, the rich symbolism of rural pursuits answered the subtly changed needs of Boston's elite.

12. Jaher, *Urban Establishment,* pp. 78–84. See also Jaher, "Businessman and Gentleman: Nathan and Thomas Gold Appleton—an Exploration in Inter-generational History," *Explorations in Entrepreneurial History* 4 (Fall 1966): 17–39.

13. See the excerpts from the *Monthly Anthology and Boston Review* included in Lewis P. Simpson, ed., *The Federalist Literary Mind: Selections from the* Monthly Anthology and Boston Review, *1803–1811* (Baton Rouge: Louisiana State University Press, 1962), pp. 47–74. The quotation is from [John Sylvester John Gardiner], *Monthly Anthology and Boston Review* 3 (January 1806): 18.

# FIVE

## The Moral Dimensions of Horticulture

A S recommended by agricultural reformers like Lowell and Quincy in the 1810s and 1820s, horticulture represented the practical farmer's adaptation to modernization. If farmers were urged to grow apples and sea kale, it was because the unprofitability of growing wheat in New England had to be acknowledged and because a growing urban and industrial population required fruit and vegetables for its sustenance. As practiced by members of the Boston elite themselves, however, horticulture had no such practical overtones. As we have seen in chapter 1, the cultivation of fruits, flowers, vegetables, and ornamental trees had been part of the rural regime of the earliest gentleman farmers of the Republic. We need only recall Theodore Lyman's elaborate greenhouses at the Vale, Joseph Barrell's many importations of plants from English nurseries, and Fisher Ames's dedication to his peach trees.

Later gentleman farmers, such as John Lowell, were also avid horticulturists and, unlike their predecessors, took pains to communicate relevant intelligence and to distribute new plants to a larger community of enthusiasts. Other members of the elite did not undertake experimental agriculture but nevertheless enjoyed gardening on their suburban retreats. Among these early merchant-horticulturists were Thomas C. Amory, whose summer house in Brookline, acquired in about 1803, was famous for its ornamental grounds;[1] Benjamin Bussey, who from 1806 on undertook

---

1. Mary Caroline Crawford, *Famous Families of Massachusetts*, 2 vols. (Boston: Little, Brown, 1930), 2:124–25; Samuel Aspinwall Goddard, *Recollections of Brookline, Being an Account of the Houses, the Families, and the Roads, in Brookline, in the Years 1800 to 1810* (Birmingham, Eng.: E. C. Osborne, 1873), p. 6.

an extensive reforestation program at Woodland Hill, his estate in Roxbury;[2] Thomas Lee, whose Brookline gardens and greenhouses were open to passersby;[3] the Perkins brother, James, Samuel, and Thomas, all three of whom settled on Brookline estates in the first decade of the nineteenth century;[4] and Ebenezer Preble, who imported no fewer than 150 varieties of fruit trees to his Watertown estate in 1805.[5] For these men gardening was a pastime appropriate to their stations in life, inasmuch as it had been adopted by the British landed classes and was regarded as a rational, and therefore socially sophisticated and morally acceptable, amusement.

By about 1830, however, and increasingly over the next few decades, members of the Boston elite supervised horticultural enterprises on a much grander scale, to the point where the phenomenon can no longer be counted as quite the same thing. The polite cultivation of a small orchard or a few dozen pots of flowers simply cannot compare with the rows of greenhouses or the hundreds of varieties of a single fruit found on some later estates. Some of these horticultural operations had to be seen—or at least must be described—to be believed.

Probably the most prominent of Boston's amateur horticulturists was the China merchant Thomas Handasyd Perkins (fig. 31). Perkins acquired an estate in Brookline in 1800, and over the next several decades he managed to squeeze horticulture into a busy life of maritime commerce and Federalist politics. He imported fruits, flowers, and trees, laid out a magnificent garden, and collected an impressive collection of farming and garden-

2. Marshall Pinckney Wilder, "The Horticulture of Boston and Vicinity," in Justin Winsor, ed., *The Memorial History of Boston, including Suffolk County, Massachusetts, 1630–1880*, 4 vols. (Boston: James R. Osgood, 1881), 4:618; Charles Arthur Hammond, " 'Where the Arts and the Virtues Unite': Country Life near Boston, 1637–1864" (Ph.D. diss., Boston University, 1982), pp. 128–35, 349–55. Bussey's estate, bequeathed to Harvard College, formed the basis of the Arnold Arboretum. See also entry for Bussey in the Appendix.

3. Report on Native Flora, in John Lewis Russell, *Report of the Transactions of the Massachusetts Horticultural Society, for the Year 1837–8, with Preliminary Observations* (Boston: Tuttle, Dennett and Chisolm, 1839), pp. 32–34; *Magazine of Horticulture, Botany, and All Useful Discoveries, and Improvements in Rural Affairs* 3 (January 1837): 29–30; Frances Rollins Morse, *Henry and Mary Lee: Letters and Journals, with Other Family Letters, 1802–1860* (Boston: privately printed, 1926), pp. 21–28; A. J. Downing, *A Treatise on the Theory and Practice of Landscape Gardening, Adapted to North America; with a View to the Improvement of Country Residences*, 2d ed. (New York: Wiley and Putnam, 1844), pp. 41–42; John Gould Curtis, *History of the Town of Brookline Massachusetts* (Boston: Houghton Mifflin, 1933), p. 210.

4. Goddard, *Brookline*, pp. 4, 6–7; Wilder, "Horticulture of Boston," pp. 625–26; Downing, *Landscape Gardening*, pp. 40–41. On Thomas Handasyd Perkins, see notes 6–11, below.

5. Wilder, "Horticulture of Boston," p. 633n; Preble, "Management of Fruit Trees," *Massachusetts Agricultural Repository and Journal* 4 (January 1816): 84–87.

31. *Thomas Handasyd Perkins*. Portrait by Gilbert Stuart, 1822. (Courtesy Frick Art Reference Library.)

ing books.[6] On his frequent business trips abroad, Perkins visited private estates, commercial nurseries, and botanical gardens.[7] Even Perkins's firm bore the boss's horticultural interests in mind when conducting business. Company letter books record orders for plant materials from around the world. Perkins's agent in Smyrna was to procure not only opium but also cantaloupe seeds.[8]

Although he did not retire completely until 1838, at age seventy-four, Perkins began to wind down his business affairs by the 1820s.[9] It was time to spend some of the wealth he had accumulated in rum, slaves, and opium.[10] Not a small portion of that fortune went toward the Brookline gardens—no less than ten thousand dollars a year, even now a considerable sum. Sometime in the mid-1820s, Perkins constructed a three-hundred-foot-long greenhouse devoted to grapes, peaches, and nectarines. Then in 1831 he built yet another greenhouse of the same length, this one differentiated into a twenty-foot-high center section for flowers and two somewhat lower wings subdivided into rooms for peach and grape cultivation. This second structure was warmed by a coal-fired furnace, a greenhouse-heating apparatus unique in America. Six years later, on the eve of his retirement, Perkins constructed two new structures, each one hundred feet long, to force grapes. With such state-of-the-art horticultural facilities, Perkins was able to cultivate an impressive array of fruits and flowers: pineapples; a huge assortment of camellias, including one named after his chief gardener, William H. Cowan; new grape varieties presented to Perkins by Sir Joseph Paxton, gardener to the duke of Devonshire and designer of the Crystal Palace; and the *Enkianthus quinqueflorus,* a rare Chinese plant (the only one in the United States) obtained from a famous London nurseryman for the huge sum of six guineas. Other reminders of the Chinese sources of Perkins's wealth embellished the Brookline estate, from the Chinese tiles that decorated a garden wall, to the bamboo furniture and Chinese wall-

6. L. Vernon Briggs, *History and Genealogy of the Cabot Family, 1475–1927,* 2 vols. (Boston: privately printed, 1927), 1:372; Wilder, "Horticulture of Boston," p. 625; Thomas Handasyd Perkins, Inventory of Property, Thomas Handasyd Perkins Papers, reel 4, vol. 29, Massachusetts Historical Society (hereafter MHS), Boston; Carl Seaburg and Stanley Paterson, *Merchant Prince of Boston: Colonel T. H. Perkins, 1764–1854* (Cambridge: Harvard University Press, 1971), pp. 390–91.

7. See, for example, Diary of Thomas Handasyd Perkins, 23, 27 September 1811, 14 May 1812, 12, 23, 24, 26 June, 1 July 1823, 6 June 1826, Perkins Papers, 3:8–11, 14.

8. Briggs, *Cabot Family,* 2:553, 565.

9. Thomas G. Cary, *Memoir of Thomas Handasyd Perkins; Containing Extracts from His Diaries and Letters* (Boston: Little, Brown, 1856), p. 239.

10. On Perkins's business enterprises, see Briggs, *Cabot Family,* 2:469–83, 523, 525, and Jacques M. Downs, "American Merchants and the China Opium Trade, 1800–1840," *Business History Review* 42 (Winter 1969): 418–42.

paper, depicting peacocks in a garden, in the dining room, to the Chinese engravings of flowers and birds that covered the walls of the garden's unusual pavilion, a Grecian temple used as a billiard room.[11]

Perkins was at the center of a family horticultural clan. When Samuel Cabot married Perkins's daughter Eliza, he not only entered the family business but also adopted the family pastime. In 1834 Perkins built a country house for the couple on land adjoining his property, and while in the early 1840s the Cabots forsook this summer residence for cooler seaside cottages, by 1843 they were back on Perkins's territory.[12] "Your father has gone to Brookline," wrote Eliza Cabot to her son, "not to enjoy its beauties but to save his taxes."[13] For whatever reason, the Cabots remained in Brookline, where Samuel immersed himself in gardening, indulging his particular love of roses, laurels, and sweetbriers.[14] By 1846 Eliza Cabot could report to her son: "Your father is well and busy cutting and slashing away the trees."[15]

And then there was the old man's nephew, John Perkins Cushing. Cushing spent most of his life in China—all but a few months of the years 1803 to 1831—working for his uncle's firm. When he returned, it was with a retinue of Chinese servants and seven million dollars, probably the largest fortune in New England of his generation. He proceeded to marry the daughter of a prominent clergyman and to lay out a grand estate in Watertown. Belmont, as Cushing named the sixty-acre estate, was described in its day as "a residence of more note than any other near Boston . . . chiefly, on account of the extensive ranges of glass, the forced fruits, and the high culture of the gardens" (fig. 32). Running the agricultural (for Cushing also took up stockbreeding) and horticultural operations required ten to fifteen laborers, in addition to the services of David Haggerston, a first-rate professional gardener. Cushing must have regarded Belmont as something

11. Briggs, *Cabot Family*, 1:298, 372; Wilder, "Horticulture of Boston," p. 625; Caroline Gardiner Curtis, *Memories of Fifty Years in the Last Century* (Boston: privately printed, 1947), pp. 30–35; *New England Farmer* (hereafter *NEF*) 10 (30 November 1831): 156; ibid. 11 (27 February 1833): 262; *Horticultural Register and Gardener's Magazine* 1 (March 1835): 106–8; ibid. 2 (February 1836): 41–43; *Magazine of Horticulture* 3 (January 1837): 28–29; Report of the Nursery and Fruit Department, in Russell, *Transactions . . .*, *1837–8*, pp. 30–31; Seaburg and Paterson, *Perkins*, pp. 390–91.
12. Briggs, *Cabot Family*, 1:293, 295, 297–98, 305, 309.
13. Eliza Cabot to J. Elliot Cabot, 30 April 1843, quoted in ibid., 1:296. Cabot had retired from active business when Perkins & Co. closed down in 1838 and sought to conserve and increase his fortune only through investments. In 1834 Cabot had valued that fortune at $340,000, mainly in the form of Perkins & Co. and manufacturing stock, with lesser amounts in railroad, canal, and insurance investments (ibid., 1:284–86).
14. Ibid., 1:296, 298.
15. Eliza Cabot to J. Elliot Cabot, 1 October 1846, quoted in ibid., 2:689.

32. *Belmont, Seat of John Perkins Cushing.* Reprinted from A. J. Downing, *A Treatise on the Theory and Practice of Landscape Gardening,* 2d ed. (New York, 1844). (Courtesy Yale University Library.)

akin to the great estates of England, for like the English aristocracy, he opened his gardens to the public once a week in the summertime.[16]

If Thomas Handasyd Perkins stood at the head of one horticultural clan, Joseph Lee stood at the head of another. "Like many old sea-captains," wrote his son, Lee " . . . took a great interest in his garden, not only during his residence at Beverly, but even in his extreme age he could often be seen in the garden of his son-in-law, Judge [Charles] Jackson . . . directing the gardener, or, saw in hand, high on the ladder, pruning or grafting his pear trees."[17] When the elder Lee died in 1831, he left behind three sons who inherited his enthusiasm for horticulture.[18] We have already seen Thomas, gardening in Brookline.[19] But there was also George, a sea captain who

16. Ibid., 1:284, 313–21, 384, 512, 524–25, 527, 529, 577; Diaries of John Perkins Cushing, 1834–56, 7 vols., John Perkins Cushing Papers, Boston Athenaeum; *Dictionary of American Biography* (hereafter *DAB*), s.v. "Cushing, John Perkins"; Wilder, "Horticulture of Boston," p. 633; G. Frederick Robinson and Ruth Robinson Wheeler, *Great Little Watertown: A Tercentenary History* (Cambridge, Mass.: privately printed, 1930), p. 79; *Farmers' Cabinet and American Herd-Book* 6 (June 1842): 338–39; *Horticultural Register* 1 (February 1835): 69–71; *Magazine of Horticulture* 3 (March, September 1837): 102–5, 346–48. The quotation is from Downing, *Landscape Gardening,* p. 40.

17. Henry Lee, quoted in Morse, *Henry and Mary Lee,* p. 14.

18. See Henry Lee's comment to this effect in ibid., p. 15.

19. See note 4, above.

retired to an estate in West Cambridge to busy himself with his garden and greenhouse. "Uncle George," wrote the captain's sister-in-law to her son, "when he can spare time from his peaches, melons, and squashes, feels and expresses great interest about you."[20]

Finally there was Henry, whom we encountered earlier as an India merchant and die-hard free trader. Even after he lost a congressional election to Nathan Appleton, Lee continued to press his economic ideas in print, but by 1850, when he came into possession of a Brookline estate, he seemed ready to leave it all behind. "Gardening seems to have usurped the place in his affection formerly held by economic research," wrote his biographer.[21] Thus when his granddaughter described his study at the Brookline house, she noted that it "almost always smelt of fruit." In the office could be found "his desk for writing, and a table against the east window, with boxes of metal and wooden tags for his fruit trees, and bits of red chalk, pencils, etc. There were drawers to the left as one entered, in which Grandfather kept ripening pears, and apples stood about on mantelpiece or shelf. On the bookshelves above the drawers were books and pamphlets on horticulture and gardening."[22]

For their generation, the Lee brothers were relatively modest in their horticultural undertakings. Compare Henry's garden with, for example, those of Horatio Hollis Hunnewell. Hunnewell, a prominent banker, purchased a five-hundred-acre estate in Wellesley in 1852, and proceeded with landscape improvements a couple of years later. Starting with nothing but a "hideous sandy plain," he laid out elaborate Italian gardens, complete with parapets, balustrades, statuary, vases, and topiary. He erected no fewer than twelve greenhouses, six for flowers and six for fruits, in addition to a conservatory attached to the main house. He planted bed after bed of ornamental flowers, and even the many fruit and vegetable gardens were enclosed with ornamental hedges. Hunnewell installed a steam engine, at a cost of twelve hundred dollars, to power the gardens' numerous fountains (fig. 33). And along the estate's avenues, he planted numerous trees, both native and exotic.[23]

20. Morse, *Henry and Mary Lee*, pp. 19–20; Mary Lee to Henry Lee, Jr., 20 September 1838, in ibid., p. 268. Lee's horticultural diligence paid off; in 1837, we find him submitting a 130-pound squash to a Massachusetts Horticultural Society exhibition (Russell, *Transactions . . . , 1837–8*, p. 98).

21. Kenneth Wiggins Porter, *The Jacksons and the Lees: Two Generations of Massachusetts Merchants, 1765–1844*, 2 vols. (Cambridge: Harvard University Press, 1937), 2:1487.

22. Morse, *Henry and Mary Lee*, p. 305.

23. Norfolk Agricultural Society, Report of the Visiting Committee, in Charles L. Flint, ed., *Abstract of Returns of the Agricultural Societies of Massachusetts, 1856* (Boston: William White, 1856), pp. 161–63; Norfolk Agricultural Society, Report of the Supervisory Commit-

33. *Gardens at the Hunnewell Estate.* Engraving by James Smillie. Reprinted from A. J. Downing, *A Treatise on the Theory and Practice of Landscape Gardening,* 6th ed. (New York, 1859). (Courtesy Yale University Library.)

Equally extravagant in his own way was Frederic Tudor, the man famous as the Ice King for the fortune he made selling New England ice to the tropics. Tudor's goal was to establish a thriving fruit and flower garden on a windy, salty promontory on the shores of Nahant. It appeared almost as foolish an undertaking as shipping ice to the equator—and it was quite as successful. The Ice King's solution was to enclose the entire garden with high double-pale fences, and eventually Louis Bonne of Jersey pears, as large as ten inches in circumference, flourished on what Tudor called his "remarkable peninsula."[24]

---

tee, in Charles L. Flint, ed., *Abstract of Returns of the Agricultural Societies of Massachusetts, for 1860* (Boston: William White, 1861), pp. 93–95; *The Horticulturist and Journal of Rural Art and Rural Taste,* n.s., 8 (February 1857): 65–66; *Magazine of Horticulture* 23 (August 1857): 367–80; 24 (January 1858): 42–44; 25 (October 1859): 459–62; "Rural Taste in North America," *Christian Examiner* 69 (November 1860): 342; A. J. Downing, *A Treatise on the Theory and Practice of Landscape Gardening,* 6th ed. (New York: A. O. Moore, 1859), pp. 442–45; Wilder, "Horticulture of Boston," pp. 631–32; L. H. Bailey, ed., *The Standard Cyclopedia of Horticulture,* 3 vols. (New York: Macmillan, 1930), 2:1581; *DAB,* s.v. "Hunnewell, Horatio Hollis."

24. Wilder, "Horticulture of Boston," p. 638; Curtis, *Memories of Fifty Years,* pp. 64–65; Albert Emerson Benson, *History of the Massachusetts Horticultural Society* (Boston: Massachusetts Horticultural Society, 1929) (hereafter, Benson, MHS), pp. 105–6; Frederic Tudor to B. Guild, 20 January 1842, Massachusetts Society for Promoting Agriculture Papers (hereafter MSPA Papers), drawer D, folder II, number 68, MHS.

If Hunnewell was extravagant in the elegance of his horticultural operations, and Tudor in the perverseness of his, Marshall Pinckney Wilder (fig. 34), a successful commission merchant in Boston, beat both of them in sheer scale. Wilder's estate in Dorchester, Hawthorn Grove, could easily have been mistaken for a commercial enterprise. The nurseries alone contained thousands of fruit trees, including at one time an astonishing nine hundred varieties of the pear. Wilder's floricultural specialty was the camellia, of which he cultivated three hundred varieties under glass.[25] It is a testament to both his own energy and that of his extensive gardening staff that Wilder devoted a scant few hours a day to the supervision of such an enormous operation. "After breakfast and family duties," wrote one horticultural editor in 1855, "he goes forth to see that each man is at his post, to drop a word of encouragement to the industrious and the faithful, and by his own example to encourage and instruct them, now training a vine, or giving a finishing touch to a boquet, then wielding the spade or the pruning knife, hybridizing a Camellia, planting a tree, inserting a bud, sketching a flower, or gathering the first fruit of a new variety of Pear for subsequent study, delineation, and description."[26] By ten o'clock, he was off to Boston to sell cotton and wool.[27]

The new enthusiasm for horticulture crystallized in the establishment of the Massachusetts Horticultural Society in 1829, the fifth such society in the United States.[28] Its most significant prototype, however, was probably

25. John H. Sheppard, "Memoir of Hon. Marshall Pinckney Wilder," *New England Historical and Genealogical Register* 21 (April 1867): 9–120; Andrew P. Peabody, "A Memorial Address on the Late Marshall Pinckney Wilder, President of the New England Historic Genealogical Society" (Boston: New England Historic Genealogical Society, 1888); "Calls at Gardens and Nurseries: Hawthorn Grove, Col. M. P. Wilder," *Magazine of Horticulture* 9 (May 1843): 187–89; "Biographical Sketches of Distinguished American Horticulturists. Marshall Pinckney Wilder, of Dorchester, Mass.," *Horticulturist*, n.s., 5 (March 1855): 111–15; Norfolk Agricultural Society, Report of the Supervisory Committee, in Flint, *Agricultural Societies . . . 1860*, pp. 89–93; Bailey, *Cyclopedia of Horticulture*, 2:1603; *DAB*, s.v. "Wilder, Marshall Pinckney."
26. "Biographical Sketches of Distinguished American Horticulturists. Marshall Pinckney Wilder," p. 114.
27. Ibid., pp. 113, 114.
28. The standard histories of the MHS are Benson, *MHS*, and Robert Manning, *History of the Massachusetts Horticultural Society, 1829–1878* (Boston: Massachusetts Horticultural Society, 1880)—hereafter Manning, *MHS*. See also *Proceedings on the Establishment of the Massachusetts Horticultural Society* (Boston: Isaac R. Butts, 1829), and *NEF* 7 (9 January, 27 February, 20 March 1829): 198, 250, 278. On other horticultural societies in America, see U. P. Hedrick, *A History of Horticulture in America to 1860* (New York: Oxford University Press, 1950), pp. 499–513; Ann Leighton, *American Gardens of the Nineteenth Century: "For Comfort and Affluence"* (Amherst: University of Massachusetts Press, 1987), pp. 101–5; James Boyd, *A History of the Pennsylvania Horticultural Society, 1827–1927* (Philadelphia: Pennsylvania Horticultural Society, 1929); and Hamilton Traub, "Tendencies in the De-

34. *Marshall Pinckney Wilder.* Reprinted from the *Horticulturist* 3 (July 1848). (Courtesy Yale University Library.)

not American at all, but the Horticultural Society of London (later the Royal Horticultural Society), established in 1804.[29] Both John Lowell and Samuel G. Perkins were corresponding members of the HSL, and Lowell in particular was fully aware of HSL developments through his extensive correspondence with that society's president, Thomas Andrew Knight.[30]

In fact, the HSL and the MHS had a great deal in common. Making allowances for the social differences between England and the United States, the membership profiles of the two societies were roughly similar. Both attracted the economic and social elite. In the case of the HSL, this meant a mix of titled gentlemen and rich merchants and manufacturers once removed from the source of their wealth, such men as the earl of Dartmouth and John Wedgwood, son of the Quaker potter Josiah Wedgwood.[31] In the case of the MHS, this meant a cross-section of the Boston elite, from merchants to industrialists to lawyers and doctors.[32] In this respect, Boston's horticultural society was not so different from the MSPA. But what was a new departure—and the same can be said of the HSL[33]— was the inclusion of *practical* men in the society, that is, gardeners, seedsmen, and nurserymen (fig. 35).[34] At least in Boston, practical horticulturists were by no means excluded from the work of the society; they held

velopment of American Horticultural Associations," *National Horticultural Magazine* 9 (January 1930): 18–26.

29. Harold R. Fletcher, *The Story of the Royal Horticultural Society, 1804–1968* (London: Oxford University Press, 1969), pp. 1–76.

30. It was Knight who first brought Lowell to the attention of the HSL. "Read an extract of a letter from Mr Knight," reads the HSL minutes of 21 August 1822, "stating that Mr. Lowel of Mombry [Roxbury!], near Boston, Massachusets, had requested him to obtain for him Parts 5 & 6 of the 1st volume of the Transactions of the Society." In light of Lowell's recent presentation of "a valuable work" to the HSL's library, he was presented with the entire first volume. By 1823 the society appeared to be more familiar with the Bostonian. That May Knight successfully recommended "John Lowell, Esq of Roxbury near Boston in N. America" for election as a corresponding member. Perkins is first acknowledged in the HSL minutes in March 1823, when he was sent a box of strawberries in thanks for a box of plants received by the HSL. In January 1824 the HSL sent him some "Esculent Vegetable seeds." His election to membership is not recorded. Horticultural Society of London, Council Minutes, 21 August 1822, 24 March, 2 May, 26 May 1823, 2 January 1824, Lindley Library, Royal Horticultural Society, London.

31. Fletcher, *Royal Horticultural Society*, pp. 19–41.

32. For a membership list of the MHS, see Manning, *MHS*, pp. 500–525.

33. Fletcher, *Royal Horticultural Society*, pp. 19–36. Among the founding members of the HSL, for example, were William Forsyth, gardener to King George III; William Townsend Aiken, the royal gardener at Kew; and James Dickson, a nurseryman and seedsman who lived over his business premises.

34. Manning, *MHS*, pp. 500–525. Among the most important of these practical members were Charles M. Hovey (Hovey & Co., Cambridge), Joseph Breck (Joseph Breck & Sons, Brighton), and Robert Manning (Pomological Garden, Salem). On nurseries in America, see Hedrick, *Horticulture*, pp. 197–212, and Leighton, *American Gardens*, pp. 67–82.

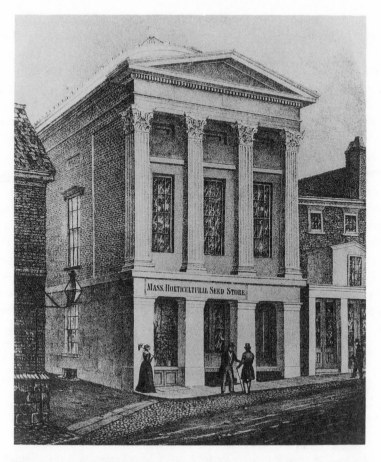

35. *Horticultural Hall.* This building, erected in 1845, accommodated MHS meetings on the second floor and related business enterprises on the first. Reprinted from Robert Manning, *History of the Massachusetts Horticultural Society* (Boston, 1880). (Courtesy Yale University Library.)

offices and often contributed the bulk of the offerings to the society's numerous exhibitions. But let there be no misunderstanding. The elite dominated the affairs of the MHS, established both its public and private image, set its very tone.

In its activities, the Massachusetts Horticultural Society again differed little from either its London counterpart or the MSPA. This similarity was predictable; all three organizations shared assumptions on the best way to advance knowledge. The MHS collected and disseminated horticultural information, mainly through the society's published transactions. It established a horticultural library. It distributed new plants received from foreign sources—for the society's corresponding secretary skillfully courted ambassadors, naval officers, and overseas horticulturists—free to MHS members, no doubt a practice that worked to the pecuniary benefit of the society's professional nurserymen. And most prominently of all, it sponsored weekly, seasonal, and annual exhibitions at which premiums were awarded for prize fruits, vegetables, and flowers.[35]

As with the MSPA's Brighton show, the MHS's annual exhibition also provided an occasion for an elaborate dinner hosting Boston's wealthiest and most prominent men. At the very first exhibition, held at that mercantile landmark the Exchange Coffee House in 1829, 160 people sat down to a "sumptuous dinner, prepared by Messrs. Johnson & Castlehouse," caterers. At that celebration, about one hundred baskets and dishes of fruit were displayed. By 1845 the scene had changed. Now the dinner, hosting 600, was held at Faneuil Hall, especially decorated for the occasion with plaques, festoons, flowers, and even trees set between the hall's pillars (fig. 36). Elaborate floral arrangements—including a Gothic pyramid, a Chinese temple, and a Newfoundland dog executed in hollyhocks and moss—also graced the festival. No fewer than fourteen hundred dishes of fruit were on display, including 240 varieties of pear from a single exhibitor. The self-congratulatory hymns, speeches, and toasts ("OUR MERCHANT PRINCES,—Their ships have ploughed the sea, and furrowed the ocean; their enterprise garners up rich crops, which their liberality now dispenses with an unsparing hand") must have gone on for hours.[36]

The MHS struck out on its own, and in fact initiated a national movement, when in 1831 it established Mount Auburn Cemetery (fig. 37). This was the first so-called rural cemetery in America, that is, a graveyard located in a nonurban, naturalistic setting, designed to meet not only a practical but an aesthetic end. As originally conceived by the MHS, Mount Auburn was to be not only a burial place but also an experimental garden (probably along the lines of the HSL's garden at Chiswick), but the garden

35. This profile of the MHS's activities emerges mainly from the society's published transactions, and secondarily from Manning's *MHS*. Originally the premiums took the form of either cash or prize plates and medals, but in 1840 an MHS committee recommended that cash premiums be done away with entirely. The reasoning in this case, as it had been with the MSPA, was that premiums were to inspire a laudable spirit of emulation, not a greedy scramble for money. Subcommittee report, 20 March 1840, Massachusetts Horticultural Society, Boston.

36. Description of the MHS festival of 1829, in H. A. S. Dearborn, *An Address Delivered before the Massachusetts Horticultural Society, on the Celebration of Their First Anniversary, September 19, 1829,* 2d ed. (Boston: T. Buckingham, 1833), pp. 23–25; Description of the MHS festival of 1845, in *Transactions of the Massachusetts Horticultural Society for the Years 1843–4–5–6* (Boston: Dutton and Wentworth, 1847), pp. 94–97, 112.

36. *Massachusetts Horticultural Society Dinner, Faneuil Hall.* Reprinted from the *Horticulturist* 3 (November 1848). (Courtesy Yale University Library.)

simply never took shape. Furthermore, it was not long before the cemetery plot owners and the horticulturists found themselves in conflict over the proper disposition of money and power. By 1834 the horticultural society had parted ways with Mount Auburn, but not before establishing financial arrangements that yielded the MHS a substantial income for years.[37]

The horticultural society probably drained away some of the energy that had formerly gone into the MSPA. Many of the agricultural society's members had all along been primarily horticulturists,[38] and it seems reasonable that they would have turned their energies to a new society that focused on their specific interest. More critically, however, the styles in rural pursuits, the sense of what sort of countryside activity was most appropriate to the elite, were changing. When the subject of horticulture was first broached in the MSPA's publications, in an article written in 1810 by John Lowell, it was only with hesitation. "A Society has been formed in Great Britain, within a few years past," wrote Lowell of the HSL, "for the purpose of promoting horticultural improvements, a branch of agriculture if not as extensively useful as some others, at least claiming the merit of

37. Jacob Bigelow, *A History of the Cemetery of Mount Auburn* (Boston: James Munroe, 1860); Manning, *MHS,* pp. 69–118; Barbara Rotundo, "Mount Auburn Cemetery: A Proper Boston Institution," *Harvard Library Bulletin* 22 (July 1974): 268–79.

38. John Lowell to the MSPA, 20 January 1813, MSPA Papers, D–I–4.

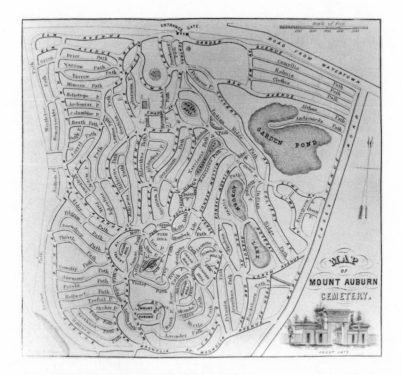

37. *Map of Mount Auburn Cemetery.* In line with its historical roots in the MHS, the cemetery's paths were given horticultural names. Reprinted from Jacob Bigelow, *A History of the Cemetery of Mount Auburn* (Boston, 1860). (Courtesy Yale University Library.)

contributing to our comforts and innocent luxuries."[39] Lowell felt obliged to apologize for horticulture because it was not of obvious utility. Within a decade, Lowell would point to the very practical reasons that horticulture should be undertaken by the Massachusetts yeomanry, but when horticulture became the latest vogue in rural pursuits among the Boston elite after about 1830, it was not because its utility had been established. One need only recall Perkins's six hundred feet of fruits and flowers under glass or Wilder's three hundred varieties of camellias to sense that. In fact, the horticultural vogue was just the opposite. It concerned the preference for the beautiful over the practical, for ornament over utility.

When they imported tea and pig iron, manufactured calicoes and woolens, built bridges and railroads, and financed and insured these enterprises,

39. *Papers for 1810, Communicated to the Massachusetts Society for Promoting Agriculture* (Boston: Russell and Cutler, 1810), p. 105.

members of the Boston elite were being quite practical; they were making money. Boston's wealthy men never questioned the morality of making money, but they did increasingly feel obliged to prove that they did not value money as an end in itself and that they could value something without monetary value altogether. Either they had to assert their transcendence of materialism or they had to purge themselves of it. The first required proof, and the second, reform. Horticulture was useful to the Boston elite because it promised both.

By virtue of their interest in horticulture, members of the elite hoped to establish their freedom from materialism. Certainly the opposite was true; so long as "the mind is absorbed at the shrine of Mammon," read the MHS *Transactions,* the products of horticulture, worth but little and good for less, will be "neglected or despised."[40] In that case, the treasuring of a flower's beauty or a fruit's perfection was prima facie evidence of an ability to appreciate what had no market value and no apparent use. "Surely," insisted one writer for Boston's *Horticultural Register,* the horticulturist "looks beyond the mere profit of his labors and rejects the insinuation, that his every act is an act of cold calculating indemnity for toil and attention."[41] He exists on a higher moral plane. "We have got beyond mere utility," remarked Caleb Cushing—who had just negotiated a commercial treaty with China—as he surveyed the MHS exhibit of 1845. "We have learned to admire art, to appreciate painting and sculpture, and to look upon fruits and flowers as models of delicacy and beauty."[42] In other words, we have arrived at ornament, beauty for beauty's sake. A writer for the *New England Magazine* echoed these sentiments. "In the march of civilization," read an article on horticulture in 1831, as man progresses "towards an exalted state of refinement, . . . to the demands of utility, are successively added those of comfort and embellishment." Enter then the fine arts— painting, sculpture, architecture, and, not the least, "the genius of Horticulture."[43] "*Agriculture, Manufactures, Commerce, and Horticulture,*" toasted manufacturer Samuel Appleton. "The first gives us *food,*—the second *clothing,*—the third gives us *riches,*—the fourth adds grace and ornament to the others."[44]

40. *Transactions . . . 1843–4–5–6,* introduction, p. 10.
41. "Horticultural Pursuits," *Horticultural Register* 1 (November 1835): 107.
42. Description of the MHS festival of 1845, in *Transactions . . . 1843–4–5–6,* p. 111.
43. "Horticulture," *New England Magazine* 1 (August 1831): 144–46.
44. Description of the MHS festival of 1832, in Thaddeus William Harris, *A Discourse Delivered before the Massachusetts Horticultural Society, on the Celebration of Its Fourth Anniversary, October 3, 1832* (Cambridge: E. W. Metcalf, 1832), p. 57.

What lay beyond the materialism of a commercial society, then, might not be the dreaded fifth stage of decay and decline but one of cultural refinement as symbolized by horticulture. If horticulture represented the final triumph over materialism instead of defeat at its hands, then the passage from utility to ornament was nothing other than the victorious entrance into the highest stage of civilization. Thus when Henry Dearborn, president of the MHS in 1829, sketched the history of the human race, he proceeded from "the wild and erratic pursuits of the savage" to the "quiet avocations of the husbandman" to the "triumphant labors of the accomplished horticulturist."[45]

Significantly, however, between the stages of agriculture and horticulture as described by Dearborn was a period of luxury and extravagance. Only when Solomon's commercial fleets had brought back the riches of the world, and only when the children of Israel had been rebuked for their materialism, were the famous gardens, vineyards, and orchards of ancient Israel created.[46] To the members of the MHS, such talk must have had a good deal of resonance, some of it disturbing, for the materialistic civilization of the past looked distressingly similar to that of antebellum Boston. Was not the China trade, the source of wealth for many a Boston horticulturist, the modern equivalent of Solomon's fleets? Were not the Boston elite, children of God's new Israel, seemingly obsessed with making money? Could one legitimately say that materialism had been transcended so long as fortunes in Turkish opium and Lowell textiles continued to be made?

Identification with horticulture, however, assured Boston's industrialists and merchants that the historical stage of materialism was a thing of the past. The very practice of horticulture was evidence of an advanced civilization and the formation of a horticultural society an emblem of cultural refinement. "Ladies and gentlemen," announced the textile millionaire Abbott Lawrence at the horticultural festival of 1842, "The exhibition here to-night, altogether, is the best proof that can be presented of a high state of civilization and refinement." Just what scene did Lawrence survey? Festoons of flowers, floor-to-ceiling bouquets of dahlias, table after table piled high with exquisite fruits—"the *tout ensemble,*" remarked the *Transactions*

45. Dearborn, *Address,* p. 3. A similar chronology is outlined in Norfolk Agricultural Society, "Report of the Committee on Orchards," in Charles L. Flint, ed., *The Agriculture of Massachusetts, as Shown in Returns of the Agricultural Societies, 1853* (Boston: William White, 1854), pp. 106–7.
46. Ibid., pp. 4–7. A similar sequence is traced in "Horticulture," *New England Magazine,* pp. 144–46.

breathlessly, " . . . presented a scene of unsurpassed beauty and moral sublimity."[47]

The self-assurance that came with identifying horticulture as an emblem of refinement is only half the picture, for the brash pronouncements of disinterestedness were matched by the prescription of horticulture as a moral antidote. This prescription was essentially the same as that recommended to American society as a whole in the antebellum era. Horticulture was being peddled as a cure not only for the moral ills of the Boston elite but also for what ailed America in general. Leaders of the broader horticultural movement, most notably Andrew Jackson Downing of Newburgh, New York, were convinced that the practice of horticulture would save America from materialism, restlessness, even intemperance, dangers that obsessed Americans of the antebellum era.[48] When prominent Bostonians attributed curative properties to horticulture, however, they were responding to moral demands specific to the elite social ethos, and they clearly identified the man in need of a cure as a member of that elite.

This is a truly desperate man. Now we see him "panting and stirring in the ranks of Fashion," now engaged in "exclusive and unremitted," even "feverish," business pursuits. How "sordid and selfish" he has become! So consumed is he by a single-minded ambition to accumulate wealth that he has become debilitated in body as well as in mind.[49] At night he cannot sleep, and by day he is plagued with a thousand ills. "Let him who is engaged in the racking cares of commerce, say in what frame of mind *his* eyes close in sleep, and what are the anxieties of his waking hours. Let the manufacturer tell of his feverish dreams by night, and his dyspeptic symptoms by day. . . . follow these men—look at their daily walks and occupations—and then turn to the horticulturist."[50]

We find the horticulturist asleep in bed, dreaming of fields and orchards. Up before dawn, he breathes in the "aroma of a thousand plants." Surveying his horticultural domain, he stops to give kind words to his "contented laborers." Here is a man whose "dreams are not harassed by

47. Description of the MHS festival of 1842, in *Transactions of the Massachusetts Horticultural Society for the Year 1842–43* (Boston: Dutton and Wentworth, 1843), pp. 19–20, 30.

48. Tamara Plakins Thornton, "Cultivating the American Character: Horticulture as Moral Reform in the Antebellum Era," *Orion Nature Quarterly* 4 (Spring 1985): 10–19.

49. *Horticultural Register* 4 (1 January 1838): 33; [John C. Gray], "[Review of] Kenrick's *American Orchardist*," *North American Review* 47 (October 1838): 448; [George Lunt], "Address Delivered before the Society on 15th May, 1845, at the Dedication of Their Hall," in *Transactions . . . 1843–4–5–6*, transactions for 1845, p. 8; John C. Gray, *An Address Delivered before the Massachusetts Horticultural Society, at Their Sixth Anniversary, September 17, 1834* (Boston: J. T. Buckingham, 1834), pp. 5–6.

thieves that rob the vaults, the keys of which are tied to the wrists of the cashier for safety." Could the same be said of Boston's merchants? Here is a man virtuous and pure, with "no fears of the deep curse which rests on him who has injured the widow and the fatherless." Could the same be said of Boston's textile kings?[51]

Horticulture would reform these pathetic merchants and manufacturers by improving their bodies, minds, and souls. "The pursuits of horticulture are salutary to the physical & moral nature of man," commented Vice President of the MHS Zebedee Cook in 1830. "They impart vigor to the body, and expansion and elevation to the mind."[52] John C. Gray agreed. "Mankind have found by experience," he stated to an MHS audience in 1834, "that the contemplation of what is graceful or beautiful, serves to correct & refine the taste, to expand & elevate the understanding, to soften & purify the heart."[53] Best then to quit the countinghouse and mill office for the suburban retreat. But if it was unrealistic to expect Boston's first men to desert their occupations altogether for a life of rural bliss, then at least the adoption of horticulture as a summer or after-hours pastime could be recommended without reservation. The man of affairs cannot lose with horticulture, remarked George Lunt, an MHS speaker, "for if it acquire him no other possession, it will at least bring him that priceless one of an innocent heart and a gentle mind."[54] Indeed, he continued, there is "scarcely a change more striking than to leave the noisy streets of the 'dim and treeless town' for the pleasant garden. . . . Instead of the tumult and intemperate haste of the crowded haunts of men, we rest with the repose of nature, broken only by murmurs that are delicious, and the warbled music of the skies. . . . We forget the debasing competitions of wealth and fame, and enter into the innocent pursuits of the guileless creatures of the air."[55]

We see now why the antebellum MHS was an exclusively male organization. The role of horticulture, after all, was to counter the money-making, power-hungry drive, something to which women, safely quarantined from the marketplace and forum, were not susceptible. It was only with the Civil War—1864 to be exact—that women were allowed into the horticultural society as anything more than guests at the annual dinners and occasional

50. *American Quarterly Review* 21 (June 1837): 366–67.
51. Ibid., pp. 367–68.
52. Zebedee Cook, Jr., *An Address Pronounced before the Massachusetts Horticultural Society, in Commemoration of Its Second Annual Festival, the 10th of September, 1830* (Boston: Isaac R. Butts, 1830), p. 5.
53. Gray, *Address*, p. 8.
54. [Lunt], "Address," p. 8.
55. Ibid., pp. 14–15.

exhibitors of flower arrangements, and it is from this year that the MHS's gradual transition away from a male self-reform association can be dated.[56]

We also see why the horticultural society became involved in the business of establishing a rural cemetery. Since during the business day, the man of commerce or industry would be out of range of the purifying influence of his suburban garden, some other institution would have to fill the need. One MHS official recommended that horticultural exhibitions be located in business districts for this purpose,[57] but the real solution was Mount Auburn. The cemetery's beautiful landscape, its gravestones' inspiring inscriptions, and its infusion with the promise of a life hereafter would impress visitors with just how ultimately meaningless are the material rewards of this world by comparison with the transcendent beauty of nature, the legacy of a virtuous life, and the glory of reunion with one's Maker (fig. 38). In his consecration speech of 1831, Joseph Story intoned: "The rivalries of the world will here drop from the heart; . . . and selfishness and avarice will be checked; the restlessness of ambition will be rebuked." In an address before the MHS, Zebedee Cook made the same point. "It is there," he stated of Mount Auburn, "that the heart is chastened, and the soul is subdued, and the affections purified and exalted. It is there that ambition surveys the boundaries of its powers, its hopes, and its aspirations." A walk through Mount Auburn, continued a writer for the *Christian Review,* serves "to moderate the aspirations of ambition" and "to allay vanity and frivolity . . . in a word, to give to life its true and awful significance."[58]

Mount Auburn's link with the MHS provides a critical clue as to the function of rural cemeteries in the antebellum era. Recently historians have examined the cemetery movement for what it reveals about contemporary attitudes toward religion, death, the city, and the natural environment.[59]

56. Manning, *MHS,* pp. 500–525 (MHS membership list).

57. Ezra Weston, Jr., *An Address Delivered before the Massachusetts Horticultural Society, at Their Eighth Anniversary Dinner, September 17, 1836* (Boston: Tuttle, Weeks, and Dennett, 1836), pp. 5–6.

58. Joseph Story, *An Address Delivered on the Dedication of the Cemetery at Mount Auburn, September 24, 1831* (Boston: Joseph T. and Edwin Buckingham, 1831), p. 20; Cook, *Address,* pp. 26–28; "Thoughts Connected with Rural Cemeteries," *Christian Review* 13 (March 1848): 11. See also "Mount Auburn," *New England Magazine* 1 (September 1831): 236–39; "Mount Auburn Cemetery," *North American Review* 33 (October 1831): 397–406; and "The Moral Influence of Graves," in Wilson Flagg, *Mount Auburn: Its Scenes, Its Beauties, and Its Lessons* (Boston: James Munroe, 1861), pp. 34–38.

59. Especially noteworthy discussions of the rural cemetery movement include Neil Harris, *The Artist in American Society: The Formative Years, 1790–1860* (Chicago: University of Chicago Press, 1966), pp. 200–208; Thomas Bender, "The 'Rural' Cemetery Movement: Urban Travail and the Appeal of Nature," *New England Quarterly* 47 (June 1974):

38. *Scene at Mount Auburn.* Reprinted from Cornelia W. Walter, *Mount Auburn Illustrated* (New York, 1850). (Courtesy Yale University Library.)

The rural cemetery's association with metropolitan elites, however, has remained something of a mystery. What purpose did it serve for this class? If we acknowledge the origins of America's first and foremost rural cemetery in an organization dedicated to the moral purification of a local elite, the picture becomes clearer. Rural cemeteries were elite institutions because the rich needed to be purged of materialism and the powerful of ambition, and what better way to do that than to impress on them the insignificance and evanescence of this world's rewards? Inasmuch as the rural cemetery took on the character of an elite self-reform movement, we might rethink the meaning of the movement it in turn spawned—the parks movement. It is no coincidence that America's first park advocates and designers—Downing, Vaux, Cleveland, and of course Olmsted—sprang from horticultural circles.[60] Perhaps it was hoped that urban parks would

196–211; Stanley French, "The Cemetery as Cultural Institution: The Establishment of Mount Auburn and the 'Rural Cemetery' Movement," *American Quarterly* 26 (March 1974): 37–59; and David Schuyler, "The Evolution of the Anglo-American Rural Cemetery: Landscape Architecture as Social and Cultural History," *Journal of Garden History* 4 (July–September 1984): 291–304.

60. Years before he designed Central Park, Frederick Law Olmsted, then a gentleman farmer, was writing to Downing's *Horticulturist* for advice on fruit trees (*Horticulturist* 2

do more than uplift and control the masses;[61] perhaps they would also engender self-control among the rich and powerful.

In characterizing horticulture as a moral antidote, then, Bostonians were crediting horticulture with the ability to cultivate man morally, intellectually, and physically. "He who cultivates a garden, and brings to perfection flowers and fruits, cultivates and advances at the same time his own nature," moralized Ezra Weston to an MHS audience in 1836. In 1845 Joseph Breck presented a toast to the same group. To "Horticulture and Mental Culture," he intoned. "The one the *cause,* the other, the *effect.*"[62] When Boston's prominent citizens characterized horticulture as evidence of refinement, they were denying any tendency to crude materialism. When instead they followed Weston's and Breck's lead and characterized horticulture as a refining agent, they sought to establish the means by which they had overcome materialism. In either case, horticulture provided a way to live up to the moral strictures of the elite ethos.

In their identification with horticulture, members of the Boston elite sought to define themselves not only as individuals but as a class. They were aware that, to many antebellum Americans, horticulture—at least at first glance—seemed an undesirable pursuit precisely because of its class associations. A writer for Boston's *Horticultural Register* noted "a secret recoil" at the idea of gardening. Some feared that its introduction into America "would prove inimical to that virtue and simplicity of manners, which alone can establish and perpetuate our institutions."[63] Was there not something antirepublican about horticulture? Was it not, after all, just the sort of thing good-for-nothing aristocrats do? According to John C. Gray, a Boston millionaire and MHS member, "some readers may remark that horticulture can form the chief business of life with very few; that generally it deserves no better name than that of an amusement; that, even in this

---

[August 1847]: 100). Olmsted's design partner, Calvert Vaux, got his start in America as Downing's partner. And another early landscape architect, Horace W. S. Cleveland, was secretary of the New Jersey Horticultural Society in the 1840s (Horace W. S. Cleveland to the Massachusetts Horticultural Society, 20 September 1848, Massachusetts Horticultural Society). Brenda Bullion discusses the historical (though not the ideological) link between horticultural activity and the emergence of landscape architecture in America in "Hawthorns and Hemlocks: The Return of the Sacred Grove," *Landscape Journal* 2 (1983): 114–24.

61. For a representative interpretation of the postbellum parks movement as a movement to control the masses, see Geoffrey Blodgett, "Frederick Law Olmsted: Landscape Architecture as Conservative Reform," *Journal of American History* 62 (March 1976): 869–89.

62. Weston, *Address*, p. 7; *Transactions . . . 1843–4–5–6*, transactions for 1845, p. 113.

63. *Horticultural Register* 3 (1 April 1837): 121.

point of view, it is better adapted to a country abounding in men of wealth and leisure, than to an economical and industrious community like ours."[64]

Of course, Boston's elite were not necessarily against engaging in a pastime that imparted a distinctly aristocratic tinge. Indeed, one of the admirable aspects of the Horticultural Society of London was that it was not merely an association of professional gardeners but one "patronized by the purses, and encouraged by the presences of princes, noblemen, and gentlemen of fortune."[65] If the MHS could not enroll peers of the realm, then at least it could boast of its lords of the loom and merchant princes. Such anglophilia, however, had no secure place in republican America. If the MHS members ever sighed over the HSL membership list, they quickly realized that such sentiments could not influence their public posture. On the defensive, Boston's elite set out to prove that horticulture was really a republican pastime. It took some imagination to republicanize horticulture, but they were equal to the challenge.

A major theme of the republicanizing campaign was that, from the urban flowerpot to the suburban estate, the rewards of cultivation were available to all, rich and poor alike. Horticulture was thus, in the words of Sen. Robert C. Winthrop, "a Republican Fine Art."[66] The very products of horticulture acquired moral significance. Fruits became republican luxuries—innocent and inexpensive. To "the art of Horticulture," toasted John C. Gray, "which furnishes us with cheap but splendid ornaments; May it never want encouragement in a Republican and economical country."[67]

Inasmuch as fruits were republican luxuries, they addressed a traditional republican bugaboo, dependence on foreign luxuries. In horticultural terms, independence translated into cultivating native plants. "We have been for too long accustomed to rely on foreign nurseries for fruit trees and other plants," argued Vice President Zebedee Cook. It has been the fashion, he continued, to underrate all domestic products, horticultural as

64. [Gray], "Review," p. 447.

65. *NEF* 8 (30 January 1829): 221. Like its London counterpart, the MHS distinguished between "ordinary members" and "practical gardeners" in its membership rolls. Bylaws of the Massachusetts Horticultural Society, Articles 18, 30.

66. Dearborn, *Address,* p. 10; *Horticultural Register* 1 (1 January 1835): 2; ibid. 4 (1 January 1838): 32; *Report of the Twentieth Annual Exhibition of the Massachusetts Horticultural Society, and Third Triennial Festival, Held at Faneuil Hall, September 19, 20, 21, 22, 1848* (Boston: Tuttle and Dennett, 1848), p. 36.

67. Description of the MHS festival of 1829, in Dearborn, *Address,* p. 27; [Gray], "Review," pp. 445–46.

well as manufactured. Cook suggested that public nurseries be established. President Dearborn advocated subsidized plant expeditions into the American wilderness.[68] There was even the expectation that in the New World plants would thrive as never before. Just as man had been reborn in the Republic, so would trees, fruits, flowers, and vegetables. Even the Europeans were looking to America's "fresh soil" for the regeneration of exhausted "vegetable races."[69]

Did elite Bostonians identify with an ultimately republican or an ultimately aristocratic pursuit? The answer is not one or the other, precisely because their social status was so ambiguous. How after all does one characterize an American elite? If, in the republican spirit, it is egalitarian, it really offers little to those interested in social recognition. If instead it is aristocratic, then it will have a hard time justifying itself in republican America. The advantage of horticulture was that it offered an alternative criterion for an American elite, one that in some measure resolved the tensions between republicanism and aristocracy. That criterion was cultivation.[70]

Cultivation, as we have seen, characterized horticulturists either because they had of their own will risen far enough above materialism to appreciate horticulture or because horticulture had purified them of their money-making fervor. These were just the sort of men to comprise a legitimate American elite. They were not basing their claims to high social status on inherited wealth or blood line, as did Old World aristocrats. In America, a man need only be cultivated—morally, mentally, and physically—to take his rightful stand at the head of society. Horticulture insured just such a morally pure, mentally strong, and physically vigorous class of men.

Hence, not the least bizarre aspect of Boston's horticultural enthusiasts is that they felt they had something in common with their fruits, flowers, and vegetables. Both were the choice products of cultivation. As Nathan Appleton explained at an MHS anniversary dinner, cultivation is "the only process of obtaining Fruit, whether applied to Mind or Matter." Harvard College was described as a nursery that produced premium-quality fruits,

---

68. Cook, *Address*, pp. 23–25; Dearborn, *Address*, p. 22. Cook's and Dearborn's comments echo the Whig policy of government protection and support of domestic economic enterprises.

69. Gray, *Address*, p. 14; A. J. Downing, "Some Remarks on the Superiority of Native Varieties of Fruits," *Transactions of the Massachusetts Horticultural Society* 1 (Boston: Wm. D. Ticknor, 1847–51), transactions for 1847, p. 30.

70. On the links between the ideal of self-cultivation and Unitarian moral philosophy, see Daniel Walker Howe, *The Unitarian Conscience: Harvard Moral Philosophy, 1805–1861* (Cambridge: Harvard University Press, 1970), pp. 93–120.

and Edward Everett was praised as "a noble specimen of the fruit of New England culture."[71]

In a society that nominally subscribed to egalitarian ideals, the notion of cultivation thus legitimized the ranking of one "variety" over another. Theoretically, this notion could have been taken a step further in a radically new direction. If improvement in the horticultural world was partly a question of inherited distinction, it might be so in the human world as well. Cultivate an Edward Everett over a lifetime, and he becomes a legitimate leader of society. Perhaps an entire class could be cultivated over several lifetimes, as one cultivates a prize variety of fruit. Perhaps a class, established by virtue of self-improvement, could finally improve itself into a species.

Antebellum horticulturists did not actively pursue this line of inquiry. The cultivation analogy functioned on the level of individual fruit and individual man, and improvement was understood more as moral uplift than genetic engineering. But it is intriguing to consider that when the "sciences" of ethnology and social Darwinism introduced new concepts— race, species, inherited traits—Boston's horticulturists may have been particularly predisposed to assimilate such ideas. Horticulture may have provided not only a resolution of aristocratic and republican principles but a link between the Jeffersonian notion of a natural aristocracy and the Spencerian notion of society's fittest.

Certainly the enthusiasm for horticulture marked the transition from the value placed on utility to that placed on ornament. When it was first introduced to the Boston elite, the cultivation of flowers, fruits, vegetables, and ornamental trees was represented as if not quite as virtuous as experimental farming, then at least a "blameless luxury"[72] with potential for practical application. Gradually, however, utility was edged out of the picture. The rivalry between the claims of utility and those of ornament may even explain why Bostonians tended to favor pomology over the cultivation of either vegetables or flowers. Vegetables were simply too prosaic—what was the glory in a radish?—whereas flowers were solely ornamental, and therefore possibly a dangerous luxury after all. Fruits represented just the right combination of utility, still valued in a republican

71. Description of the MHS festival of 1831, in Malthus A. Ward, *An Address Pronounced before the Massachusetts Horticultural Society, in Commemoration of Its Third Annual Festival* (Boston: J. T. and E. Buckingham, 1831), pp. 38, 39; *Transactions . . . 1843–4–5–6,* transactions for 1845, p. 99.

72. Thomas G. Fessenden, "The Feast of Fruits and Flowers," in Description of the MHS festival of 1831, in Ward, *Address,* p. 40.

nation and a mercantile society, and beauty, proof that the Boston elite could indeed appreciate something of no market value.

By the end of the antebellum era, however, any lingering doubts about the legitimacy of ornament seem to have vanished. The elaborate and costly horticultural domains created in the 1840s and 1850s had little to do with utility and economy. But an element of irony was visible in some of these gardens. Designed to demonstrate an appreciation of ornament, a transcendence of materialism, many instead became themselves displays of wealth, the horticultural version of conspicuous consumption. Ornate flowerbeds, colossal greenhouses, exotic trees—somewhere along the line these transformed from evidence that the horticulturist had risen above the acquisitive fever to acquisitions in themselves. Think, for example, of the growing trend to give the price tags on horticultural purchases, such as Perkins's six-guinea flower (fig. 39) or Hunnewell's twelve-hundred-dollar water pump. Think, too, of Hunnewell's magnificent estate in Wellesley. As described by Marshall Pinckney Wilder, it sounded like a collection of costly items designed to satiate every frivolous, sensual desire. "The whole," wrote Wilder, " . . . constitutes a place unsurpassed in this country for the acquisition of everything new or old in horticulture to please the eye, charm the senses, or gratify the taste."[73] Perhaps these extravagant displays indicate a relaxation of the elite ethos, an easing of conscience and of the need to prove legitimacy, a first, tentative step into the postbellum sensibility of unapologetic authority.

73. Wilder, "Horticulture of Boston," p. 632n.

39. *Enkianthus quinqueflorus*. Reprinted from Pierre Joseph Redouté, *Choix des plus Belles Fleurs* (Paris, 1833). (Courtesy Library of Congress.)

# SIX

## Agriculture in an Age of Ornament and Nostalgia

" *I* have devoted 28 years to the cause of agriculture," wrote a gloomy John Lowell in 1833. "It is enough for one man." The following year he closed a career as sometime corresponding secretary, recording secretary, trustee, and president of the MSPA and left the work of agricultural reform to a younger generation of gentleman farmers.[1] But the issues that had seemed so urgent to men like Lowell—the shameful state of Massachusetts agriculture, the resulting depopulation of the Commonwealth, the need for farmers to adapt to a modernizing economy and society—no longer gripped the hearts of the Boston elite. Experimental agriculture as a species of civic duty was a dead letter among these gentleman farmers and their agricultural society. It became instead a private statement about the farmers themselves, both as individuals and as members of the elite. After a brief and troubled generation of public activity, Boston's gentleman farmers turned inward once more.

A shift in the meaning of rural pursuits soon evidenced itself in the MSPA. During the 1830s, the society underwent a molting process, shedding its responsibility for the botanical garden, its sponsorship of the Brighton fairs, and its publication of a regular journal. In 1836 it even reduced the number and value of premiums it offered. But though the MSPA either eliminated or reduced its traditional activities, it was by no means out

1. Lowell to John Heard, Jr., 13 February 1833, Massachusetts Society for Promoting Agriculture Papers (hereafter MSPA Papers), drawer D, folder I, number 53, Massachusetts Historical Society (hereafter MHS), Boston; *Centennial Year (1792–1892) of the Massachusetts Society for Promoting Agriculture* (Salem, Mass.: n.p., n.d.), pp. 141–45.

to make itself defunct. It instead decided to focus its energies and resources on a single field of endeavor—stockbreeding.

Although the MSPA had imported livestock as early as 1817, only in the mid-1830s did the society formally decide to devote itself almost exclusively to this activity.[2] The ostensible purpose of large-scale cattle importation was to improve Massachusetts livestock, a goal that could only be achieved if the foreign breeds were disseminated throughout the Commonwealth. And the MSPA did make attempts toward this end. It offered the offspring of its own stock to county societies, sold off some of the cattle (much of it to MSPA trustee and future president George W. Lyman) on the condition that it remain in Massachusetts, and gave away pairs of purebreds, again to the county societies.[3]

The first importations, undertaken in 1836, were relatively modest: one bull and three cows of the Ayrshire breed, representing an outlay of $1,170.[4] By 1845, however, the MSPA was ready for a more ambitious importation project. This time, it sent to Britain its own agent, who purchased cattle from no less than the celebrated Thomas Coke, earl of Leicester, along with some Scottish purchases that included a bull named Prince Albert and the more patriotically named cow, Flora McDonald.[5] By

2. This decision is first recorded in 1835 (*Centennial Year*, p. 100), but it was repeated over the decades. See, for example, Elias Phinney to the MSPA, 28 December 1846, MSPA Papers, C–XLII–40. For periodic confirmations of the society's almost exclusive focus on stock importation and breeding in this era, see Report of the Massachusetts Society for Promoting Agriculture, in *Transactions of the Agricultural Societies in the State of Massachusetts, for the Year 1849* (Boston: Dutton and Wentworth, 1850), pp. 1–3; and Report of the Trustees of the Massachusetts Society for Promoting Agriculture, in Charles L. Flint, ed., *The Agriculture of Massachusetts, as Shown in Returns of the Agricultural Societies, 1853* (Boston: William White, 1854), pp. 268–84.

3. "Abstract of the Records, from 1792 to 1858," in *Transactions of the Massachusetts Society for Promoting Agriculture*, n.s., 1 (1858): 117, 120–22; *Centennial Year*, p. 110; Committee report, 12 June 1847, MSPA Papers, C–XXIV–50; Committee report, 9 February 1850, MSPA Papers, C–XXIII–59.

4. "Abstract of the Records," pp. 104, 106; P. C. Brooks to B. Guild, 10 April 1840, MSPA Papers, C–XXIII–30; Bill of Lading, Baring Brothers to P. C. Brooks, 17 June 1836, MSPA Papers, C–XXIII–8.

5. "Abstract of the Records," p. 113; Committee of the Trustees to Alexander Bickett, 30 May 1845, MSPA Papers, C–XXIV–7; Baring Brothers to MSPA, 3 July 1845, MSPA Papers, C–XXIII–419; H. W. Keary to Alexander Bickett, 4 August 1845, MSPA Papers, C–XXIV–10; List of Imported Stock, MSPA Papers, C–XXIV–3; Report of the Committee on Imported Stock, 11 October 1845, MSPA Papers, C–XXIV–32; Phinney to the MSPA, 28 December 1846. On learning "that it was by your Lordship's personal kindness & Interest" that the MSPA procured the North Devon cattle, the agricultural society conferred honorary membership on the earl of Leicester. The MSPA also promised to send seeds, plants, or pamphlets "as yr Lordship will express a wish to receive." MSPA to the earl of Leiscester, n.d., MSPA Papers, A–XI–82.

1846 the MSPA had no fewer than twenty-five full-blooded animals under its care, and it purchased many more over the next years.[6] It was an expensive undertaking, but one the MSPA regarded as of the utmost importance. No longer was the superiority of imported stock tentatively, defensively, bashfully forwarded. Where among native stock, asked Elias Phinney of their advocates, can you find a cow whose progeny can compare with our imported animals? "What has become of the famous 'Oakes Cow,' " inquired Phinney, referring to the celebrated Danvers milker, ". . . and a host of other *accidental* good cows, descended from a medley of all races . . . ?" The answer was plain. "All found their way to the shambles." And their offspring? "All gone the same way; not a solitary one of them found to be worth the expense of rearing." In light of this incontrovertible evidence, Phinney hoped that all the bellyaching over "expending a few thousand dollars" on imported stock would cease.[7]

   If the MSPA could afford to relinquish its sponsorship of cattle shows and to decrease the number and value of premiums it offered, this was largely because, by the 1840s, county agricultural societies, now dominant on the Massachusetts agricultural scene, assumed these tasks.[8] Although they in some measure replaced the MSPA of an earlier generation, however, county societies in no way duplicated it. The Essex Agricultural Society, for example, was one of the oldest (established in 1818) and, by this period, one of the richest of the county societies. In its early years, it focused on such issues typical of that era of agricultural reform as cultivating root crops and draining salt meadows. Gradually, however, its concerns became more ornamental, more polite. In 1835 fruits and flowers first appeared at the Essex cattle shows. The major interests of members in the 1840s consisted of stock raising, pomology, and tree culture. The society's transactions of the following decade seemed custom-made for the gentleman's library:

6. Elias Phinney, "Description of Stock Recently Imported by the Massachusetts Society for Promoting Agriculture, with Pedigree," excerpted in "Abstract of the Records," pp. 118, 122, 145–46; *Centennial Year*, pp. 112, 118–19.

7. Elias Phinney, "Description of Stock," pp. 118–19. On Phinney's management of MSPA cattle on his Lexington farm, see "Visit to the Farm of Elias Phinney, Esq., Lexington, Mass.," *Genesee Farmer* 9 (21, 28 September 1839): 301–2, 309; "The Farm of E. Phinney, Esq.," *The Cultivator*, n.s., 5 (April, May 1848): 105–7, 137–40; and "Further Sketches of Mr. Phinney's Farming," ibid., n.s., 6 (May 1849): 140–42.

8. The best evidence of the great activity of the county societies can be found in their transactions. For specific acknowledgment of their assumption of roles once associated with the MSPA, see Report of the Massachusetts Society for Promoting Agriculture, in *Transactions of the Agricultural Societies . . . 1849*, pp. 1–3. On their history, see Donald B. Marti, *To Improve the Soil and the Mind: Agricultural Societies, Journals, and Schools in the Northeastern States, 1791–1865* (Ann Arbor, Mich.: University Microfilms International, 1979), pp. 32–44, 80–87.

huge octavo volumes filled with agricultural burlesques and poetry sprinkled with classical and literary allusions. On the eve of the Civil War, practical farmers constituted at most a third of the society's members, and, according to the institution's historian, the Essex group "bore the earmarks of a literary club, or a coterie of fine gentlemen."⁹

The gradual alienation of the agricultural societies from the practical concerns of the Massachusetts yeomanry did not go unnoticed or unlamented by the older generation of agricultural reformers. As early as 1831 Gorham Parsons sensed the MSPA's waning commitment to practical farmers. "I have always had doubts of Gentleman Volunteers (for so they may be considered) undertaking too much responsibility," he wrote on the occasion of the society's split with the botanical garden. "Public spirit and patriotism will sometimes tire."¹⁰ Three years later, in 1834, Parsons felt called upon to prod the volunteers out of their torpor. It seems the MSPA had received a new kind of seed-sower from Europe and had no definite plans to disseminate information about the machine to practical farmers. "It does seem to me you gentleman Trustees owe something to the public," insisted Parsons, adding that demonstrating the machine would afford a valuable opportunity "of showing that you are alive to the Agricultural Interests of the Country," something evidently in doubt.¹¹ In 1836, when the MSPA decided against sponsoring a cattle show, Parsons wrote despondently: "I fear the younger part of you gentleman Trustees . . . forget the importance of aiding the agricultural interest of the state."¹²

Parsons had reached this conclusion when making arrangements for the previous year's cattle show dinner. What specifically appalled him then was the exorbitant cost of the meals. "They ought not to be of a character to cost more than one dollar . . . ," he wrote the society's assistant secretary. After all, any practical farmer:

9. Thomas Franklin Waters, *The History of the Essex Agricultural Society of Essex County, Massachusetts, 1818–1918* (Salem, Mass.: Trustees of the Essex Agricultural Society, 1918), pp. 3–28, quotation on p. 25. The records from the Norfolk and Middlesex societies indicate that the Essex society was no exception in its increasing isolation from the concerns of practical farmers. See, for example, *Transactions of the Agricultural Societies in the State of Massachusetts, for 1852* (Boston: White and Potter, 1853), pp. 674–79, 698–701; [Charles L. Flint], *Fourth Annual Report of the Secretary of the Massachusetts Board of Agriculture, together with the Reports of Committees Appointed to Visit the County Societies* (Boston: William White, 1857), pp. 287–89, 291–93, 309–11; and [Charles L. Flint], *Sixth Annual Report of the Secretary of the Massachusetts Board of Agriculture, together with Reports of Committees Appointed to Visit the County Societies* (Boston: William White, 1859), pp. 117–18, 121–22, 145–47.
10. Parsons to B. Guild, 11 March 1831, MSPA Papers, D–VII–66.
11. Parsons to John Heard, Jr., 29 August 1834, MSPA Papers, C–XXXV–35.
12. Parsons to Benj. Guild, 25 November 1836, MSPA Papers, C–XXX–51.

knows the worth of money by the earning it, and will turn a dollar over half a dozen times and examine that shilling before he will pay more than one dollar for a dinner. . . . Such prices destroy the Cattle Show and defeat the objects intended by the first promoters of the Massachusetts Society for the *Promotion of Agriculture.* . . . What must many of the Gentlemen think who subscribed for the new [Cattle Show] Hotel from pure Patriotic motives, to accommodate the visitors of the Cattle Show, to accommodate the Drovers, to benefit the Farmers of the State, and to promote the public welfare[?][13]

As finally arranged, however, the meal cost a full $1.75. Parsons described it sarcastically as "a dinner fit for the epicures of the City hardly lacking anything that is rare (perhaps Ortolan excepted and the Rice Bird I believe has gone South)."[14]

It was precisely this increasing estrangement from the goals and values of the early MSPA that motivated E. Hersey Derby to resign his trusteeship in 1837. Derby was disgusted with "the rapid growth of luxury among us," evidenced in the ever more elaborate "business" dinners, hosted by the trustees on a rotating basis. "I have no right, nor have I the wish to dictate to others," wrote Derby in the panic year of 1837, "but it seems to me, that greater simplicity of style, (while it would better suit the present state of our Country, and the object of our Association) would be equally consistent with social enjoyment." Derby agreed to remain on the board so long as his fellow trustees made no objection to partaking of "a plain, substantial, old fashioned, agricultural dinner" chez Derby.[15] Derby did in fact stay on, but at least one member of the board thought him a bit ridiculous in his objections. When it came Josiah Quincy's turn to entertain the trustees, he inquired of Benjamin Guild, the MSPA's assistant secretary: "Are the sumptuary laws to be enforced this year? And if so what are they[?]" Quincy wanted Guild to send him a bill of fare. "I am desirous of giving as good a dinner as is *lawful,* but like the apostle I am unwilling that my meats should cause a brother to offend."[16] Alas, the menu is lost to history.

If the transformation in the nature of Boston's elite agricultural societies did not go unobserved by some of its older members, not surprisingly neither did it escape the notice of the Commonwealth's practical farmers. Since its formation in the previous century, the MSPA had come under

13. Parsons to B. Guild?, 1 October 1835, MSPA Papers, C–XXXV–53.
14. Parsons to Benj. Guild, 2 October 1835, MSPA Papers, C–XXXV–44. The ortolan is a small European bunting prized as a culinary delicacy; rice birds, the best known of which is the bobolink, are similarly valued.
15. E. Hersey Derby to P. C. Brooks, 28 June 1837, MSPA Papers, C–XXIII–24.
16. Josiah Quincy to B. Guild, 29 June 1837, MSPA Papers, D–II–11.

attack as a suspiciously elitist organization of good-for-nothing book farmers, squandering public funds on extravagant entertainments. The society's change in style—its increasing isolation from public concerns and the increasing gentility of its private ones—only fueled the fire. When in February 1857 a public meeting was convened in Boston to consider the wisdom of establishing a state agricultural society separate from the MSPA, the resentment spilled over once more.[17] Up stood Mr. Loomis of Springfield. "The State society," he said, referring to the MSPA, "had been called ancient and honorable, but was it not so more for ornament than for use?" Loomis conceded that it "had done some good, surely, but not the amount that was sufficient for the requirements of the times. It was too contracted in numbers. . . . the State society, to be influentially operative, and do credit to the whole State, should not be narrowed in its numbers, and contracted in its views, as the Massachusetts Society had been."[18]

More direct in his remarks was Mr. Lewis of Framingham. He noted, first of all, that most people were totally ignorant of the MSPA. (In fact, many of those attending the meeting were unaware that a state agricultural society existed.)[19] What Lewis himself claimed to know about the society was that "it had a respectable existence . . . in State Street, and was likely to be a money-making concern." Of the six hundred dollars it received from the state every year, "some said it was spent in good dinners." Personally, he was glad to see citizens of the western part of the state come to this meeting and demand to know just where that money went. Lewis favored the replacement of the MSPA with a new state society. "It would not be a bad thing," he stated bluntly, "that the incorporation of some Young American blood should speedily take place among the old-fogy, aristocratic, but respectable members of the society."[20]

Those were fighting words, and M. P. Wilder, then president of a host of local and national agricultural and horticultural societies, felt called upon to respond. The MSPA members were "men of the strictest integrity," he

17. This meeting may represent just one of many challenges for control of elite-dominated institutions with ostensibly public purposes. See Ronald Story's discussion of the challenge to elite domination of Harvard and similar controversies over the Athenaeum and Mount Auburn in *The Forging of an Aristocracy: Harvard and the Boston Upper Class, 1800–1870* (Middletown, Conn.: Wesleyan University Press, 1980), pp. 135–59, 168–70.

18. Report of a meeting held on 5 February 1857, in [Charles L. Flint], *Fifth Annual Report of the Secretary of the Massachusetts Board of Agriculture, together with the Reports of Committees Appointed to Visit the County Societies* (Boston: William White, 1858), p. 13. Loomis's comments, along with others made at this meeting, were recorded by a newspaper reporter and are thus an accurate paraphrase but not a verbatim transcription.

19. Ibid., p. 11.

20. Ibid., p. 9.

insisted, who would never dream of spending society funds in any but the most unimpeachable manner. Nor was it precisely true that it was difficult to join the society. "Members from all quarters could be admitted," although, conceded Wilder, suddenly vague, there was some sort of rule that required some knowledge of the candidates for membership. Lewis replied, somewhat pacified. He was not out to destroy the MSPA, only to infuse it with some vitality. "If this meeting was the means of causing any rattling among the dry bones," he remarked, "it would do about all it had a design to do." But Benjamin French, then vice president of the horticultural society, was not mollified.[21] Returning to Lewis's earlier statements, he branded as "fabulous" the "tales about feastings and drinkings of wine which were paid out of the public funds." French was willing to admit that "the complaints were getting loud" and the MSPA "becoming a little too conservative," but he had no doubt that its members would require little prodding to do their best by agriculture.[22] At this point, it seems to have occurred to the more disgruntled participants that if nothing else, the MSPA did have "a good store of funds." The meeting thus concluded with a resolution not to "alienate those kind and patriotic feelings which have so uniformly characterized the past and present trustees of an ancient and honorable state society," and a further resolution that the state board of agriculture, and not a second state society, should hold exhibitions funded either from the public treasury (unlikely) or by private munificence (that is, the MSPA).[23]

However much their advocates might deny it, Boston's agricultural societies did change radically from the 1830s onward. They were simply no longer interested in serving the yeoman farmer and regenerating Massachusetts agriculture, goals that underlay most of the MSPA's efforts in the 1810s and 1820s. Instead, they devoted themselves to a polite species of agriculture, far removed from the realities of practical farming in Massachusetts. Out went mangel-wurzel and manure, and with them, disinterested benevolence and public-spirited reform. In came stockbreeding and horticulture.

The polite, cultivated approach to rural pursuits was also evident on the

21. On French and his agricultural activities, see "Mr. French's Farm, Braintree, Mass.," in *The Cultivator*, n.s., 1 (December 1844): 368.

22. Ibid., pp. 10–11.

23. *Springfield Daily Republican*, 7 February 1857, p. 4. The mercantile *Boston Daily Advertiser* smoothed over the incident when it reported: "An unsuccessful attempt was made in this city yesterday to organize a second State Agricultural Society. It is generally believed, however, that the excellent society now in existence, covers the necessary ground" (6 February 1857, p. 1).

suburban farms of the Boston elite. As the activities of the agricultural societies reflected, gentleman farmers of this era concentrated their energies almost exclusively on stockbreeding.[24] Even more intriguingly, in this period Boston's gentleman farmers first took an active interest in a new endeavor—breeding horses. By the 1850s we find Quincy A. Shaw breeding racehorses on his farm in West Roxbury. Another Boston horsebreeder to get his start in the 1850s was Henry S. Russell, whose Milton estate was famous not only for its ornamental gardens but also for the "Smuggler" breed of racehorses raised there (fig. 40). Meanwhile, the MSPA kept up with the change in taste. In 1850 an MSPA committee recommended that society funds be appropriated to import studhorses. In 1846 and again in 1853 it sponsored a series of lectures on horse anatomy, an undertaking that involved importing a complete horse skeleton from France at a cost of $800. Also in 1853 the society saw fit to grant $250 worth of premiums to the National Exhibition of Horses. By 1863 it had come full circle, authorizing the importation of five horses from Normandy at the cost of something over $7,000.[25]

A major change in the meaning of rural pursuits had clearly come about. The fascination with stockbreeding, parallel to the vogue for horticulture, is one indication of what this change involved. As we saw in the previous chapter, this was an age in which utility was spurned for ornament. The sure sign of a truly cultivated person was the ability to appreciate what could not be assigned a monetary value—beauty, perfection, quality—precisely the traits characterizing a prize dahlia or a full-blooded Ayrshire. Horticulture appealed to the elite as a cultural symbol of individual and class "breeding"; if anything, the symbolism of animal breeding was even stronger. Reflecting on the bare facts of the situation—the importation of choice specimens of the animal kingdom, from Britain no less; the careful breeding of these animals with handpicked individuals of equally

24. Noteworthy stockbreeders include, for example, Marshall P. Wilder and John P. Cushing, encountered in the previous chapter, George B. Loring and Thomas Motley, Jr. (see biographies in the Appendix), and George W. Lyman, the son of Theodore Lyman of the Vale. On Lyman, see *Centennial Year*, p. 110, and Marshall Pinckney Wilder, "The Horticulture of Boston and Vicinity," in Justin Winsor, ed., *The Memorial History of Boston, Including Suffolk County, Massachusetts, 1630–1880*, 4 vols. (Boston: James R. Osgood, 1881), 4:635.

25. Charles L. Flint, ed., *Abstract of Returns of the Agricultural Societies of Massachusetts, for 1860* (Boston: William White, 1861), p. 83; Wilder, "Horticulture of Boston," pp. 624–25; Hamilton Bushey, *The Trotting and the Pacing Horse in America* (New York: Macmillan, 1904), pp. 62–63, 98–99, 107, 288; Report of a committee on the appropriation of MSPA funds, 16 November 1850, MSPA Papers, C–XLII–64; Report on the Subject of Procuring a Figure Showing the Whole Anatomy of the Horse, 24 December 1846, MSPA Papers, C–XLII–38; "Abstract of the Records," pp. 115, 124–25; *Centennial Year*, pp. 106–9, 122–24.

40. *The Champion Trotting Stallion* SMUGGLER. Currier and Ives. (Courtesy Yale University Art Gallery, Mabel Brady Garvan Collection.)

impeccable lineage; the celebration of their perfection; even the execution of their portraits (fig. 41)—it is hard to resist the impression that the Boston elite was in some metaphorical sense recreating the process whereby they came to stand at the head of *their* kingdom, the one called Boston. Again, the conclusion to be drawn is not that the Boston elite engaged in any sort of deliberate genetic engineering, only that the concept of breeding was laden with meaning, was of innate interest and significance to a class anxious to establish itself as well-bred.[26]

The new enthusiasm for racehorses is equally telling. In an earlier generation, horse breeding had been considered too removed from the practical concerns of the Massachusetts yeomanry, in other words, too polite, to warrant attention. In 1820 the MSPA's journal commented that "it is to be doubted whether the Massachusetts Agricultural Society, considering the interests of the state which they are bound to consult, ought to encourage the raising of pleasure horses," since "they are mere articles of luxury."[27] When, by the 1850s, Boston's elite agricultural circles under-

26. For a thought-provoking discussion of stockbreeding among British landowners, see Harriet Ritvo, *The Animal Estate: The English and Other Creatures in the Victorian Age* (Cambridge: Harvard University Press, 1987), pp. 45–81.

27. *Massachusetts Agricultural Repository and Journal* 6 (July 1820): 181.

41. *Alice, Jersey Cow Owned by the State.* Reprinted from [C. F. Flint], *Third Annual Report of the Secretary of the Massachusetts Board of Agriculture* (Boston, 1856). (Courtesy Yale University Library.)

went a distinct change of heart on the subject of breeding horses, it was probably not because horses had somehow ceased to be "mere articles of luxury" but, more likely in this age of ornament, precisely because they were. In this respect, horse breeding was similar to both stockbreeding and horticulture. But an additional factor was present, one that involved breeding racehorses in particular. The Boston elite had heretofore rejected the enthusiasm for horse races among the British aristocracy as the darker, decadent side of the landed classes, wholly inappropriate to a thrifty and virtuous republic. Thus it would seem that the new interest in the breeding of racehorses represented a shift in elite sensibilities, a waning of the traditional hostility toward and suspicion of aristocratic values.

Certainly attitudes toward the Boston elite's entrepreneurial roots changed, at least among many of the youngest members of that elite. In the generation after the Revolution, and for years afterwards, Boston's merchants and industrialists remained proud of the entrepreneurial traits—

frugality, industry, sobriety—that they so assiduously cultivated. In the post–1840 generation, however, the sons of self-made (or almost self-made) men felt differently. Francis Lowell Lee, for example, dreaded his inevitable initiation into the world of commerce. "I must say that I cannot contemplate a mercantile life with any great pleasure at present," he wrote Henry Lee, Jr., in 1843. Architecture or medicine—learned professions— appealed to him more.[28] Amos Adams Lawrence, the son of the textile magnate, was more resigned to his destiny. Writing in the mid-1830s as a senior at Harvard, he stated his plan to become a merchant, but "not a plodding, narrow-minded one pent up in a city, with my mind always in a counting-room."[29]

For second- and third-generation men like Lee and Lawrence, rural occupations, with their overtones of "cultivation," were tremendously attractive. By 1848 Lee had abandoned mercantile life to take up farming in Westport, New York.[30] Lawrence, meanwhile, had decided that the way out of a "plodding, narrow-minded" existence as a merchant was a country life. In his Harvard diary he had stated that alongside a mercantile career, "I would be at the same time a literary man in some measure and a farmer. That is, I would live in the country a few miles from town (excepting when devoted to business, which would be in the forenoons), and there I would read and work on my farm."[31] The dream did not fade. In September 1839, now a young merchant living in Boston, Lawrence wrote dreamily: "The autumn has come on, & the country is beautiful. I wish I could stay in it all the time, away from the turmoil of the city. But that may perhaps come, by and by." Later that autumn, he wrote, "I am not so ambitious to be rich as to

28. Lee to Henry Lee, Jr., 29 September 1843, quoted in Kenneth Wiggins Porter, *The Jacksons and the Lees: Two Generations of Massachusetts Merchants, 1765–1844,* 2 vols. (Cambridge: Harvard University Press, 1937), 2:1531. Another member of Lee's generation held the same opinion. Wrote his mother, Mary, in the same year: "Pat [Patrick Tracy Jackson, Jr.] . . . happened to hear something of Frank [Francis Lowell Lee] going into a store & really entered a most earnest protest against it—he was puzzled for an answer when I asked what he shd. do? & said be a Physician—but how can you expect him to study said I? he has himself said he could not venture to trust himself—no he must be a merchant & trust to becoming interested in the science of his profession at some future period." Mary Lee to Henry Lee, Jr., 30 May 1843, quoted in ibid.

29. Diary of Amos A. Lawrence, quoted in William Lawrence, *Life of Amos A. Lawrence, with Extracts from His Diary and Correspondence* (Boston: Houghton Mifflin, 1888), p. 23.

30. Porter, *Jacksons and Lees,* 2:1532–33; *New England Historical and Genealogical Register* 76 (July 1922): 215.

31. Diary of Amos A. Lawrence, quoted in Lawrence, *Amos A. Lawrence,* p. 23.

live in a city & work like a slave fr. morning till night for money, money," probably a fair, though perhaps unconscious, description of his father's life. "I have not great wants," he continued, "& think I can live well in the country."[32]

And that is precisely what Lawrence did. In 1851 he and his brother, William, purchased a ninety-acre tract of land in Brookline, two and a half miles west of Boston. The property was called Cottage Farm after the small house that already existed there, but when Lawrence built his own residence, he named it after the adjoining piece of property, Longwood. He hired George M. Dexter, an architect who had made a study of English country houses, to design Longwood, and the result recalled Old England far more than New. The house was built of stone and featured tremendous, open fireplaces and a great hall. To the south and west of the house stretched a lawn; to the north, a grove of oaks; and to the east, a fruit garden, including a grape trellis, tended by Mr. Maloney, the Irish gardener. This was also a working farm, complete with cows, horses, and hens.[33]

At Longwood, Lawrence could be found "almost every day in the year superintending the plowing, sowing, and reaping, planting nurseries of fruit-trees, pruning and grafting, overseeing the dairy, and giving play to his taste for farming and country life."[34] This is not the usual picture we have of the man. Instead, Lawrence is remembered as a prime mover behind the New England Emigrant Aid Company, a supporter of John Brown, and the Union party's candidate for governor in 1860. Apart from his involvement in the turmoil that led to the Civil War, he is known simply as a textile magnate. Yet Lawrence's devotion to rural pursuits was common for his generation and points to a widespread change of view experienced by the maturing elite. This was the desire of the youngest members of this class to go beyond the entrepreneurial values that had nourished their predecessors. It was not merely a question of demonstrating that mercantile traits were consistent with high-mindedness and benevolent generosity. It was a question of going beyond those traits and, in some cases, even rejecting them. Not all sons and grandsons of the elite evidenced this desire by taking up life as a gentleman farmer, but in its late

32. Diary of Amos A. Lawrence, 4 September, 7 November 1839, Amos A. Lawrence Papers, MHS.

33. Lawrence, *Amos A. Lawrence,* pp. 60–62; William Lawrence, *Memories of a Happy Life* (Boston: Houghton Mifflin, 1926), pp. 2–7.

34. Lawrence, *Amos A. Lawrence,* p. 217.

antebellum incarnation, gentleman farming can often be linked with this new penchant to go beyond the bourgeois to the aristocratic.

Even as the realities of practical farming in Massachusetts figured less and less in agriculture as pursued by the Boston elite, practical farmers themselves achieved a central place in elite rhetoric. Of course, there was nothing novel about upper-crust Bostonians discussing the common farmers of Massachusetts; recall the condemnation of the practical farmer as sloppy and inefficient, the handwringing over emigration, the insistence that the state's farmers should stay right where they were that peppered the agricultural addresses of the late 1810s and 1820s. But there was something new in the 1840s and 1850s. These themes dominated elite rhetoric on agriculture as they never had before. And this rhetoric took on an increasingly authoritarian tone, evident even in the titles of agricultural addresses and essays of this period: "The Pleasures and Profits of Farming, and the Folly of Quitting It," for example, or "The Duty of the Farmer to His Calling," or "Why a Massachusetts Farmer Should Be Content."

The main message elite Bostonians wished to convey was that farmers should stay on their farms.[35] As in an earlier generation, when emigration lay uppermost in the minds of elite agricultural reformers, this might mean that farmers should not move west. (For a brief period, the West referred to was not that of Midwestern farms but of the California Gold Rush.)[36] Speakers and writers emphasized that nothing could be more priceless than New England institutions and the morally exquisite society they engendered and epitomized.[37] Even ignoring the virtues of New England, there were the vices of New England emigrants to convince Massachusetts farmers to stay put. Only "the idle and unthrifty . . . emigrate from their homes to the Far West," proclaimed one speaker before the Essex Agricul-

35. For a discussion of the antiemigration theme as it developed over the course of the nineteenth century, see Hal S. Barron, *Those Who Stayed Behind: Rural Society in Nineteenth-Century New England* (Cambridge: Cambridge University Press, 1984), pp. 31–50.

36. "[Review of] Colman's *European Agriculture*," *Christian Examiner* 46 (March 1849): 289–90.

37. George S. Hillard, "Why a Massachusetts Farmer Should Be Content," an address to the Norfolk Agricultural Society, in Flint, *Agricultural Societies . . . 1860*, p. 54. See also, for example, Emory Washburn, "The Massachusetts Farmer," an address to the Worcester [Agricultural] Society, in Charles L. Flint, ed., *The Agriculture of Massachusetts, as Shown in Returns of the Agricultural Societies, 1854* (Boston: William White, 1855), pp. 459–60, and George S. Boutwell, "The Profits and Wastes of Agriculture," an address to the Housatonic Agricultural Society, in *Hunt's Merchants' Magazine* 31 (1853): 695.

tural Society in 1860, "in hopes to find in its virgin soils some excuse for negligence and unthrift."[38]

Though the antiemigration theme lingered on throughout the antebellum period, it increasingly took second place to another message, namely, that the farmer must not abandon agriculture for commerce, manufacturing, or the learned professions. Part of the argument was that though merchants, manufacturers, lawyers, and doctors might become very wealthy, even spectacularly so, their road to fortune was by no means as secure as that traveled by the farmer.[39] "I bethink me of many who started with me in life," related the Reverend Charles Babbidge to the Middlesex Agricultural Society in 1857, "some of them beguiled with the hope of commercial prosperity, some dazzled with professional renown to be acquired, and others content to work that mine of wealth that lies within twelve inches of the surface of a farm." And what of these fellow travelers? "Of my early acquaintances," reported Babbidge sadly, "many lie buried in the ocean; others, worn out with fruitless toils, and discouraged by repeated failures, live, and that is all; worse than this, I have seen those upon whom God had bestowed every desirable gift, yield to the temptations that early success brought with it, and then go down, covered with disgrace, to untimely graves." And what of those who chose farming? Time has proved "the wisdom of their choice." They are to be found "surrounded with the peace and plenty of their own honestly-acquired domains," not wealthy, but living in comfort and contentment, "waiting patiently and hopefully for the sunset of life."[40]

To leave the farm was a sign not merely of poor judgment but of a reprehensible disinclination for physical toil. Such laziness was not to be tolerated. "He who would 'thrive by the plough,'" warned merchant George R. Russell in 1851, "must leave his gloves with his Sunday coat. He

38. John L. Russell, "Agriculture an Art," an address to the Essex Agricultural Society, in Flint, *Agricultural Societies . . . 1860,* p. 2.

39. See, for example, "Colman's *European Agriculture,*" pp. 286–87; George S. Boutwell, "The Pleasures and the Profits of Farming, and the Folly of Quitting It," an address to the Middlesex Agricultural Society, in *Transactions of the Agricultural Societies in the Commonwealth of Massachusetts, for the Year 1850* (Boston: Dutton and Wentworth, 1851), p. 375; Washburn, "The Massachusetts Farmer," pp. 462–64; and George B. Loring, "Report of the Committee on Farms," Essex Agricultural Society, in Charles L. Flint, ed., *Abstract of Returns of the Agricultural Societies of Massachusetts, 1857* (Boston: William White, 1857), pp. 127–28.

40. Charles Babbidge, "Agricultural Heart-Work," an address to the Middlesex Agricultural Society, in Flint, *Agricultural Societies . . . 1857,* pp. 28–29. On Babbidge, see the *New England Historical and Genealogical Journal* 5 (April 1851): 158.

must not expect to walk daintily over the earth, in holiday garb, and have her productions spring up in his footsteps. He who courts her favors, must go manfully to the work."[41] Avoiding hard work was more than unwise, even more than lazy. It went against the social order. "There is a growing propensity among our young men," stated one agricultural speaker in 1849,

> to live without manual labor, or with the least possible quantity. Hence, we see multitudes of them, despising the vocation of their ancestors, seeking for clerkships, and secretaryships, and agencies; or dashing, without capital or talent, into trade or manufactures, and obtaining from the credulity of others, the borrowed means of sporting a carriage, and arraying their persons in the extreme of fashion. These young people should be instructed, that, of the whole population, nature designs but a small proportion for merchants and master mechanics, for fine gentlemen and ladies; that the great mass of mankind must, of course, be laborers,—not necessarily slaves and serfs, but independent laborers.[42]

Nor did agricultural commentators try to minimize just how much hard work farming in Massachusetts required. Members of the elite were the first to admit that New England's climate was harsh and its soil poor, yet they insisted that New Englanders should be grateful for such adverse conditions. The Reverend George Ellis counted "that continual demand for industry and hard labor" as one of the "blessings" of New England agriculture. "Industry and effort are severe conditions sometimes," he admitted, "but how rich their gains . . . !" Citing Holland, Switzerland, England, and now New England as examples, Ellis claimed that "all the

41. George R. Russell, "The Progress of Agriculture, and the Necessity for Its Further Progress," an address to the Norfolk Agricultural Society, in *Transactions of the Agricultural Societies in the State of Massachusetts, for 1851* (Boston: Dutton and Wentworth, 1852), pp. 605–6. For expressions of similar sentiments, see "[Review of Henry] Colman's *Agricultural Address,*" *North American Review* 49 (July 1839): 241, and "[Review of Henry] Colman's *Agricultural Addresses,*" *Christian Examiner* 30 (March 1841): 128.

42. Lilly Eaton, "The Privileges and Duties of Farmers," an address to the Middlesex Society of Husbandmen and Manufacturers, in *Transactions of the Agricultural Societies in the State of Massachusetts, for the Year 1849* (Boston: Dutton and Wentwoth, 1850), p. 370. A similar endorsement of a fixed social hierarchy characterized the thought of a professional elite of this period, psychiatric hospital superintendents. They argued that insanity was the ultimate result of the foolish but, in a society exalting social and economic mobility, nonetheless irresistible attempt to rise above one's station. Intriguingly, both failure and success at this attempt were regarded as leading to unbearable psychological strain. David J. Rothman, *The Discovery of the Asylum: Social Order and Disorder in the New Republic* (Boston: Little, Brown, 1971), pp. 108–29.

useful discoveries and inventions have come from parts of the globe where hard labor in agriculture has been essential to support life," for "where the hardest labor has been necessary, precisely there, has been the most of thrift, and happiness and virtue."[43] (One might add that the unspoken corollary to this celebration of cold and stony New England was the disparagement of the warm and fertile South as a lazy, dissolute, not to say wicked, culture.[44])

Thus the elite agricultural speakers acknowledged, as Charles Babbidge did in 1857, that farming "is work, work, work, morning, noon and night, year in, and year out, to-day in a mud hole and to-morrow in a manure heap." From the point of view of elite agricultural commentators, the problem with this back-breaking labor was not that it was unpleasant—that was unavoidable—but that it made the farmer restless and dissatisfied. "No wonder that farmers' sons flee from the old homestead as if it were the city of the plague," exclaimed Babbidge. In the opinion of one writer for the *Atlantic Monthly,* the solution was to reform rural life above its present level, epitomized for this one observer by the stench of stewing soap grease, boiling cabbage, and perspiring hired men that fills the farmhouse's combined kitchen and parlor. To the brutish life of labor must be added intellectual interest in the form of scientific agriculture, emotional bonds in the form of community life, and, not the least, aesthetic pleasure in the form of a beautified homestead and a higher standard of personal deportment and cleanliness. Here, of course, the farmer was blamed for the discontent arising from his degraded existence, for it is he who would "willingly go so far into essential self-debasement" as to "contemn beauty and those who love it, and to glory above all things in brute strength and brute endurance."[45]

For other commentators, the compensations to hard work that would allay a farmer's discontent were nothing so tangible as a genteel farmhouse parlor. As Charles Babbidge explained: "You must not undertake to deal

43. George E. Ellis, "Rewards of Agriculture," an address to the Middlesex Agricultural Society, in *Agriculture of Massachusetts . . . 1854,* pp. 448–49. For other examples of this line of argument, see Charles Francis Adams, "What Can Be Done for the Farming of Norfolk County?" an address to the Norfolk Agricultural Society, in *Transactions of the Agricultural Societies . . . 1850,"* pp. 430–41; J. M. Merrick, "Agricultural Societies," an address to the Norfolk Agricultural Society, in *Agricultural Societies . . . 1855,* pp. 423–24; and George B. Loring, "New England Farming," an address to the Hampshire, Franklin and Hampden Agricultural Society, in Charles L. Flint, ed., *Abstract of Returns of the Agricultural Societies of Massachusetts, 1858* (Boston: William White, 1859), pp. 57–58.
44. See, for example, Russell, "Agriculture an Art," p. 3, for a discussion of how "the physical, moral and intellectual conditions of a people depend on climatic characters."
45. "Farming Life in New England," *Atlantic Monthly* 2 (August 1858): 334–41.

with the members of a farmer's household, as we sometimes deal with whimsical children, telling them that they are not sick, and will be better by and by. Farmers, male and female, must work, and must make up their minds to it. And to do it cheerfully, they must have their attention directed to the advantage and blessings of their particular calling in life."[46] Those advantages and blessings were such intangibles as security, self-reliance, exposure to natural beauty, and even a hearty appetite.[47] Only when farmers were content with such abstract compensations would the problem of farm abandonment be solved. Those who accepted their lot in life, though it be one of grueling labor, would not think of pulling up stakes for the West or, far worse, of taking their chances in the cities and mill towns of Massachusetts.

What is most striking about this rhetoric is not so much its message—intimations of social control were present in earlier decades—but its strident tone. It is hard to believe that what motivated these men to castigate farmers for laziness and social climbing in the harshest of terms was a genuine fear of economic competition. Could members of this ever more powerful elite have seriously felt threatened by the appeal of commerce and industry to farmers' sons? Surely something else was at stake. Emigration from Massachusetts, and the loss in power and influence that population drain represented and engendered, did linger as a concern among the elite. But other, more subtle anxieties must have been at work.

Members of the elite felt anxiety for themselves. At the same time that yeoman farmers were condemned for their alleged aversion to adversity and their economically and morally ruinous attraction to the easy life, some elite Bostonians were sounding precisely the same warnings with respect to their own class. Luxury, went the Brahmin admonition, threatens to emasculate us. Whereas our fathers and grandfathers proved their mettle in the struggle for wealth and power, we, born to advantage, are prone to deteriorating into what Oliver Wendell Holmes termed "cheap dandyism." Holmes regretted that no ritual of hardship, such as military duty, served to strengthen the elite, to give it "pluck," as he termed it. "Our young men must gild their spurs," he wrote, "but they need not win them."[48] Whom, then, was one agricultural speaker really addressing when he stated that true men wish not for golden spoons but for iron ones—lazy farmers or

46. Babbidge, "Agricultural Heart-Work," p. 25.
47. Ibid., pp. 25–27.
48. Oliver Wendell Holmes, *The Autocrat of the Breakfast-Table* (Boston: Phillips, Sampson, 1858), p. 304.

Harvard dandies?[49] In their castigation of Massachusetts farmers as soft and spoiled, elite Bostonians may have really been addressing fears for their own class. At the very least, we can see that members of this class had their own reasons for celebrating the virtues of the strenuous life.[50]

Then, too, there may have been a very real fear that, in the absence of a vigorous young generation of Brahmins, New England had better preserve its ultimate source of moral strength and identity, the yeoman class. "Let us hold fast to the sheet anchor and stay of nations," pleaded Caleb Cushing before the Essex Agricultural Society in 1850, for the farmer retains "the stewardship of our nationality."[51] This message could take on overtones of not only republican ideology but also nativism and even romantic racism, as when it was feared that degraded Irish hired hands would soon replace Yankee yeomen on Massachusetts farms[52] and as when Massachusetts farmers were especially praised as "the descendants of the Puritans," true to "the hardy virtues . . . of their adventurous Anglo-Saxon ancestors."[53]

What would happen if this stock ceased to exist? Agriculture, argued George B. Loring, a physician and gentleman farmer, "supplies the raw material out of which the leaders of our race are created." Here "their growing powers were moulded" and "they inherited the natural powers which lie at the foundation of their success."[54] Perhaps these "natural powers" of rural life were all that New England could rely on, now that the merchant-manufacturing class of Boston found itself morally weakened by luxury and artifice. If so, the disappearance of the hardy yeoman stock boded ill for Massachusetts. In his eulogy to Daniel Webster, Boston merchant George S. Hillard described the deceased statesman's life as "an eminently New England life" and the man himself as one of a "race of

49. Henry F. Durant, "Dignity of Labor," an address to the Norfolk Agricultural Society, in Charles L. Flint, ed., *Abstract of Returns of the Agricultural Societies of Massachusetts, for 1859* (Boston: William White, 1860), pp. 59–73.

50. On the Brahmin anxiety over an emasculated elite and attraction to the strenuous life, see George M. Frederickson, *The Inner Civil War: Northern Intellectuals and the Crisis of the Union* (New York: Harper and Row, 1965), pp. 32–35, 72–73, 153–56, 164–65.

51. Caleb Cushing, "The Relation of Land to the Prosperity and Happiness of the United States," an address to the Essex Agricultural Society, in *Transactions of the Agricultural Societies . . . 1850*, pp. 364–65, 369.

52. Marshall P. Wilder, an address to the Norfolk Agricultural Society, in *Transactions of the Norfolk Agricultural Society, for 1849* (Boston: Coolidge and Wiley [1850?]), p. 44. See also "Farming Life in New England," p. 341.

53. Wilder, address to the Norfolk Agricultural Society, p. 46; "Colman's *Agricultural Address*," p. 243.

54. George B. Loring, "The Social and Civil Position of the Farmer," an address to the Franklin Agricultural Society, in Flint, *Agricultural Societies . . . 1858*, p. 83.

intellectual Scandinavians, that swarmed out from the frozen North to reap the harvests of opportunity and pluck the clusters of success in more genial fields." By Hillard's own admission, however, this was a vanishing race. "The child of to-day," he explained, " . . . cannot have the same elements flow into his life, because New England is not now what it was then."[55] Brahmins regarded the threatened New England yeomanry much as we today look toward the disappearing Amazon vegetation, as a source of natural cures for the diseases of civilization.

And something even more subtle might have been at work in the harsh rhetoric of the Boston elite—a resistance to the change in Massachusetts from an agrarian to an industrial society, now that the elite had made that change irreversible and inevitable. Let us look, for example, at the agricultural survey of Massachusetts undertaken in the late 1830s and early 1840s by the Reverend Henry Colman, a Unitarian minister and gentleman farmer. Colman's survey was commissioned by the state house of representatives but was subscribed to largely by such members of the Boston gentry as industrialist Abbott Lawrence, China merchant John P. Cushing, and Justice Joseph Story. It focused on a revealing sample of counties: highly urbanized, commercialized, and industrialized ones, such as Middlesex and Essex, and counties that by comparison were frontier areas, Berkshire and Franklin.[56]

Colman's commentary on farming in the Commonwealth reflects that same clash of tradition and the modern order. Typical of the narrative is Colman's description of a farm he visited in one of the valleys of Franklin County. Here he found "an humble unpainted cottage," surrounded by flowers and shrubs and exhibiting perfect order and harmony. Outside, remarked Colman, "no growling sow, with her hungry and squealing litter, disputes your entrance. . . . The extended row of milk-pans are glittering in the sun; and the churn and the pails are scrubbed to a whiteness absolutely without a stain." Inside the cottage, Colman found skeins of home-spun linen adorning the kitchen, a bass-viol in the corner to accompany morning and evening hymns, and a thrifty and industrious farm family, complete with "the aged grandmother" occupying what Colman called her "chair of state." Here, concluded Colman, was "the true poetry of rural life."

55. Speech of George S. Hillard, in [John Clark], ed., *In Memory of Daniel Webster* (Boston: *Boston Courier* Office, 1856), p. 45.

56. Donald B. Marti, "The Reverend Henry Colman's Agricultural Ministry," *Agricultural History* 51 (July 1977): 524–39; Henry Colman, *First Report on the Agriculture of Massachusetts. County of Essex, 1837* (Boston: Dutton and Wentworth, 1838), p. 5.

Colman's task, of course, was not to recite poetry, even rural poetry, but to evaluate the state of farming in the Commonwealth. Given the continuing decline of New England agriculture, his recommendations should ostensibly have been directed toward economic viability and prosperity. But dollars-and-cents considerations were not uppermost in his mind. Instead, he wished to preserve the social and economic basis of the yeoman's moral qualities, even if that meant economic struggle and hardship.[57] Thus Colman advocated the cultivation of wheat in Massachusetts, even as he admitted the greater economy of purchasing western wheat, simply because it represented and engendered independence and self-sufficiency.[58] For the same reasons, he urged farm women to persist in such traditional household activities as baking bread, and particularly spinning and weaving.[59] "Though the supply of our own great wants from our own farms might seem, however, in some cases to be a *pecuniary loss,*" he wrote, "it is always in the end a *moral gain,* with which the pecuniary loss is not to be put in competition."[60] Conversely, of course, Colman rejected factory-made goods as "showy but flimsy products," and the leisure made possible by the purchase of such goods as "the idleness and frivolities of pride and luxury." He was even willing to endorse the use of female agricultural labor in the field as at least preferable to female labor in textile mills. To Colman, Rochester flour, Waltham sheetings, and Lowell mill girls were equally threatening signs of modern times.[61]

Obviously Colman's model Franklin County farm was fast becoming a thing of the past, and to no one was that more obvious than Colman himself. It was precisely the farmer's stubborn refusal to be an economic and cultural anachronism that incited Colman's wrath. Farmers today are too lazy and greedy to run a farm the old-fashioned way, he insisted. Their folly and their sin, he added in a typical swipe at modernity, is in yearning to imitate "city millionaires," the unproductive merchants and bankers of the metropolis, the same ones, of course, who were Colman's patrons and readers. Instead of working hard, investing all their capital in their farms,

57. Henry Colman, *Second Report on the Agriculture of Massachusetts. County of Berkshire, 1838* (Boston: Dutton and Wentworth, 1839), p. 138; Colman, *Fourth Report of the Agriculture of Massachusetts. Counties of Franklin and Middlesex* (Boston: Dutton and Wentworth, 1841), pp. 159–60; Colman, "Report on the Culture of Wheat in Massachusetts, 1838," in *Third Report of the Agriculture of Massachusetts, on Wheat and Silk* (Boston: Dutton and Wentworth, 1840), pp. 53–54.

58. Colman, "Report on the Culture of Wheat," pp. 51–54.

59. Colman, *Fourth Report,* pp. 156–60. See also Colman, *Second Report,* pp. 137–38.

60. Colman, *Second Report,* p. 138.

61. Ibid.; Colman, *First Report,* p. 36.

and living a life of humble self-sufficiency, he argued, farmers today squander borrowed money wheeling and dealing in real estate and buying up Texas scrip.[62]

What Colman wanted to do was to freeze the yeoman in time, preserving him—and New England—from the disturbing realities of modernization. Nor was he the only one. It is astonishing how many agricultural speakers—men who by virtue of their personal involvement in trade and manufacturing knew better—characterized Massachusetts as a fundamentally agricultural state, whether defined in moral, social, or even economic terms.[63] Such claims may have had a sound basis a generation earlier, but by the late antebellum period, Massachusetts had without question become irrevocably detached from its agricultural roots. Of course it was precisely because the Commonwealth was drifting ever further from its agrarian past—and set adrift, one must add, by Boston's merchants and manufacturers—that the farmer became ever more mythologized as a symbol of that past. He became the symbolic bulwark against change. So long as the yeoman stayed where he had always been, on a little farm in Massachusetts, the enormous social and economic changes set in motion by the mercantile-manufacturing elite—the expansion of cities, the growth of manufacturing, the massive influx of foreign immigrants—could not touch the essence of New England civilization. Massachusetts as an economy and a society might change altogether, but as a moral concept it would remain unaltered. In the resistance to change and the idealization of the yeoman, we see an elite unable to accept the changes it had engendered.

Thus, in the words and deeds of the agricultural societies, there is a decided split in the attitude toward Massachusetts farmers. As the elite turned inward, the societies abandoned practical agriculture as ungentlemanly. Yet as the agrarian origins of New England society receded further into the past—a change for which the elite bore direct responsibility—the yeoman took on increasing symbolic importance as guarantor of the moral foundation of that society. The farmer was no longer a real person, as he had been in the days of Lowell and Quincy. He was neither an object of

62. For Colman's condemnation of modern farmers, see for example, his *First Report,* pp. 90–91; *Third Report,* pp. 92–95; and *Fourth Report,* pp. 424–30. For his references to merchants and manufacturers as unproductive men and "city millionaires," see his *Third Report,* pp. 55–57, 146, and his *Fourth Report,* pp. 158–59. The reference to speculations in real estate and Texas scrip is from the *Fourth Report,* p. 426.

63. See, for example, Loring, "New England Farming," p. 46; Loring, "The Social and Civil Position of the Farmer," pp. 81–91; and I. H. Wright, "The Position of Agriculture," an address to the Middlesex South [Agricultural] Society, in *Agriculture of Massachusetts . . . 1854,* pp. 452–53.

benevolence nor of reform, but instead of nostalgia, perhaps the fate of all doomed species. When through his real world actions—emigration to the West or migration to cities and mill towns—he challenged the symbolic role he had been assigned, he became an object of control. Either way, he was of concern only as he conformed to or rebelled against that role.

Because the ordinary farmer of Massachusetts was nothing *but* a symbol to elite Bostonians, they "played" yeoman in a way that earlier generations neither could nor did. Retirement to a country estate at the end of a business career was thus depicted not only as evidence of personal refinement but also as a longed-for return to the peaceful life of a farmer. "The stripling," commented Charles T. Russell at a county fair in 1850, "just mounted at the counting house desk, or for the first six months, fingering laces, or measuring off cambrics and ginghams, or it may be, just emerging from college walls, looks back to the farm as an escape from drudgery. The merchant, the manufacturer, the professional man, on the crowded and heaving ocean of middle life, turns to it, as the sailor, to his distant home."[64] It made no difference, of course, that most such men had no farm to "look back" to or that the only "home" they had ever known was a Boston town house.

No individual epitomized the simultaneous self-characterization as both landed aristocrat and simple yeoman better than the Marshfield Farmer himself, Daniel Webster. Webster first acquired the Marshfield property known as Green Harbor in 1832 (fig. 42). What began as a modest enough 160-acre farm expanded over the years into a spread of no fewer than fourteen hundred acres, encompassing thirty buildings and requiring the labor of twenty-five men, most of them tenant farmers. It has been estimated that Webster spent a total of ninety thousand dollars on the estate—an enormous sum for that era—sometimes at the rate of twenty-five hundred a month, about the same amount of money he was simultaneously borrowing.[65] It took that kind of money to turn what had been a marginal New England farm into a squire's estate. Webster not only acquired more land, he also renovated a modest eighteenth-century farmhouse into an elegant residence; transformed the farmstead into a proper English country landscape, complete with ornamental geese, peacocks, and llamas; undertook numerous agricultural experiments, most inspired by British agricultural

64. Charles T. Russell, "Agricultural Progress in Massachusetts for the Last Half Century," an address to the Hampden County Agricultural Society, in *Transactions of the Agricultural Societies . . . 1850*, pp. 410–11. See also "[Review of A. J.] Downing on Rural Architecture," *North American Review* 56 (January 1843): 1–2.

65. Irving H. Bartlett, *Daniel Webster* (New York: W. W. Norton, 1978), p. 208.

42. *Green Harbor, Seat of Daniel Webster.* Reprinted from Charles Lanman, *The Private Life of Daniel Webster* (New York, 1852). (Courtesy Yale University Library.)

reformers; and stocked his barns with imported livestock of impeccable pedigree.[66]

As early as his days as Christopher Gore's law clerk, Webster had been attracted to an aristocratic way of life. He liked good wines, fine dining, and elegant company.[67] The English landed aristocracy particularly appealed to him, as a class invariably endowed with style and at least potentially with a sense of public duty. If, on his journey through Britain in 1839, Webster did not approve of every extravagance indulged in by the English aristocracy, he was certainly attracted by their elegant manner of living. Part of this style of life, of course, was a fashionable interest in experimental agriculture. It was entirely in character, then, for Webster as something of an American squire to attend a meeting of the Royal Agricultural Society,

66. On Green Harbor and Webster's activities as a gentleman farmer, see Webster's biography in the Appendix.
67. Bartlett, *Webster,* pp. 74–75, 122, 200.

compose a memorandum on new methods of field drainage, and make careful note of local farming conditions.[68]

But Webster as the country gentleman and Marshfield as the manor are only half the story. Squire Webster, as his Marshfield overseer always referred to him,[69] also cultivated an image as the Farmer of Marshfield, a sturdy yeoman at heart. The pomp, the glory, the power of political life were not really what Webster desired; they were instead the sacrifices he made to serve the public. "Nothing affords him more true pleasure," wrote one agricultural writer in 1849, "than the personal supervision of the farming operations on his estate, and social and familiar discussion of the principles of good husbandry with his brethren of the plow. He retires from the noise and bustle of the world, and the wearing duties of public life, during a winter at Washington, to his pleasant and modest country seat, with much delight. . . . Here . . . none can be more cheerful and familiar in all that pertains to agreeable companionship, than the yeoman,—the Farmer of Marshfield."[70]

And the part of the yeoman he played. It was Senator Webster, whose huge estate boasted vast orchards and an acre-large flower garden, who commented disingenuously in 1845 at a horticultural society dinner: "We, who belong to the class of farmers, are compelled to bring nothing but our applause to those whose taste, condition, and position enable them to contribute these horticultural excellencies which we see around us."[71] What part of the yeoman image was deliberately cultivated by Webster himself and what part was ascribed to him by others, how much was fact and how much fiction, are almost impossible to determine. There are stories of Webster as he "descant[ed] upon the goodness and beauty of his Alderney cows"; pitched hay faster than his hired hands; insisted that his horses be buried standing up and in their halters; and, during his last fatal illness, called for his "favorite yoke of Syrian oxen" to be passed before his window.[72] This is the man who, while feeding ears of corn to his cattle,

68. Ibid., pp. 158–61; C. H. Van Tyne, ed., *The Letters of Daniel Webster* (New York: McClure, Phillips, 1902), pp. 647–51; Rexford B. Sherman, "Daniel Webster, Gentleman Farmer," *Agricultural History* 53 (April 1979): 483.

69. Bartlett, *Webster,* p. 208.

70. "Sketches of Farms: The Farm of the Hon. Daniel Webster," *The Cultivator,* n.s., 6 (January 1849): 9.

71. Description of the MHS festival of 1845, in *Transactions of the Massachusetts Horticultural Society for the Years 1843–4–5–6* (Boston: Dutton and Wentworth, 1847), p. 102.

72. Charles Lanman, *The Private Life of Daniel Webster* (New York: Harper and Brothers, 1852), p. 71; Bartlett, *Webster,* p. 214; Speech of Edward Everett, in *In Memory of Daniel Webster,* p. 30.

allegedly remarked to his son, "I had rather be here than in the Senate," and who in truth wrote his farm agent from Washington: "Amidst the toil of law, & the stunning din of politics, any thing is welcome, which calls my thoughts back to Marshfield, tho' it be only to be told which way the wind blows."[73] The same statesman who supposedly addressed the steward of his New Hampshire estate as "Brother Farmer" was in fact toasted in 1832 at an MSPA dinner as "Our senator in Congress—a New Hampshire farmer."[74]

Webster's manipulation of his Marshfield image should come as no surprise. As much as he was by temperament drawn to men of wealth and power and to their elegant mode of living, Webster could not afford to cultivate an exclusively aristocratic image, lest he lose his popularity with the voters. Representing his life at Marshfield as a return to his yeoman roots was a stroke of political brilliance. But it may have been more than that. Webster's career was in large part based on his evocation of myths and manipulation of symbols. The American union was one such symbol, of course, but so too was New England's rich heritage. As memorable as his "Liberty and Union" speech were his addresses at the dedication of Plymouth Rock and of the Bunker Hill monument. Both of these dedication speeches drew tremendous power by evoking images of New England's moral glory. In the gallery of New England heritage, the Massachusetts yeoman hangs next to the Pilgrim Fathers and Boston's Revolutionary war heroes, much as the portrait of Webster as the Marshfield Farmer hangs side by side with that of him as preserver of the Union (fig. 43). In the same way that Webster's oratory heightened the power of important cultural symbols, his cultivation of a yeoman image elevated the power of that cultural icon.

John Lowell was about as likely to have represented himself as the Farmer of Roxbury as he was to have imported Peruvian llamas for his fourteen-acre farm. A man of one mind, he knew perfectly well he was neither yeoman nor aristocrat but a member of a commercial elite responsible to the larger populace. Members of the generation that followed Lowell, however, were of two minds. They could not quite face what they had done to the society they headed. Having torn Massachusetts from its agrarian roots, they maintained a rhetorical attachment to the sturdy yeo-

73. Peter Harvey, *Reminiscences and Anecdotes of Daniel Webster* (Boston: Little, Brown, 1877), p. 277; Webster to Charles Henry Thomas, 4 February 1836, in Charles M. Wiltse, ed., *The Papers of Daniel Webster: Correspondence*, 6 vols. (Hanover, N.H.: University Press of New England, 1974–84), 4:82.
74. Harvey, *Webster*, p. 295; *Centennial Year*, p. 74.

43. *The Marshfield Farmer.* Reprinted from Peter Harvey, *Reminiscences and Anecdotes of Daniel Webster* (Boston, 1877). (Courtesy Yale University Library.)

man, the symbolic representative of virtues they themselves had destroyed. Yet they fretted less over their public duties than over their private characters, which they sought to elevate by pursuing the rich associations of an ornamental, aristocratic, "well-bred" agriculture. If the true harvest of this agriculture was symbolic, it was still a bumper crop.

# Epilogue

"GOD Almighty," stated John Winthrop in 1630 on the deck of the westward-sailing *Arbella,* "in His most holy and wise providence hath so disposed of the condition of mankind as in all times some must be rich, some poor; some high and eminent in power and dignity, others mean and in subjection." For Winthrop, a fixed social hierarchy was divinely ordained; there was no need to mince words on the subject, no reason to sidestep the fact of a permanent underclass or to defend the legitimacy of a social, economic, and political elite.

One hundred fifty years after Winthrop landed in Massachusetts Bay Colony, the rich, the high, and the eminent of Boston may well have envied the confidence with which John Winthrop had stated the blunt facts of hierarchy, power, and subjection. In the America of the early Republic and the antebellum era, the notion of an elite was distinctly problematic. At the close of the Revolution, prominent Bostonians considered themselves to be a national ruling class, but in republican America, what was to define them as a legitimate political elite? What was the source of their authority? Long before the age of Andrew Jackson, they had lost national political prominence, but they retained local political and cultural dominance while accumulating ever greater social pretensions along with their fortunes. Yet in a society in which faith in the equality of opportunity and the perfectibility of all men precluded a closed caste, how could this social and economic elite justify itself? And for the individuals within the elite, grown rich on trade, finance, and manufacturing, how was a moral transcendence of wealth to be demonstrated?

Members of the Boston elite were not without answers to these questions. The first generation settled the problem of legitimacy by claiming to be a natural aristocracy, the only kind of aristocracy acceptable in republican America. To elite Bostonians, those who could be expected to belong to this justifiedly privileged class were men like themselves—men of education and gentility, wealth and prominence, epitomizing the mercantile virtues of thrift, sobriety, and industry. When these same people acquired country estates, it was to solidify their image as the men at the apex of society, for other images of other powerful elites lurked in the background. These were the country house owners of Britain—noblemen, country squires, and landed merchants and professionals—subgroups of the elite that were socially, economically, and morally distinct from one another, and in that sense projecting distinct and even conflicting images. No matter. Landed Bostonians tapped into the symbolism of all three groups. If they rejected the decadence of the British nobility, they nevertheless savored its stability and permanence, power and prestige. If they refused to accept the hereditary status of the country gentry, they nonetheless embraced the elegant simplicity and the enlightened benevolence of the gentry's style of living. And if they might ideally prefer settled station over the nouveau achievements of the landed merchants and professionals, they still looked to the bankers and lawyers settled on Thames estates as moral way stations between ostentatious aristocrats and boorish men of business. These men represented an ideal of personality and of living that they yearned to approximate in their private characters and lives. Rational and restrained, genteel and cultivated—it was an ideal befitting an aristocracy in America.

Members of the postrevolutionary elite settled on country estates and took up gentleman farming as private men. If they wished to tap the symbolic possibilities of rural pursuits as public men, they joined the Massachusetts Society for Promoting Agriculture. Here they defined themselves against the public at large, the Massachusetts citizenry, the yeoman farmers of the Commonwealth. In the early years of the MSPA, members of the agricultural society, many of whom were in fact gentleman farmers, claimed no personal expertise of agriculture and denied any personal benefit from agricultural improvement. The expressions of humble disinterestedness were their own reward, for they offered elite Bostonians something precious in the postrevolutionary world, a public stance of unselfish virtue. Furthermore, it was virtue magnified manifold, because the objects of MSPA benevolence, agriculture and the farmer, were themselves freighted with moral content. Yet if MSPA members claimed no right or ability to dictate to farmers based on their own agricultural expertise, they did stake a claim for leadership on their mercantile identities. Who but the merchant, they insisted, has the broad experience needed to gather and assess the latest in agricultural knowledge? These claims for social leadership had nothing to do with disinterested virtue; they did not rely at all on the moral weight of agriculture and the farmer. Instead, they rested on the Boston elite's understanding of themselves as an elite legitimized by mercantile talent, wealth, and social standing.

By the War of 1812, MSPA members were far more explicit about the importance of commerce and the merchant to the progress of agriculture. To be sure, the standard rhetoric was retained: agriculture continued as the basis of wealth, just as the farmer continued as the pillar of republican virtue. But at the same time, commerce was boldly represented as *the* progressive force in agriculture, just as the gentleman farmer—alias the merchant—was credited with initiating progressive change in the common farmer's routine. And MSPA members of the middle generation were much less coy in criticizing practical farmers than were their postrevolutionary counterparts. Pillars of virtue the yeomanry may have been, but so were they lazy, wasteful, hidebound, blind to improvement—in short, not much different from Old World peasants. What they needed, of course, was the leadership of the Boston elite, but with the same fickleness and foolishness that led them to reject Boston Federalists as their political leaders, they rejected Boston's agricultural reformers as their mentors in farming. Elite Bostonians could only shake their heads in wounded bewilderment that they should be thus rejected, thus martyred.

There was certainly an irony in the condemnation of practical farmers as peasantlike in their mentality, for the agricultural reformers' ultimate message to the Massachusetts yeomanry was that, in their expectations for themselves, they must reject the New World sense of unlimited possibilities for an Old World sense of fixed station. This conviction was born of a realization that Massachusetts was fast becoming anglicized, experiencing such Old World problems as overpopulation and emigration and such Old World phenomena as urbanization and industrialization. This was not an easy realization for many elite Bostonians. Many were personally responsible for some of those dramatic changes. Yet some had economic, social, and ultimately psychological difficulties adjusting to the displacement of commerce as the foundation of Boston wealth and prominence. Once the new order was embraced, however, as it was by about 1830, proper Bostonians found their elite position only strengthened by a generation of adjustment. It was thus both as agricultural reformers and as leaders of society that they

urged the practical farmers of Massachusetts to accept a decidedly middling and, even more critically, a decidedly fixed status in a permanent
social hierarchy.

Thus two hundred years after the *Arbella* arrived in Boston, the undisguised endorsement of social stasis and hierarchy was advanced once
more. In embracing this point of view, prominent Bostonians were certainly out of the mainstream of American thought. After all, we remember
the Jacksonian era as a time when the egalitarian, perfectionist ideals of
social mobility and unlimited opportunity dominated the American outlook. In identifying with rural pursuits, Bostonians sought to tap into a
reservoir of associations that were valuable precisely because, as widely
accepted cultural symbols, they had meaning for all Americans. The ultimate irony is that in the process, they put forth an ideology that was
anything but broadly endorsed.

By the 1840s and 1850s, agricultural commentators assumed an even
more severe stance toward the practical farmer; the insistence that the
yeoman farmer stay put became more strident, harsh, even threatening. At
the same time, however, Boston blue bloods mythologized the practical
farmer into a nostalgic image of the self-sufficient yeoman. Both approaches
to the husbandman were unrealistic, and both sought to freeze him in time
and place in order to defy the realities of modernization. It was as if the
wealthy merchants, manufacturers, financiers, and railroad magnates of
Boston could not quite face what they had done—displaced the farmer
economically and socially, severed the last links to an agrarian past—and so
the farmer became nothing more than a symbol to be manipulated toward
psychological ends. In both approaches to the farmer, social control as well
as nostalgia, elite Bostonians demonstrated their increasing alienation from
mainstream American thought. Belief in a fixed social hierarchy carried
little currency in antebellum America. Belief in the self-sufficient farmer as
the basis of society was far removed from the realities of smokestack, steam
whistle America.

But antebellum Bostonians distanced themselves ideologically from
more than the bulk of the American populace; they distanced themselves as
well from the postrevolutionary sources of their own outlook. In their
desire to prove their individual and collective transcendence of materialism,
members of the Boston elite edged ever closer to endorsing an ideal of
aristocracy and rejecting their mercantile roots. Elite Bostonians of the late
eighteenth and early nineteenth centuries had also endorsed a concept of
aristocracy, but one based on an image of a legitimate aristocracy as one
epitomizing mercantile virtues and values. When they participated in rural

pursuits, antebellum Bostonians had a very different aristocracy in mind, one that valued the beautiful above the practical, ornament above utility— one that more nearly resembled the nobility of Old England than the business entrepreneurs of New England.

Members of the Boston elite thus claimed to have transcended their commercial roots when they transcended materialism. They saw themselves as having arrived at a stage of civilization beyond commerce, and if the commercial stage had been characterized by luxury and materialism, this triumphant fifth stage was marked by cultivation. It was just this cultivation that provided members of Boston's elite with legitimacy as individuals and as a class. Here was a criterion for privileged status that was certainly more aristocratic than public virtue or mercantile wisdom yet, in that it was not strictly hereditary, did not ignore egalitarian republicanism either. It thus remained acceptable in antebellum America. By the eve of the Civil War, however, there were signs aplenty that at least some members of the Boston elite were ready to jettison any pretensions to egalitarian republicanism altogether; they were ready to endorse aristocracy plain and simple. We see this in the introduction of the term *Brahmin,* in Nathan Appleton's newly acquired "family crest," and of course in the undisguised fascination with "breeding" involved in the twin passions for ornamental horticulture and pedigreed livestock.

And what of the postwar period? The fate of the Brahmins in the Gilded Age has been marked by historiographical controversy. Frederic Cople Jaher maintains that Boston blue bloods, horrified equally by boorish parvenu industrialists and immigrant masses, retreated into a slough of despond and disgust. Repelled by business culture and popular culture alike, they turned to mugwumpery as a political means of controlling the dangerous excesses of rich and poor. Many shunned careers in commerce and manufacturing for fields untainted with any suggestion of money-making—education, religion, medicine, philanthropy, and culture—and even those who continued in business did not do so in the same compulsive, entrepreneurial spirit of a Thomas Handasyd Perkins or an Amos Lawrence. The rejection of mercantile roots for aristocratic culture took its most blatant form in the pronounced anglophilia of postbellum patricians. This era witnessed the establishment of elite academies along the model of the British public school, the founding of exclusive country clubs devoted to such upper-class British pastimes as polo, fox hunting, and golf, and the final stage in the transition from Unitarianism, the merchant's creed, to the conservative, ritualistic, hierarchical, and ultimately English Episcopalianism as *the* elite faith. For Jaher, the postbellum Brahmin continuum began with Henry Lee Higginson, a culturally refined investment banker who helped establish the Boston Symphony Orchestra, continued with such cultural lights as art historian Charles Eliot Norton, and ended with Henry Adams, the prophet of Brahmin despair.[1]

Other historians disagree with this representation. Both Gabriel Kolko and Peter Dobkin Hall stress the continuing vitality of Brahmin business culture. They point to blue-blooded Boston's involvement in and leadership of investment banking, western mining ventures, and major business corporations. Henry Lee Higginson, Kolko insists, was not, as the myth would have it, a "sensitive lover of music who wished to sit down at the footsteps of his office every morning and cry before entering." Instead he was a contented investment banker whose "taste in music ran to the ninety-minute balanced program" and whose main impact on the Boston Symphony Orchestra was to transform it into an efficient business organization. As for Henry Adams, his alienation from American culture was real enough but can hardly be considered representative of his class.[2]

The issue is not really whether the Boston elite ceased to be a business aristocracy, as Jaher claims it definitely did, and as Kolko and Hall insist it most definitely did not. This class had always based its status on business wealth, and in the postbellum era, as Kolko and Hall demonstrate, it proved itself eager to perpetuate and increase that wealth with new financial and industrial enterprises. Business activity and business values are two different phenomena, however, and I would argue that even if Higginson's musical tastes smacked too much of the shopkeeper, the impulse that drove him to nurture a symphony orchestra did not. Even in the days of powdered wigs and knee breeches, Boston's merchants sought to balance the mercantile virtues with those of the cultivated, landed gentleman. By the end of the antebellum era, that need for a counterweight to mercantile values had proceeded so far that many a blue blood sought to transcend and a few even to reject their entrepreneurial origins. In this respect, the Gilded Age entailed only an intensification of prewar trends.

1. Frederic Cople Jaher, "The Boston Brahmins in the Age of Industrial Capitalism," in Jaher, ed., *The Age of Industrialism in America: Essays in Social Structure and Cultural Values* (New York: Free Press, 1968), pp. 188–262. See also James McLachlan, *American Boarding Schools: A Historical Study* (New York: Charles Scribner's Sons, 1970), pp. 136–298.

2. Gabriel Kolko, "Brahmins and Business, 1870–1914: A Hypothesis on the Social Basis of Success in American History," in Kurt H. Wolff and Barrington Moore, Jr., eds., *The Critical Spirit: Essays in Honor of Herbert Marcuse* (Boston: Beacon Press, 1967), pp. 343–63, and Peter Dobkin Hall, *The Organization of American Culture, 1700–1900: Private Institutions, Elites, and the Origins of American Nationality* (New York: New York University Press, 1984), pp. 220–39. The quotations are from Kolko, "Brahmins and Business," pp. 353, 354.

What changed in the Gilded Age was not the relevance of business to elite identity—that had posed a problem even before the Civil War—but the meaning of aristocracy to that same class. Upper-crust Bostonians had always understood themselves as an aristocracy, but, in response to both popular ideology and an internal ethic, they had also always taken pains to redefine that term away from its associations with Old World nobility. Theirs was to be not a class based on hereditary status but one legitimized by some alternate criterion such as public virtue or personal cultivation. By the postbellum decades, however, they were ready to jettison these moral definitions of aristocracy for a more blatantly biological one.

Rural pursuits of the Gilded Age reflected these struggles with class identity. The enthusiasms that first appeared in the 1840s and 1850s—for ornamental horticulture, pedigreed livestock, and racehorses—dominated the postbellum period. But now the full implications of biological breeding, once limited to the symbolic level of cultivation, began to be drawn in earnest. Perhaps the best illustration of this subtly altered, greatly heightened interest in breeding is afforded by the horticultural career of Francis Parkman.

Parkman is best known, of course, as an early historian of the American wilderness and secondarily as a critic of northern culture as dangerously emasculated by business values.[3] Recently, much has been made of both his historical writings and his social commentary as they reflect Parkman's anxiety over the virility of northern elites, such as his own Brahmin class, and his personal quest to prove his mettle.[4] His interest in horticulture, strongest during the 1860s and 1870s, has been largely dismissed as therapy for Parkman's crippling physical—many today would say hysterical—ailments.[5] In this sense, flower gardening appears as something of a lapse in Parkman's mentality, for it seems to represent an indulgence in an almost feminine pleasure and a surrender to physical limitations. To be

3. See, for example, Parkman to the *Boston Daily Advertiser,* 30 June, 4, 14 July 1863, in Wilbur R. Jacobs, ed., *Letters of Francis Parkman,* 2 vols. (Norman: University of Oklahoma Press, 1960), 1:159–65.

4. Harold Beaver, "Parkman's Crack-up: A Bostonian on the Oregon Trail," *New England Quarterly* 48 (March 1975): 84–103; Francis Jennings, "Francis Parkman: A Brahmin among Untouchables," *William and Mary Quarterly,* 3d ser., 42 (July 1985): 305–28; Kim Townsend, "Francis Parkman and the Male Tradition," *American Quarterly* 38 (Spring 1986): 97–113.

5. Henry Dwight Sedgwick, *Francis Parkman* (Boston: Houghton, Mifflin, 1904), pp. 234–43, 337; Charles Haight Farnham, *A Life of Francis Parkman* (Boston: Little, Brown, 1910), pp. 27–34; Howard Doughty, *Francis Parkman* (New York: Macmillan, 1962), pp. 208–10. For details of Parkman's horticultural activities, see his biography in the Appendix.

sure, Parkman's interest in horticulture does present us with intriguing discontinuities. We may contrast Parkman as he self-consciously described the hardships he withstood on the Oregon Trail with Parkman as he lectured on floriculture to young ladies. We may contrast his public letter of 1863 condemning commerce as an emasculating and brutalizing influence on northern culture with his private announcement, on establishing a commercial nursery on his Jamaica Plain estate in 1862, that "turning tradesman has agreed with me so far."[6] Here, however, it is important to note the single set of ideas that guided Parkman in his historical writing, cultural critique, and horticultural philosophy.

For Parkman, horticulture was nothing more and nothing less than an exercise in breeding superiority (fig. 44). It was the use of human art to aid Nature "in the daily miracle by which she works beauty out of foulness." Accordingly, the major purpose of a horticultural society was to reward excellence. "The great function of this society," he stated in his first address as president of the MHS, "is to recognize and to requite with honor and profit every form of horticultural merit according to nature and degree." Horticulture in America, he continued, faces special stumbling blocks. "It shares the tendency which belongs to all our democratic civilization to diffuse itself widely without rising very high. It is for us to strive by every means to break that barren routine and repetition into which it is so much inclined to fall; to wean the cultivator from the beaten tracks and teach him that eminence in special cultures, and not a feeble mediocrity in all, is the best condition of his enjoyment and his success."[7]

The continued superiority of the Brahmin "variety" was crucial to Parkman, and it appears that his concept of the development of that variety was close to, if not in fact, biological. In examining Parkman's *Book of Roses,* published in 1866, the reader can hardly escape the impression that human beings, not flowers, are the true subject of some critical passages. Parkman himself stated unambiguously that "like all things living, in the world of mind or matter, the rose is beautified, enlarged, and strengthened by a course of judicious and persevering culture, continued through successive generations." Horticulture, he insisted, is "no leveller." Success is contingent on "rigid systems of selection and rejection." The good horticul-

6. Parkman to Mary Parkman, 4 April 1862, Francis Parkman Papers, Massachusetts Historical Society, Boston.

7. *Transactions of the Massachusetts Horticultural Society, for the Year 1875. Part I* (Boston: Tolman and White, 1875), pp. 6, 7–8. Parkman thus fretted over the routine award of premiums for plants that represented no improvement over previous winners. *Transactions of the Massachusetts Horticultural Society, for the Year 1878. Part I* (Boston: Massachusetts Horticultural Society, 1878), pp. 6–7.

44. *Lilium parkmanni.* Years of painstaking hybridization resulted in this splendid blossom, Francis Parkman's horticultural triumph. (Courtesy Massachusetts Historical Society.)

turist, continued Parkman in increasingly suggestive language, "chooses those marked out by conspicuous merit; protects them from the pollen of inferior sorts; intermarries them, perhaps, with other varieties of equal vigor and beauty; saves their seed, and raises from it another generation."[8] Could Parkman have been describing some of his ancestors, who rose to wealth and power through native business talent, shunned the less successful as marriage partners in favor of other elite Bostonians, Salemites, or perhaps Philadelphians, and fathered offspring expected to repeat the same process?

Certainly when Parkman moved into a discussion of the very beginnings of superior varieties, he appeared to account for the humbler colonial

8. Francis Parkman, *The Book of Roses* (Boston: J. E. Tilton, 1866), pp. 95–96.

origins of many members of his own class. "All the roses of our gardens have some wild ancestors of the woods and meadows," he explained, perhaps referring to the "wilds" of Essex County and rural New England, "from whom, in the process of successive generations, their beauties have been developed, sometimes by happy accidents, but oftener by design. Thus have arisen families of roses, each marked with traces of its parentage. These are the patricians of the floral commonwealth, gifted at once with fame, beauty, and rank."[9]

Parkman's interest in horticulture demonstrates the new place rural pursuits assumed in elite culture after the Civil War. For Parkman, as for postbellum Bostonians in general, horticulture involved something quite other than an intensification of the antebellum interest in "cultivation." Parkman focused narrowly on the plants themselves, and on the process of their breeding, but not, as with the antebellum MHS, on the moral state of the breeder. Horticulture as a science of heredity confirmed a new aristocratic ethos that, by the time of Henry Cabot Lodge and the Immigration Restriction League of the 1890s, flirted with eugenics.[10] It was therefore of special *interest,* but it was no longer of special *use.* It was not used to send cultural messages—either to the horticulturists themselves or to society at large—on such outdated issues as the theoretical legitimacy or moral worthiness of an American aristocracy.

Other developments in postbellum horticulture further suggest its declining importance as a tool of self-characterization and self-justification. For one, horticulture as a movement had passed its heyday. High-toned periodicals no longer covered horticulture as a topic of general interest to the elite. The MHS, finding itself in debt, was forced to cut back on its premiums. An attempt to revive the elaborate horticultural festivals of antebellum days was a social and financial flop; so few tickets were purchased that a few faithful members were forced to buy large numbers and distribute them gratis.[11] Of even greater significance than the waning

9. Ibid., pp. 96–97. Here, Parkman resembles his contemporary, Oliver Wendell Holmes, in his characterization of the Brahmin class as the result of biological refinement. "Money kept for two or three generations transforms a race," wrote Holmes, and not "merely in manners and hereditary culture, but in blood and bone." Wealth buys a healthy diet, favorable environment, and good medical care; and in making marriage choices, the wealthy "can afford the expensive luxury of beauty." The result is a "congenital and hereditary" caste. Oliver Wendell Holmes, *Elsie Venner,* 2 vols. (Boston: Ticknor and Fields, 1861), 1:13–17; Holmes, *The Autocrat of the Breakfast-Table* (Boston: Phillips, Sampson, 1858), pp. 303–4.

10. On the currency of racial thinking and eugenics among the Boston elite, see John Higham, *Strangers in the Land: Patterns of American Nativism, 1880–1925,* rev. ed. (New York: Atheneum, 1985), pp. 101–5, 138–44, 152.

11. *Transactions of the Massachusetts Horticultural Society, for the Year 1875. Part II* (Boston: Tolman and White, 1876), p. 176; *Transactions of the Massachusetts Horticultural*

popularity of horticulture was its acceptance as a female pastime in the postbellum era. In 1864 the Massachusetts Horticultural Society accepted its first female member. By the 1870s, Boston's female horticulturists were planning how to cheer up slum sections of the city with window boxes, and young ladies attended lectures on flowers at Harvard's Bussey Institution.[12] Horticulture had lost its meaning as an antidote to materialism and therefore its special importance to the money-makers of the world, male businessmen. Released from the task of defining elite identity, horticulture was free to take on new connotations.

Rural pursuits in general, not just horticulture, were drained of their symbolic power in the postwar decades. Agricultural fairs, once tense contradances between Boston gentlemen and common farmers, degenerated into little more than country club outings. By 1885, for example, the Essex Agricultural Society was offering premiums for gentleman's driving horses. At the society's annual fair fifteen years later there were no livestock and no farm products, but members of the blue blood Myopia Hunt Club demonstrated their equestrian skills.[13] Similarly, country estate living lost many of its earlier connotations when it became nothing more than a patrician flight from Boston and its immigrant masses to the pristine suburbs. Residence in a North Shore community was less an embrace of a rural and agricultural style of living than a rejection of the city as a place for the wellborn to live.

As elite Bostonians distanced themselves from the entrepreneurial outlook of their forefathers and the democratic, capitalistic tendencies of contemporary America, the link between country life and class identity underwent a parallel transformation. Through their rich cultural associations, rural pursuits had provided a powerful means for Boston's merchants, financiers, industrialists, and professional men to characterize themselves as individuals and to justify themselves as members of an elite. Thus they attempted to establish their legitimacy as a privileged class in republican America, to cope with the economic and social changes for which they bore direct responsibility, and to prove their personal transcendence of material-

---

*Society, for the Year 1877. Part I* (Boston: Massachusetts Horticultural Society, 1877), pp. 6–7.

12. Robert Manning, *History of the Massachusetts Horticultural Society, 1829–1878* (Boston: Massachusetts Horticultural Society, 1880), pp. 500–525 (MHS membership list); Albert Emerson Benson, *History of the Massachusetts Horticultural Society* (Boston: Massachusetts Horticultural Society, 1929), pp. 70, 201–2, 267, 436, 439.

13. Thomas Franklin Waters, *The History of the Essex Agricultural Society of Essex County, Massachusetts, 1818–1918* (Salem, Mass.: Trustees of the Essex Agricultural Society, 1918), pp. 35, 40.

ism and boorishness. By the postbellum era, however, as an undisguisedly aristocratic outlook replaced an entrepreneurial one, elite Bostonians no longer faced the same imperatives. Under these circumstances, country estate living, gentleman farming, and the practice of horticulture became less useful to the elite. Rural pursuits faded from the elite scene as widely used, widely understood tools of self-characterization and self-justification. They became a matter of cultural habit rather than of cultural expression. If George Cabot's potatoes, Josiah Quincy's carrots, Nathaniel Ingersoll's pigs, and Thomas Handasyd Perkins's fruits can be interpreted as a body of cultural statements, postbellum rural pursuits more closely resemble an upper-class vernacular, figures of speech idiosyncratically employed by the Brahmin caste. But in the years between the Revolution and the Civil War, when rural pursuits still constituted a form of class expression, it was a rich and curious and telling story they had to relate.

# *APPENDIX*

# *Rural Biographies of Selected Elite Bostonians*

ADAMS, CHARLES FRANCIS (1807–86), diplomat

Adams owned over a thousand acres of land in various farms in the town of Quincy. His principal farm, at Mount Wollaston, ran to some four hundred acres and was run by his son. Here he kept fifty head of livestock, some of them imported. Adams leased another two-hundred-acre farm, which he drained at great expense, later claiming that the improvements had indeed been cost-effective. Adams was a member of both the MSPA and the MHS and in 1850 addressed the Norfolk Agricultural Society at its annual fair. [Charles L. Flint, ed., *Abstract of Returns of the Agricultural Societies of Massachusetts, for 1860* (Boston: William White, 1861), pp. 73–75; Adams, "What Can Be Done for the Farming of Norfolk County?" *Transactions of the Agricultural Societies in the Commonwealth of Massachusetts, for the Year 1850* (Boston: Dutton and Wentworth, 1851), pp. 426–43.]

ADAMS, JOHN (1735–1826), lawyer and statesman

Adams is of course best known as the second president of the United States, but from 1805 to 1813 he was also president of the MSPA. He had a long-standing interest in agriculture. In 1759, having just purchased a "Common Place Book of Husbandry and Gardening" covering every topic from turnips to quince trees to salt meadow to dung, Adams wrote in his diary: "Husbandry may be studied by me either as a Phylosopher inquisitive into the secrets of Nature in Vegetation, Generation, and of Art in Manufacture or as a Politician and Patriot, desirous of promoting the Improvement of

Laws &c. for the Interest of the Public, or as a Private Man, selfishly [thirsting?] after Profit, in order to make money." Adams did not grow rich on the produce of any of his Braintree farms: the first, a forty-acre farm inherited in 1761, the second, his thirty-five-acre family homestead, purchased of his brother in 1774, or the third, purchased in 1787. Nevertheless, he seemed to enjoy the supervision of agricultural operations immensely. In 1762 he rose before sunrise to write in his diary that his thoughts were "running continually from the orchard to the Pasture and from thence to the swamp, and thence to the House and Barn and Land adjoining." "Sometimes," he continued, "I am at the orchard Ploughing up Acre after Acre"; at other times, he was digging stones in the pasture, burning bushes in the swamp, buying fencing materials in town, plowing the upland with six yoke of oxen, carting gravel, or introducing new English grasses into the meadow. In 1774, while riding on the court circuit, he confided in his wife that "Time, on these tedious Peregrinations, hangs heavily," and that his "Fancy and Wishes and Desires" were among the "Fields, Pastures and Meadows" of Braintree "as much as those of the Israelites were among the Leeks, Garleeks and Onions of the Land of Goshen." As president, Adams rued his inability to keep abreast of agricultural progress. When in 1799, Secretary of State Timothy Pickering (whom Adams later fired) sent Adams a copy of John Bordley's agricultural treatise, Adams replied: "I have a great opinion of Mr. Bordleys Experience, Skill and knowledge in Husbandry and should have great delight in trying his Experiments, if I was not obliged to recollect and apply to myself President Washingtons words to me, a few days before he went out and I came in. 'Sir, I have read nothing these Eight Years, but the Papers that have been brought me from day to day.'" Given his falling out with the Massachusetts Federalist establishment, it is not surprising that Adams was atypical in his attitudes toward rural pursuits. He refused to accept membership in European agricultural societies and would not even acknowledge the letters and packets of Scottish agricultural reformer Sir John Sinclair; he looked askance at English country seats as decadent (see chapter 1, pp. 36–37); and he may even have regarded those of his Boston neighbors in the same light. Referring to his fellow members on the MSPA's Board of Visitors for the professorship of natural history at Harvard, he wrote: "These are all real gentlemen, all but me very rich, have their city palaces and their country seats, their fine gardens and greenhouses and hothouses, etc., etc., etc." Under the circumstances, it is remarkable that Adams functioned as MSPA president in the politically tumultuous years leading up to the War of 1812. Later MSPA members liked to point out the apolitical nature of the society, but in fact the tensions that divided Boston statesmen were reflected in the agricultural association. As long as Adams remained president of the MSPA, for example, it was impossible to invite Timothy Pickering to society functions. [Diary of John Adams, Spring 1759, 24 October 1762, 28 February 1774, in L. H. Butterfield, ed., *Diary and Autobiography of John Adams,* 4 vols. (Cambridge: Harvard University Press, 1961–62), 1:80, 229–30, 2:87–88; Adams to Abigail Adams, 23 June 1774, in Butterfield, ed., *The Book of Abigail and John: Selected Letters of the Adams Family, 1762–1784* (Cambridge: Harvard University Press, 1975), p. 56; Adams to Timothy Pickering, 5 August 1799, Timothy Pickering Papers, reel 25, frame 78, Massachusetts Historical Society (hereafter MHS), Boston; Adams to John Quincy Adams, 27 December 1812, quoted in Page Smith, *John Adams,* 2 vols. (Garden City, N.Y.: Doubleday, 1962), 2:1107; Edmund Quincy, *Life of Josiah Quincy of Massachusetts* (Boston: Ticknor and Fields, 1868), pp. 264–65; Charles A. Hammond, "'Where the Arts and the Virtues Unite': Country Life near Boston, 1637–1864" (Ph.D. diss., Boston University, 1982), pp. 175–84.]

BIGELOW, TIMOTHY (1767–1821), lawyer and statesman

Even before he acquired his Medford estate in 1805, Bigelow indulged his taste for horticulture. While studying law in Worcester, he attended to a flower garden; when he removed to Groton, he cultivated both ornamental and useful plants. But the Medford estate, situated on the banks of the Mystic River, was by far his most extensive horticultural achievement. Here, under the care of gardener Martin Burridge, could be found both common and exotic trees, flowers, vegetables, and fruits, some grown in open culture, others under glass, and others along fruit walls. Some of the fruit trees in Bigelow's garden were obtained from his friend and client Theodore Lyman. Bigelow joined the MSPA in 1819 and was active as well in establishing and running the Association of the Middlesex Husbandmen. [Eliza M. Gill, "A Medford Garden and the Gardener's Notes," *Medford Historical Register* 21 (October 1918): 69–73; "An Early Tourist's Medford Home," ibid., pp. 74–77; Introduction, "Journal of a Tour to Niagara Falls in the Year 1805 by Timothy Bigelow," excerpted in ibid., p. 75.]

BOWDOIN, JAMES (1752–1811), merchant and diplomat

Bowdoin was the son of the Massachusetts governor of the same name, whose Boston garden was famous for its abundance of fruits. The son also had horticultural interests—he planted experimental orchards on both his farm in Dorchester and his estate on Naushon Island off Cape Cod—but his primary interest was in animal husbandry, particularly sheep. In his capacity as minister to Spain, he was able to import merino sheep to the United States. In 1810 he translated and published Louis-Jean-Marie Daubenton's *Advice to Shepherds and Owners of Flocks*. Naushon Island and nearby Nonimasit Island, both of which were owned by Bowdoin and supervised by tenant farmers, yielded sheep, cattle, cheese, and deer for the Boston market at the rate of about $3,350 a year. Bowdoin served as one of the trustees of the MSPA from 1792 through 1795 and donated the bank interest on $400 to the organization in 1796. [Josiah Quincy, 9 June 1801, "Account of Journey of Josiah Quincy," in *Proceedings of the Massachusetts Historical Society*, 2d ser., 4 (May 1888): 127; *Rules and Regulations of the Massachusetts Society for Promoting Agriculture* (Boston: Thomas Fleet, Jr., 1796) (hereafter *MSPA, Rules and Regulations, 1796*), p. 75; "Abstract of the Records, from 1792 to 1858," in *Transactions of the Massachusetts Society for Promoting Agriculture*, n.s., 1 (1858): 51; Marshall Pinckney Wilder, "The Horticulture of Boston and Vicinity," in Justin Winsor, ed., *The Memorial History of Boston, including Suffolk County, Massachusetts, 1630–1880*, 4 vols. (Boston: James R. Osgood, 1881), 4:612; Clifford K. Shipton, *Biographical Sketches of Those Who Attended Harvard College in the Classes 1768–1771*, vol. 17: *Sibley's Harvard Graduates* (Boston: Massachusetts Historical Society, 1975), p. 499; *Dictionary of American Biography* (hereafter *DAB*), s.v. "Bowdoin, James."]

BROWN, JAMES (1800–1855), publisher

On marrying in 1825, Brown moved from his residence in Cambridge to a rural estate named Wellington Hill in West Cambridge. In 1835 he relocated in Boston, but, due to his love for the countryside, he remained in the city only one or two years, finally leaving for Wellington Hill once more. From 1840 until his death he occupied a country seat in Watertown. Over the years, Brown gradually expanded the size of his estate by purchasing contiguous farms, until at the time of his death he owned about 140 acres of wooded, arable, and pasture land. Brown's estate was located in what Boston merchant George Hillard described as "the border land between the region of agriculture and the region of horticulture." The former region, he expanded, is one of "plain farm-houses and farms . . . a district not yet whirled into the vortex of the metropolis, where land is still sold by the acre and not by the foot, and where old manners and primitive habits are yet found." The horticultural region, by contrast, is an area of "trim gardens, ornamented pleasure-grounds, smooth-shaven lawns, fair houses, and all the indications of wealth which is drawn from the city and expended in the gratification of rural tastes." Consistent with the "middle" location of Brown's estate was his management of the farm. It was not, commented Hillard, "one of those showy, model establishments, which require a fortune to carry it on; nor was it conducted exactly as it would have been done by a sharp New England farmer, who looked at nothing but the main chance." Instead, it was managed with future and not present gain in mind, with "no extravagant expenditure, no whimsical outlay, no fantastic indulgence of unprofitable tastes." What Brown did spend his money on was the acquisition of choice cattle, both domestic and imported; the cultivation of crops according to the latest agricultural methods; and the landscaping of his grounds. He was a trustee of the MSPA during the final two years of his life and a founding member of the MHS. [George Stillman Hillard, "James Brown," in Freeman Hunt, ed., *Lives of American Merchants,* 2 vols. (New York: Office of Hunt's Merchants' Magazine, 1856; Derby and Jackson, 1858), 2:515–82.]

BUSSEY, BENJAMIN (1757–1842), merchant

From 1806 until his death in 1842, Bussey gradually accumulated an estate of over two hundred acres in Jamaica Plain named Woodland Hill and carried out an extensive program of reforestation there. He planted not only orchards, specializing in apples and cherries, but also a large variety of forest trees. The property, renamed the Bussey Institution, was given by bequest to Harvard College on the condition that it would "establish there a course of instruction in practical agriculture, in useful and ornamental gardening, in botany, and in such other branches of natural sciences as may tend to promote a knowledge of practical agriculture." It constituted the nucleus of Harvard's Arnold Arboretum. For a time, Woodland Hill, again according to terms of Bussey's bequest, was occupied by Bussey's grandson-in-law THOMAS MOTLEY, JR. (son of a Boston merchant, brother of the historian), who served the MSPA in various capacities from 1850 until well into the postbellum period. Here Motley carried out an extensive stockbreeding program, importing cattle, boarding others imported by the MSPA, and donating some of his own to that association. ["Abstract of the Records," pp. 124, 133; Wilder, "Horticulture of Boston," p. 618; *Centennial Year*

*(1792–1892)* of the Massachusetts Society for Promoting Agriculture (Salem, Mass.: n.p., n.d.), p. 112; Hammond, "Country Life near Boston," pp. 128–35, 349–55.]

CABOT, JOSEPH SEBASTIAN (1796–1874), lawyer,
East India merchant, and banker

On coming of age in 1817, Cabot inherited the ancestral Essex Street mansion, said to be the finest house in Salem when it was built in 1748, and lived here until 1863. Thereafter, he occupied another house in Salem. Cabot frequently submitted fruits and flowers to MHS exhibits—he grew no fewer than six hundred varieties of tulip in Salem—and he served as president of that society from 1852 to 1857, having become a member in 1837 and worked his way up through the posts of counsellor and vice president. He was also an organizer of the Harmony Grove Cemetery, Salem's answer to Mount Auburn, established in 1840. On his European tours, Cabot wrote papers on foreign floriculture and pomology. [L. Vernon Briggs, *History and Genealogy of the Cabot Family, 1475–1927*, 2 vols. (Boston: privately printed, 1927), 1:51–52, 2:644–48; Joseph S. Cabot, address to the MHS, *Addresses of the Retiring President and President Elect of the Massachusetts Horticultural Society* (Boston: Dutton and Wentworth, 1852), pp. 3–6.]

CODMAN, JOHN (1755–1803), merchant

In the 1790s Codman embarked on an ambitious renovation of the 280–acre Chambers Russell estate in Lincoln. He was not the owner of the estate but the coexecutor, and his fellow executor, Samuel Dexter, Jr., thought it most unwise of Codman to invest fifteen thousand dollars in expanding the mansion house and developing the surrounding grounds and farm. Codman, however, was attracted to the ideal of the English country seat—on his business trips to England, he was most impressed with, for example, the seat of his business associate Sir Francis Baring—and therefore happily turned the Russell estate, built in 1741, into a more up-to-date rural retreat for his summer enjoyment. He not only doubled the size of the mansion house but created an ornamental pond on the estate grounds, built a new farmhouse for the farm agent, initiated a ditching and draining program, and erected new fences and walls. The farm itself was devoted mainly to the cultivation of fodder crops and the raising of cattle and sheep. Codman was a charter member of the MSPA, served as a trustee from 1796 to 1799, and donated fifty dollars to the organization in 1796. [*MSPA, Rules and Regulations, 1796*, p. 75; John Codman–Catherine Amory Codman correspondence, 10 July 1800–9 March 1801, Codman Family Manuscripts Collection, Society for the Preservation of New England Antiquities, Boston, Mass.; Charles A. Hammond, "The Country Place 'Made a l'Anglaise with Ease,'" *Journal of the Society of Architectural Historians* 35 (December 1976): 312–13; Alan Emmet, "The Codman Estate—'The Grange': A Landscape Chronicle," *Old Time New England* 71 (1981): 5–23; R. Curtis Chapin, "The Early History and Federalization of the Codman House," ibid., pp. 24–46; Lynne M. Spencer, "Codman House, Lincoln, Massachusetts," *Antiques* 129 (March 1986): 626–31; Hammond, "Country Life near Boston," pp. 164–75, 356–61.]

COOK, ZEBEDEE (1786–1858), merchant, insurance company
president, and state representative

It was largely through Cook's initiative that the MHS was established, for it was he who pointed out the lack of such a society in Boston in a letter to the *New England Farmer*. As a result of this letter, Boston horticulturists met at Cook's insurance office and there founded the MHS with Cook as one of its vice presidents. He served in this capacity until 1835, when he assumed the presidency of the organization. Cook's own horticultural activities were carried out on his Dorchester estate under the supervision of his gardener, Patrick Kennedy; here he cultivated foreign grapes, apricots, peaches, and pears. [*New England Farmer* (hereafter *NEF*) 7 (9 January, 3 April 1829): 198, 295; *Proceedings on the Establishment of the Massachusetts Horticultural Society* (Boston: Isaac R. Butts, 1829), pp. 7–8; Wilder, "Horticulture of Boston," p. 619; Robert Manning, *History of the Massachusetts Horticultural Society, 1829–1878* (hereafter Manning, *MHS*) (Boston: Massachusetts Horticultural Society, 1880), pp. 56–62; *DAB*, s.v. "Cook, Zebedee."]

CRAIGIE, ANDREW (1754–1819), apothecary, financier, and
speculator

In 1791 Craigie bought the Vassall estate in Cambridge, a purchase that, in concert with other smaller acquisitions of land, made him the owner of over 150 acres of marsh, pasture, meadow, and orchard, as well as a fine mansion. He then proceeded to update the house and to transform the estate grounds into a proper Picturesque landscape. Toward this latter end, he dammed up the swamp into an irregular lake, erected a greenhouse and a combination summerhouse-icehouse-observatory, laid out gardens, and planted numerous trees. In addition to his Cambridge property, which functioned as both a fashionable estate and a working farm, Craigie also owned farms in Chelmsford, Massachusetts, and Hebron, Maine. He did in fact take an interest in gentleman farming, joining the MSPA in 1793, and in 1796 donating four hundred dollars worth of shares in the Bank of the United States to that association. He also published an article on plowing in the MSPA's journal of 1803. In his library were a number of works on husbandry, horticulture, and related sciences. One story about Craigie reported that he had received three merino sheep in 1793 and, not knowing their value as superior wool producers, "simply ate them." [*MSPA, Rules and Regulations, 1796,* p. 75; Andrew Craigie, "The Benefit of Frequent Ploughings," *Papers on Agriculture, Consisting of Communications Made to the Massachusetts Society for Promoting Agriculture* (Boston: Young and Minns, 1803), pp. 78–79; Wilder, "Horticulture of Boston," pp. 627–28; Carroll W. Pursell, Jr., "E. I. du Pont, Don Pedro, and the Introduction of Merino Sheep into the United States, 1801: A Document," *Agricultural History* (hereafter *AH*) 33 (April 1959): 86; Hammond, "Country Life near Boston," pp. 155–63, 362–75; *DAB,* s.v. "Craigie, Andrew."]

DEARBORN, HENRY ALEXANDER SCAMMELL (1783–1851),
lawyer, politician, and author

In the field of rural pursuits, Dearborn is best remembered as a founder and first president of the MHS, but he was active as well in many collateral activities. He was one of the driving forces behind the MHS's establishment of Mount Auburn Cemetery in 1831 and the subsequent establishment of a similar rural cemetery, Forest Hills, in Roxbury in 1848. He translated and published several horticultural works from French. Dearborn also had links with the MSPA. He published an account of his attempts to cultivate indigo in the society's journal in 1817 and a similar discussion of another dyestuff, woad, in 1823. Dearborn had experimented with woad during the War of 1812 with an eye to the domestic manufacture of textiles—he later tried cultivating cotton as well—but with the coming of peace and the renewal of cheap imports, the practical applications of his work received little interest. In 1823, however, RICHARD CROWNINSHIELD, a textile manufacturer and gentleman farmer, communicated to Dearborn his own successful experiments with woad and saw a bright future for its cultivation in industrializing America. Between 1809 and 1829, Dearborn's horticultural and agricultural experiments took place at Brinley Place, his father's Roxbury estate. Following his father's death, Dearborn moved to Hawthorne Cottage, also in Roxbury. Roxbury's historian Francis Drake described Dearborn's "fine old mansion" as "the constant scene of courtly manners and aristocratic display." [*Massachusetts Agricultural Repository and Journal* (hereafter *MSPA Journal*) 4 (January 1817): 289–96; ibid. 7 (June 1823): 342–47; *NEF* 1 (1 March 1823): 246; Francis S. Drake, *The Town of Roxbury: Its Memorable Persons and Places, Its History and Antiquities* (Roxbury: privately printed, 1878), pp. 231–34, 337–38; Wilder, "Horticulture of Boston," p. 622; Manning, *MHS*, pp. 67–68, 86–88, 90–91; L. H. Bailey, ed., *The Standard Cyclopedia of Horticulture*, 3 vols. (New York: Macmillan, 1930), 2:1571; *DAB*, s.v. "Dearborn, Henry Alexander Scammell."]

DERBY, ELIAS HASKET (1739–99), merchant

In the category of rural pursuits, Derby is probably best known in connection with the splendid Salem mansion, surrounded by equally splendid gardens, built for him by Samuel McIntire in 1797. Here were terraces, walks, and a large conservatory filled with exotic plants. In addition to the Essex Street estate, however, Derby also owned an experimental farm a few miles outside of Salem in the town of Danvers, and to this farm Derby frequently repaired on Sunday afternoons. McIntire's hand was here as well, as, for example, in the neoclassical summerhouse designed in 1793–94. The Danvers farm was the site of numerous farming and gardening experiments, carried out under the supervision of a German horticulturist whom Derby had brought over from Europe. "It was in these improvements," wrote Derby's son-in-law Benjamin Pickman, "that Mr. Derby found some of his most tranquil enjoyments, and they imparted delight to all who had the curiosity to visit them." After one such visit to the Danvers farm and garden, the Reverend William Bentley praised Derby for his enjoyment of "the innocence of rural life" and "the happy application of riches to facilitate agriculture." Derby joined the MSPA in 1793. [Robert E. Peabody, *Merchant Venturers of Old Salem: A History of the Commercial Voyages of a New England Family to the Indies and Elsewhere in the Eighteenth Century* (Boston: Houghton Mifflin, 1912), pp. 163–64; Benjamin Pickman, obituary of Elias Hasket Derby, *Salem Gazette*, 10 September 1799, in ibid., pp. 164–66; William Bentley, *The Diary of William Bentley, D.D.*, 4 vols. (1907; reprint ed., Gloucester, Mass.: Peter Smith, 1962), 1:180, 373–74, 2:219, 244, 341–42, 4:445; E. Griswold, "Early

American Garden Houses," *Antiques* 98 (July 1970): 82–83; *DAB,* s.v. "Derby, Elias Hasket."]

DEXTER, AARON (1750–1829), physician and professor of chemistry and materia medica at Harvard

Dexter served the MSPA faithfully from its incorporation in 1792 until just a few years before his death. He acted as its treasurer from 1792 to 1800; its second vice president from 1800 to 1807; its first vice president from 1807 to 1811; its president from 1812 to 1822; and its trustee from 1793 until 1827. In line with his profession, Dexter undertook experiments in agricultural science on his farm in Chelsea. There he carried out investigations on marl, compost, and plant nutrition. [*MSPA, Rules and Regulations, 1796,* pp. 59–60; "Abstract of the Records," pp. 19, 22, 43; Joseph Lovering, "Boston and Science," in Winsor, *Memorial History of Boston,* 4:511; *Centennial Year,* pp. 10–11.]

DOWNER, SAMUEL (1773–1854), merchant and whale oil manufacturer

On his estate in Dorchester, Downer indulged his taste for pomology, developing new types of apple, pear, and cherry. His special interest was the origin and character of native fruits. He was a founding member of the MHS and served as its counsellor from 1829 to 1835 and again in 1840 and 1841. Downer's son of the same name (1807–81), also a merchant and oil manufacturer, carried on his father's horticultural interests. [David R. Downer, *The Downers of America* (Newark, N.J.: n.p., 1900), p. 75; Wilder, "Horticulture of Boston," p. 619; *DAB,* s.v. "Downer, Samuel."]

GARDNER, SAMUEL PICKERING (1767–1843), merchant

Gardner was just one member of an extended family taken with rural pursuits. Thus in his correspondence with his uncle Timothy Pickering, Gardner ranged from a discussion of cattle breeds to a promise of obtaining pear scions from his brother-in-law John Lowell. His Summer Street garden, which he inherited in 1800, was noted for its fine specimens of pear and foreign varieties of grape, the latter grown without benefit of a greenhouse. Gardner's son JOHN LOWELL GARDNER (1804–84), also a merchant, inherited an enthusiasm for horticulture. Many a specimen from the younger Gardner's Brookline conservatories were submitted to MHS exhibitions. In wonderfully telling phrases, one eulogist described the younger Gardner as "a typical Bostonian, a representative no less of the old-time commercial spirit than of the later wealth and culture." [Samuel P. Gardner to Timothy Pickering, 19, 22 March 1825, 30 August 1828, Pickering Papers, 45:316, 317, 383; "Notice of Samuel Pickering Gardner," *Proceedings of the Massachusetts Historical Society* 2 (1835–55), proceedings of April 1844, pp. 282–83; *New England Historical and Genealogical Register* 38 (October 1884): 466; Wilder, "Horticulture of Boston," pp. 608, 627; John Gould Curtis, *History of the Town of Brookline Massachusetts* (Boston: Houghton Mifflin, 1933), p. 212.]

GODDARD, NATHANIEL (1767–1853), merchant

In the early nineteenth century, Goddard cultivated vegetables, fruit trees, and grapevines in his Summer Street, Boston, garden. In these years, Summer Street was famous for its gardens; Goddard's horticultural neighbors included Joseph Barrell, Samuel P. Gardner, James Jackson, John Welles, and Benjamin Bussey. Sometime in the 1840s, Goddard purchased property in suburban Brighton to pursue his gardening interests. Nathaniel's brother, BENJAMIN GODDARD (1766–1861), bought their father's thirty-acre farm in Brookline when he retired from business in 1813. Here the older brother devoted himself to the cultivation of both garden and farm. [Henry Goddard Pickering, *Nathaniel Goddard: A Boston Merchant, 1767–1853* (Cambridge: Riverside Press, 1906), pp. 29–31, 143–47; Wilder, "Horticulture of Boston," pp. 612–13.]

GRAY, JOHN CHIPMAN (1793–1881), lawyer and politician

Thanks largely to fortunes inherited both from his father, Salem merchant William Gray, and from his father-in-law, Boston merchant Samuel Pickering Gardner, Gray never actually practiced law. His favorite pursuits were said to be agriculture and horticulture, and these he was able to indulge at his summer estate in Cambridge. In 1827 he became a member of the MSPA, and he served as its president from 1846 to 1856. He was a founder and, from 1829 to 1833, a vice president of the MHS. Gray was a well-known speaker before agricultural and horticultural societies, addressing such topics as "the difficulties and obstacles to be encountered in agriculture," forest trees, and the New England climate. Many of these speeches were collected and published in an 1856 volume entitled *Essays, Agricultural and Literary*. [John C. Ropes, "Memoir of the Hon. John

Chipman Gray, LL.D.," *Proceedings of the Massachusetts Historical Society*, 2d ser., 4 (November 1887): 22–27; John C. Gray, "The Difficulties and Obstacles to be Encountered in Agriculture," in *Transactions of the Agricultural Societies of Massachusetts, for the Year 1847* (Boston: Dutton and Wentworth, 1848), pp. 198–208.]

INGERSOLL, NATHANIEL (1773–1838), East India merchant

Ingersoll purchased his twenty-one-acre Brookline farm in 1805. Here he cultivated fruits and vegetables for his family as well as for his livestock, which in 1824 included one cow, two horses, sixty sheep, and—what were Ingersoll's pride and joy—160 hogs. Ingersoll kept twelve sows and two boars just for breeding purposes; his efforts must have paid off, for in 1817 we find him taking Brighton premiums in both these categories. Labor on the Brookline farm was carried out by two full-time hired men with the assistance in plowing season of day laborers, but Ingersoll complained that, along with other gentleman farmers, he was forced to drive his own vegetable cart to market, since otherwise he was subjected to fraud and deception. Ingersoll served as a trustee of the MSPA from 1817 to 1818. [1817 premiums, Massachusetts Society for Promoting Agriculture Papers (hereafter MSPA Papers), drawer C, folder XXXIV, number 1, MHS; "Mr. Ingersoll's Piggery," *American Farmer* 5 (2 January 1824): 321–24; Samuel Aspinwall Goddard, *Recollections of Brookline, Being an Account of the Houses, the Families, and the Roads, in Brookline, in the Years 1800 to 1810* (Birmingham, Eng.: E. C. Osborne, 1873), p. 7.]

JACKSON, JAMES (1787–1867), physician and professor of clinical medicine at Harvard

Between 1825 and 1841, Jackson occupied a thirty-to-forty-acre estate in Waltham for portions of the year, giving up obstetrics but otherwise continuing his medical practice in order to do so. He was not the only one in his family to seek rural felicity in the town of Waltham. One brother, Judge CHARLES JACKSON, leased Gore Place for several years, while another brother, manufacturer PATRICK TRACY JACKSON, selected Waltham as the site for his country seat because his textile enterprise, the Boston Manufacturing Company, was located in that town. At his estate, Dr. Jackson cultivated fruit trees and experimented with buckthorn hedges. "Work in your garden if you have any taste for it," he advised John Murray Forbes in 1855, "but gardening is one of those fine arts, not to be polluted by those who do not love it." He served as a trustee of the MSPA from 1829 to 1831 and joined the MHS when it was established in 1829. [James Jackson Putnam, *A Memoir of Dr. James Jackson* (Boston: Houghton, Mifflin, 1905), pp. 305–6, 353, 387; John Lowell, "Live Hedges for New England," *MSPA Journal* 10 (April 1832): 411–12; Wilder, "Horticulture of Boston," p. 635.]

LORING, GEORGE BAILEY (1817–91), physician and politician

Following his retirement from medicine in 1850 and subsequent removal to a 450-acre Salem estate the following year, Loring quickly became one of the major gentleman stockbreeders of his time. His involvement with agricultural societies was extensive, beginning with his membership in the Essex Agricultural Society, extending through posts with the MSPA, the Massachusetts Board of Agriculture, and the New England Agricultural Society, and culminating in his appointment in 1881 as U.S. Commissioner of Agriculture. He also wrote prolifically on agricultural topics, delivered many addresses at agricultural fairs, and even lectured on stockbreeding at the Massachusetts Agricultural College. [(Charles L. Flint), *Fifth Annual Report of the Secretary of the Massachusetts Board of Agriculture, together with the Reports of Committees Appointed to Visit the County Societies* (Boston: William White, 1858), p. 236; Flint, ed., *Abstract of Returns of the Agricultural Societies of Massachusetts, for 1859* (Boston: William White, 1860), pp. 110–25; L. H. Bailey, ed., *Cyclopedia of American Agriculture*, 4 vols. (New York: Macmillan, 1909), 4:593; *DAB*, s.v. "Loring, George Bailey."]

LYMAN, THEODORE, JR. (1792–1849), politician

As was true of many rural enthusiasts of the antebellum period, Theodore Lyman, Jr., inherited his taste for country living and pastimes from his father. The first Theodore Lyman was an MSPA trustee and builder of the Vale in Waltham. On his father's death, the younger Lyman inherited the Waltham estate, but he also chose to build his own country seat in Brookline. In 1842 he hired the architect Richard Upjohn to build a house on the Brookline estate and improved the grounds by grading the lawn, planting trees, and constructing graperies. For many years a member and official of the MHS, Lyman bequeathed no less than ten thousand dollars to that society. That sum pales before the over seventy thousand dollars Lyman donated to the state-owned reformatory in Westborough, an institution that looked to the positive benefits of rural living to reform juvenile offenders. Lyman also left ten thousand to a similar private charity, the Boston Farm School. [Wilder, "Horticulture of Boston" pp. 626–27; Manning, *MHS*, pp. 124; *DAB*, s.v. "Lyman, Theodore."]

NEWHALL, CHEEVER (1788–1878), boot and shoe manufacturer

Newhall purchased his Dorchester farm in 1824 and spent summers there until his death. Of the estate's sixty acres, a few remained wooded, a few were devoted to ornamental landscaping, eight to ten were given over to fruit culture, and the remaining sustained twenty-five cows, eighteen to twenty hogs, one bull, four oxen, and three horses. Apples and pears were Newhall's pomological specialties, but he cultivated cherries, plums, and grapes as well. He was a founder and officer of the MHS and an early member of the American Pomological Society. When it came to animal husbandry, Newhall employed the latest scientific techniques. Thus his cattle were soiled, not pasture-fed; swine were kept mainly for the creation of fertilizer; and the farm buildings, such as his two-story hoghouses, were designed with cleanliness and efficiency in mind. Newhall showed great resourcefulness in his management of the farm; he fertilized his land with hogsheads of urine collected from several Boston hotels. He belonged to the MSPA, the Norfolk Agricultural Society, and the Massachusetts Agricultural Club. ["Farming in Massachusetts," *The Cultivator*, n.s., 2 (January 1845): 22–23; *New England Historical and Genealogical Register* 32 (October 1878): 430–31; Wilder, "Horticulture of Boston," p. 619.]

PARKMAN, FRANCIS (1823–93), historian

Parkman purchased a summer cottage with a three-acre garden in Jamaica Plain in 1852, but only in the 1860s and 1870s did he turn to gardening in earnest. His biographers have characterized Parkman's horticultural phase as a period of therapy, and Parkman himself, in an autobiographical letter written in 1864, stated: "In the severer periods of the disorder, books were discarded for horticulture, which benign pursuit has proved most salutary in its influences." As conceived by Parkman, however, the extensive gardens were far more than a source of soothing pleasures. They also constituted a profit-making operation. In 1862 Parkman went into partnership with William H. Spooner, a commercial nurseryman. Although the partnership lasted only a year, Parkman continued to invest in his gardens, spending thousands of dollars on a greenhouse, gardener's cottage, plant material, and garden equipment and hiring a continually growing staff of gardeners. Ornamental shrubbery and flowers, of which he had hundreds of varieties, were his specialty; in 1866 he published *The Book of Roses,* and in the next dozen years several more articles on floriculture followed. By 1864 he was able to turn a profit from sales. Indeed by 1868 he earned more money from his nursery operations ($529.74) than from his copyright receipts ($269.25). During this period, Parkman was a zealous member of the MHS, winning literally hundreds of premiums between 1859 and 1884, serving as chairman of its library committee (1863–74), as vice president (1871–74), and finally as president (1875–78). He was also appointed professor of horticulture at Harvard's Bussey Institution in 1871, a position that entailed delivering floricultural lectures to young ladies. His major horticultural accomplishment was the painstaking and ultimately triumphant hybridization of a new variety of lily, named the *Lilium parkmanni* in his honor. In 1876 he sold the lily to a London nurseryman specializing in American plants, reportedly for a thousand dollars (although Parkman recorded only slightly over half that sum in his account books). [Francis Parkman to Mary Dwight Parkman, 4 April 1862, Francis Parkman to George E. Ellis [1864], Francis Parkman to Anthony Waterer, 15 January 1876, in Wilbur R. Jacobs, ed., *Letters of Francis Parkman,* 2 vols. (Norman: University of Oklahoma Press, 1960), 1:146–47, 183, 2:87–88; Francis Parkman, Receipt Book for Sale of Flowers, 1859, 1874–80, Parkman Papers, MHS; Parkman, Account Books, 1859–79, 1861–66, 1866–76, Parkman Papers; Parkman, Diary of Gardening Activities, 1868–1886, Parkman Papers; Parkman, *The Book of Roses* (Boston: J. E. Tilton, 1866); Anthony Waterer, *Catalogue of Conifers, Evergreens, Roses, &c., 1877–78, Knap Hill Nursery* (London: H. M. Pollett [1878?]); *Garden and Forest* 6 (15 November 1893): 471; Albert Emerson Benson, *History of the Massachusetts Horticultural Society* (Boston: Massachusetts Horticultural Society, 1929), pp. 135–36, 183, 200; Henry Dwight Sedgwick, *Francis Parkman* (Boston: Houghton, Mifflin, 1904), pp. 234–43, 337; Charles Haight Farnham, *A Life of Francis Parkman* (Boston: Little, Brown, 1910), pp. 27–34; Howard Doughty, *Francis Parkman* (New York: Macmillan, 1962), pp. 208–10, 285, 286, 290–91.]

PICKMAN, BENJAMIN (1740–1819), merchant

Pickman was a successful but not an enthusiastic merchant; his tastes ran to the literary and the rural. When in 1780 he visited the gardens at Stowe, he commented that they "exceed anything I have ever seen and would take a volume to describe them." He inherited a farm in South Salem that had been expanded piece by piece by his father since 1754 until it reached its ultimate size of 420 acres. In 1811 the Reverend William Bentley praised the Pickman farm as "an excellent example of our best agriculture & pasturage." In 1816 he commented on its neatness and its plain but excellent buildings. Bentley noted the farm's many hogs, poultry, and cattle and its fine vegetables grown for the market but singled out the horticulture as especially impressive. [George Francis Dow, *The Diary and Letters of Benjamin Pickman (1740–1819) of Salem, Massachusetts* (Newport, R.I.: n.p., 1928), pp. 53–55, 63–64, 151–52; Bentley, *Diary*, 4:28, 166, 396–97.]

PRINCE, JOHN (1770–1843), occupation unknown

Prince was an early afficionado and long faithful advocate of merino sheep. He first purchased merinos in 1810, the height of the fever, and at the second Brighton cattle show, his merino ewes took a premium. At some point, certainly by the late 1820s, Prince moved his sheep operation to Merino Island in the middle of New Hampshire's Lake Winnipesaukee. Meanwhile, on his fifty-seven-acre estate in Roxbury, Prince cultivated fruits and flowers, kept cattle and hogs, and grew root crops (including a prize-winning field of mangel-wurzel) for his animals' subsistence. He contributed sporadically to the MSPA's journal, served as trustee (1810–11, 1833) and treasurer (1812–26) of the society, and for several years was in charge of the Brighton plowing matches. He was also a charter member of the MHS, its counsellor in 1835, and its vice president from 1837 to 1839. [John Prince, "Statement Respecting Merino Sheep," *MSPA Journal* 3 (January 1815): 183; "Account of Premiums Paid for the Exhibitions of 13 & 14 Oct 1817 at Brighton," MSPA Papers, C–XXXIV–1; Prince to B. Guild, 8 November 1826, 11 June 1828, 25 November 1830, MSPA Papers, C–XLII–27, A–XI–125, A–XVIII–24; *NEF* 1 (9 November 1822): 116; *American Farmer* 2 (19 January 1820): 340; Wilder, "Horticulture of Boston," p. 622; Bailey, *Cyclopedia of American Agriculture*, 4:606.]

SARGENT, IGNATIUS (1800–1884), East India merchant

Sargent's one-hundred-acre estate in Brookline, Pine Bank, was known primarily for its grapes. In the 1840s Sargent was exhibiting bunches of the Black Hamburg grape that weighed between four and six pounds. One horticultural editor described the Pine Bank grapes as "almost fabulous in size and weight." The father's horticultural interests were inherited by his son, CHARLES SPRAGUE SARGENT (1841–1927), professor of horticulture (1872–73) and arboriculture (1879–1927) at Harvard, director of the Harvard Botanic Garden (1872–79) and the Arnold Arboretum (1873–1927), publisher and editor of *Garden and Forest* magazine (1888–97), and author of numerous works on trees and plants. The younger Sargent continued to supervise the Brookline estate, opening its conservatories, its many native and foreign trees and shrubs, and its landscaped gardens to the public every year. Both father and son were members of the MHS, and Charles also assumed office in the postbellum MSPA. ["Visits to Country Places.—No. 7. Around Boston," *Horticulturist,* n.s., 8 (February 1857): 67; Emma Worcester Sargent and Charles Sprague Sargent, *Epes Sargent of Gloucester and His Descendants* (Boston: Houghton Mifflin, 1923), pp. 150–51, 154–58; Wilder, "Horticulture of Boston," p. 626; *DAB,* s.v. "Sargent, Charles Sprague."]

STICKNEY, JOSIAH (1789–1876), sugar manufacturer and railroad director

Stickney began his horticultural career, when, while still "a gentleman whose time was almost incessantly occupied in commercial matters," he chanced to see an exhibit of dahlias at the MHS. Thereafter, he took up floriculture in his small, urban garden. In 1844 he purchased a thirty-five-acre estate in Watertown, located along the Charles River and a five-minute walk from the suburban railroad station. Here he indulged his enthusiasm for horticulture, even undertaking a massive terracing project between the riverbanks and his Georgian mansion set high on a hill. Stickney joined the MHS in 1839, served as its vice president from 1852 to 1857, and then as its president in 1858. At one point, he made a bequest of his Watertown estate to the society, then revoked it, contributing instead twelve thousand dollars, the income of which was to be used toward the purchase of books for the MHS library. [*The Cultivator,* n.s., 9 (November 1852): 375; Wilder, "Horticulture of Boston," p. 634; G. Frederick Robinson and Ruth Robinson Wheeler, *Great Little Watertown: A Tercentenary History* (Cambridge: privately printed, 1930), p. 79.]

WARREN, JOHN COLLINS (1778–1856), surgeon and professor at Harvard Medical School

Warren inherited his taste for rural pursuits from his father, JOHN WARREN (1753–1815), also a surgeon and Harvard professor, and an MSPA member and owner of an estate in Roxbury. The younger Warren owned a farm in Brookline. The intensity of his horticultural and agricultural interests is obvious from the amount of time he devoted to them on his postretirement travels in Europe. On an 1851 trip to England, for example, he purchased trees from William Skirving's nursery in Liverpool, visited the famous greenhouses at Chatsworth, attended an exhibition of the Farnham Horticultural Society, and admired the prize livestock at the Royal Agricultural Show at Windsor. "I often wish I was with you," he wrote to his son from London, "enjoying grapes and figs; but I must say, I have never seen such strawberries as those here." Many are the size of "a billiard ball," he reported, "and of so delicate a flavor, that I eat them without cream or sugar." He had not been so lucky in France, when "an indisposition" had prohibited his sampling of the native fruit there. Nevertheless, he had maintained a horticultural schedule. "While in Paris," he wrote, "I usually arose at half-past seven; breakfasted at ten, and fagged away at the Garden of Plants and other places till dinner-time, which was at about six." [Edward Warren, *The Life of John Collins Warren, M.D., Compiled Chiefly from His Autobiography and Journals,* 2 vols. (Boston: Ticknor and Fields, 1860), 2:61, 62, 66, 71, 74, 79–80, 82, 85; Lovering, "Boston and Science," 4:519–20; Samuel A. Green, "Medicine in Boston," in Winsor, *Memorial History of Boston,* 4:566–67; Drake, *Roxbury,* pp. 412–14.]

WEBSTER, DANIEL (1782–1852), lawyer and statesman

In addition to speculating in Western land in 1836 (much to his post-Panic dismay), Webster owned farms in his native village of Franklin, New Hampshire, and the far more famous Green Harbor, his estate in Marshfield, Massachusetts. The New Hampshire holdings consisted of the original family farm, the Elms, much enlarged by the purchase of contiguous land. Although Webster entrusted the management of the farm to a local farmer in exchange for half of the farm's income, he nonetheless chose to involve himself in many of the day-to-day workings of the farm, sending detailed instructions in frequent letters. The Webster family did occasionally visit the Elms, setting up house in a wing of the farmhouse put aside for their use. The real country seat of the Websters, however, was Green Harbor, purchased in 1832. Over the years, Webster invested no less than ninety thousand dollars in the estate—and the farm never turned a profit. The Marshfield holdings were expanded from the original 160 acres to a full 1,400 acres cultivated with the labor of twenty-five men, most of them tenant farmers. The old-fashioned farmhouse (just one of thirty buildings) was enlarged and renovated into an elegant residence. The scruffy farmstead was transformed into a proper English landscape with the planting of huge numbers of ornamental trees and a full acre of flowers; the construction of a trout pond and a stone bridge over the pond to complete a circuit walk of the estate; and the importation of Indian peacocks and Peruvian llamas. Webster's Marshfield pastimes were consistent with his image as country squire—fishing, boating, hunting for waterfowl, and, probably the most important, the pursuit of experimental farming. Many of Webster's agricultural activities—carried out by his resident overseer, Charles Henry Thomas, and Porter Wright, his head farmer—bordered on the extravagant; his "scientific" application of kelp as a fertilizer, for example, involved the construction of a road to the sea and the labor of 150 teams of oxen. Guiding this and other agricultural operations at Green Harbor— the cultivation of turnips, for example—was the desire to implement reforms put forth by the aristocratic "book farmers" of Britain. As part of that reform program, and again in line with his "cultivated breed" of agriculture, Webster stocked his farm with the finest in pedigreed cattle, horses, sheep, swine, and poultry, many imported directly by Webster from England and Scotland. [(Charles Henry Charles Thomas), Appraisal of the Estate of the late Hon. Danl. Webster, Marshfield, 14 December 1852, Boston Athenaeum; M. Wiltse, ed., *The Papers of Daniel Webster: Correspondence,* 6 vols. (Hanover, N.H.: University Press of New England, 1974–84), esp. correspondence with Charles Henry Thomas; C. H. Van Tyne, ed., *The Letters of Daniel Webster* (New York: McClure, Phillips, 1902), pp. 641–89; N. Parker Willis, *Hurry-Graphs; or, Sketches of Scenery, Celebrities and Society, Taken from Life* (New York: Charles Scribner, 1851), pp. 18–19; Charles Lanman, *The Private Life of Daniel Webster* (New York: Harper and Brothers, 1852), pp. 69–75; George Ticknor Curtis, *The Life of Daniel Webster,* 2 vols. (New York: D. Appleton, 1870), 2:107–11; Peter Harvey, *Reminiscences and Anecdotes of Daniel Webster* (Boston: Little, Brown, 1877), pp. 275–79; *The Cultivator,* n.s., 3 (November 1846): 355; "Sketches of Farms: The Farm of the Hon. Daniel Webster," ibid., n.s., 6 (January 1849): 9–11; Emeline Stuart Wortley, "A Visit at Mr. Webster's," *Harper's New Monthly Magazine* 3 (June 1851): 94–96; Irving H. Bartlett, *Daniel Webster* (New York, W. W. Norton, 1978), pp. 122–23, 208–9, 211–14; Maurice G. Baxter, *One and Insepar-*

*able: Daniel Webster and the Union* (Cambridge: Harvard University Press, 1984), pp. 282–86; Merrill D. Peterson, *The Great Triumvirate: Webster, Clay, and Calhoun* (New York: Oxford University Press, 1987), pp. 385–88; and Rexford B. Sherman, "Daniel Webster, Gentleman Farmer," *AH* 53 (April 1979): 475–87.]

WELLES, JOHN (1764–1855), merchant and politician

Welles's major interest on his Dorchester farm was the breeding of livestock. It was Welles who was given charge of Admiral, the Shorthorn donated to the MSPA by Admiral Sir Isaac Coffin in 1824. Small wonder that his bulls won premiums in several Brighton shows and that in 1832 he should submit a vindication of imported stock to the MSPA's journal. He was not single-minded in his agricultural pursuits, however. Welles dabbled in everything from forest trees to asparagus. From 1817 to 1828 he served on the MSPA's board of trustees, from then until 1840 as second vice president, and as president from 1841 to 1846. [Brighton premiums for 1824, 1826, MSPA Papers, C–XXXIV–6–7, 8; *NEF* 1 (17 May 1823): 329–30; John Welles, "On Asparagus," *MSPA Journal* 10 (January 1831): 301–3; Welles, "Imported Stock," ibid. 10 (April 1832): 425–27; George F. Lemmer, "The Spread of Improved Cattle through the Eastern United States to 1850," *AH* 21 (April 1947): 82.]

# Rural Pursuits in Boston

Ever inclined to draw a generous estimate of their own importance, elite Bostonians took tremendous pains to leave voluminous records of their thoughts and actions, both trivial and significant, for posterity. In turn, posterity, often in the form of blood descendants, has seen fit to record the histories of elite individuals, families, and institutions. There is thus no clear distinction between primary and secondary source material but instead a continuum running from manuscript material through works published by and for elite individuals and institutions to biographies and histories, many of which in their celebratory tone fall into the category of antiquarian. All these prove useful. The types of sources available include manuscript collections of individuals, families, and institutions; individual and "clan" biographies, many of which are especially useful collections of personal letters, diaries, and papers; biographical dictionaries and encyclopedias of Boston (or Massachusetts) figures; "in-house" periodicals and newspapers; business histories, chronicling the origins and development of specific banks, insurance companies, railroads, and commercial and manufacturing enterprises; and institutional biographies, including the histories of charitable, cultural, educational, and social organizations associated with the Boston elite. Because this body of literature is by no means obscure and has been tapped by other historians, I will not use this essay to expand on it. For bibliographical guidance on this literature, see the bibliographical essays in Ronald Story's *Forging of an American Aristocracy: Harvard and the Boston Upper Class, 1800–1870* (Middletown, Conn.: Wesleyan University Press, 1980) and Edward Pessen's *Riches, Class, and Power before the Civil War* (Lexington, Mass.: D. C. Heath, 1973). Frederic Cople Jaher's *The Urban Establishment: Upper Strata in Boston, New York, Charleston, Chicago, and Los Angeles* (Urbana: University of Illinois Press, 1982) also provides good listings of many categories of sources in its footnote matter.

This bibliographical essay instead focuses on little known and little used sources, those that relate specifically to rural pursuits as practiced by elite Bostonians. Of course, as my footnotes indicate, much information relating to country estates, gentleman farming, and horticulture is scattered throughout the general body of Boston sources. Here I concentrate on those sources devoted entirely to rural pursuits or that make an especially critical contribution to our understanding of these pastimes.

## Manuscript Collections

By far the most important manuscript collection in the area of rural pursuits is the Papers of the Massachusetts Society for Promoting Agriculture, now deposited at the Massachusetts Historical Society in Boston. The MSPA Papers consist of thirty-three boxes of material dating from the society's establishment in 1792. The material includes correspondence, premium offerings and lists of winners, bills and receipts, committee reports, and other internal records. Although the MSPA published a relatively large amount of information on its activities in its transactions, it is impossible to arrive at any detailed understanding of the organization and its leaders without consulting these papers. This holds especially true for the MSPA's first generation of existence and for the two decades before the Civil War, when published material appeared more sporadically.

Unfortunately, the Massachusetts Horticultural Society has no corresponding manuscript collection. It appears that no systematic attempt was made to preserve its internal papers, though a few scattered items do exist at the society's library.

Of great importance in the study of rural pursuits are the private papers of individuals involved in country estate living, gentleman farming, and gardening. Many relevant manuscript collections contain highly significant but nevertheless occasional references to rural pursuits; far fewer are relatively dense with agricultural and horticultural information. Those that are include the Joseph Barrell Papers, the Timothy Pickering Papers (especially volume 45), and the Parsons-Sargent Papers, all at the Massachusetts Historical Society; the Fisher Ames Papers, at the Dedham Historical Society; and the John Perkins Cushing Papers, especially Cushing's diaries, at the Boston Athenaeum.

*Published Transactions, Surveys, and Reports*

The publications of the MSPA provide a tremendous amount of valuable information on the society, its activities, and its members. In 1793, just a year after its establishment, the society published its *Laws and Regulations of the Massachusetts Society for Promoting Agriculture,* a volume that contained, in addition to what its title suggests, notices of premiums, agricultural essays, communications to the society, and a membership list. Subsequent volumes reflect a similar mix of material. In the following two decades, the MSPA published *Rules and Regulations of the Massachusetts Society for Promoting Agriculture* (1796); five volumes of *Papers on Agriculture* (1799, 1801, 1803, and 1804 [two in this last year]); two volumes of *Papers* (1806 and 1807); *Georgick Papers for 1809; Papers for 1810;* and *Papers for 1811.* In November 1813 it published the first issue (although designated the first number of volume three) of the *Massachusetts Agricultural Repository and Journal,* which quickly became a regular series of transactions published twice yearly. The contents of this journal were varied and included items directly connected to the society, such as membership lists and Brighton fair proceedings, as well as articles reflecting the latest in agricultural thinking both at home and abroad. The journal ceased publication in 1832 (it appeared only irregularly in the preceding five years), and not until 1856 did the MSPA issue another set of transactions.

That this very successful journal could barely outlive the 1820s is due to several circumstances. First, the driving force behind the periodical— editor, compiler, and author of half its material—was John Lowell (1769– 1840), who retired from active involvement in the journal in 1830. Second, agricultural newspapers, as discussed below, occupied the same niche as the society's journal and therefore edged it out of existence. Finally, the society itself was losing its dominant place on the elite agricultural scene to county societies. This last consideration points us to another fruitful source of information on rural pursuits—namely, the published transactions of the "suburban" societies based in Essex, Middlesex, and Norfolk counties.

We find out more about all these societies, as well as elite attitudes toward farmers and farming in the Commonwealth, in Henry Colman's agricultural surveys. Colman, a Unitarian minister and gentleman farmer, was commissioned by the Massachusetts legislature in 1837 to undertake an agricultural survey of the state on the model of those carried out by Sir John Sinclair and Arthur Young in Britain. The result was four volumes that editorialized on the state of agriculture in the counties of Essex (1838), Berkshire (1839), and Franklin and Middlesex (1841) and on the culture of wheat and silk in Massachusetts (1840). Colman's works and ideas were very popular among the Boston elite. Upper-crust Bostonians were the main individual subscribers to his agricultural survey, as they were the main subscribers to his two-volume *European Agriculture and Rural Economy*, published in Boston in 1844.

Beginning in the mid-1840s, two series of extremely useful publications detailing the activities of the state and county agricultural societies appeared. Volumes in the first series, running from 1845 through 1852, are titled *Transactions of the Agricultural Societies of Massachusetts, for the Year 1845 [1846, etc.]*. These contain reports of society activities, including most prominently their agricultural fairs; agricultural essays; and addresses delivered before the societies at these fairs. The second series, running from 1853 to 1892, consists of two separate reports bound together, both edited by the secretary of the newly established State Board of Agriculture. In the period of interest here, the secretary is Charles L. Flint. The first set of reports is titled *First [Second, etc.] Annual Report of the Secretary of the Massachusetts Board of Agriculture, together with the Reports of Committees Appointed to Visit the County Societies;* the second set of reports is titled *Abstract of Returns of the Agricultural Societies of Massachusetts, 1854 [1855, etc.]*. Included in these reports are the secretary's evaluation of the state of agriculture and agricultural societies in the Commonwealth; reports of delegates appointed to visit county fairs; reports of exhibition committees; addresses delivered at the agricultural fairs; and lists of society officers. A guide to the contents of these publications as well as of Colman's reports can be found in Frederick H. Fowler, *Agriculture of Massachusetts: Synoptical and Analytical Index, 1837–1892* (Boston: Wright and Potter, 1893).

Finally, the publications of the Massachusetts Horticultural Society constitute by far the most important sources on the MHS. These date back to the society's founding in 1829, when *Proceedings on the Establishment of the Massachusetts Horticultural Society* was published. In subsequent years, the society published texts of the speeches delivered at its annual horticultural festivals, together with detailed descriptions of the festival proceedings and the toasts, songs, and poems recited at these lavish affairs. The speakers at the festivals (and, therefore, the authors of the subsequently issued pamphlets) include H. A. S. Dearborn (1829), Zebedee Cook (1830), Malthus A. Ward (1831), Thaddeus William Harris (1832), Alexander H. Everett (1833), John C. Gray (1834), John Lewis Russell (1835), Ezra Weston, Jr. (1836), William Lincoln (1837), James E. Teschemacher (1842), and George Lunt (1845). Society proceedings, including records of society meetings, lists of premium entrants and winners, and festival descriptions, are covered in a series of variously titled *Transactions* that span the years from 1837 to 1852. Separately published was the *Report of the Twentieth Annual Exhibition of the Massachusetts Horticultural Society, and Third Triennial Festival, Held at Faneuil Hall, September 19, 20, 21, 22, 1848.*

## Published Treatises

By the beginning of the nineteenth century, Americans were starting to generate their own agricultural literature to supplement the mainly British sources they were used to consulting. Most popular were newspapers, discussed below; pamphlets and books were far less important. In the field of horticulture, however, the number of American treatises was substantial. Many of the most important of these were written by Bostonians and published in their native city. Among these are Thomas Green Fessenden, *The New American Gardener* (Boston, 1828) and *The Complete Farmer and Rural Economist* (Boston, 1834); William Kenrick, *The New American Orchardist* (Boston, 1833); Robert Manning, *Book of Fruits* (Salem, 1838); Joseph Breck, *The Flower-garden; or, Breck's Book of Flowers* (Boston, 1851); and Charles Mason Hovey, *The Fruits of America,* 2 vols. (Boston, 1852–56). All these authors, with the partial exception of Fessenden, who was also a sometime lawyer, satirical poet, and Federalist pamphleteer, were professional nurserymen. Not surprisingly, their books are mainly technical works that provide little if any commentary on the moral dimensions of agriculture and horticulture. Thus, although they arise from the milieu of elite rural pursuits—Kenrick, for example, dedicated his book to "the Hon. John Lowell, LL.D." for his "disinterested and distinguished zeal"—they are not especially useful in studying rural pursuits as a cultural phenomenon. Good introductions to this literature can be found in U. P. Hedrick, *A History of Horticulture in America to 1860* (New York: Oxford University Press, 1950), pp. 467–94, and Hamilton Traub, "The Development of American Horticultural Literature, Chiefly between 1800 and 1850," *National Horticultural Magazine* 7 (July 1928): 97–103, 8 (January 1929): 7–17.

Somewhat more useful are the works of Andrew Jackson Downing, especially his *Treatise on the Theory and Practice of Landscape Gardening,* first published in 1841. Downing was not a member of the Boston elite, although blue-blooded horticulturists admired both his character and his works, and he started out in life as a relatively humble commercial nurseryman. Nevertheless, both because he sought to raise his own social status as well as that of his profession, he was not content to limit his discussions of horticulture, landscape gardening, and architecture to technical matters. His books consist substantially of moral commentary on these topics. Downing can be considered the prime mover in the middle-class vogue for horticulture, a moral reform movement that paralleled and overlapped but was not identical to elite interest in horticulture.

*Agricultural and Horticultural Periodicals*

Newspapers devoted solely to agricultural topics did not appear until 1819, when the *American Farmer,* published in Baltimore and catering largely to the southern states, was established. The first such periodical based in New England was established in 1822 and appropriately named the *New England Farmer.* Its editor until 1837 was Thomas Green Fessenden, noted above as a poet, pamphleteer, and author of agricultural and horticultural treatises. The newspaper quickly developed close ties with the MSPA, publishing articles by many of its members and covering its activities. As we have seen, it eventually contributed to the MSPA's decision to suspend publication of its own journal. Other Boston-based agricultural newspapers include the *Boston Cultivator,* the *Massachusetts Ploughman,* and the *Yankee Farmer.* Also useful are many agricultural newspapers published in upstate New York—New England moved west. Because of the cultural links between the two regions, these periodicals tended to pay special attention to the people and problems of New England. Thus we find upstate papers publishing disapproving editorials on the depopulation of rural New England and profiling such Boston gentleman farmers as Cheever Newhall, Josiah Stickney, and Daniel Webster. Included in this category are the *Genesee Farmer* (Rochester), the *New Genesee Farmer and Gardener's Journal* (Rochester), the *Cultivator* (Albany), and the *Country Gentleman* (Albany). Introductions to agricultural newspapers are provided in Albert L. Demaree, *The American Agricultural Press, 1819–1860* (New York: Columbia University Press, 1941), and Donald B. Marti, *To Improve the Soil and the Mind: Agricultural Societies, Journals, and Schools in the Northeastern States, 1791–1865* (Ann Arbor, Mich.: University Microfilms International, 1979), pp. 124–62.

Horticultural periodicals appeared later than agricultural periodicals, although agricultural periodicals often included much information relevant to the cultivation of fruits, flowers, and vegetables. In fact, the full titles of many early agricultural periodicals—*New England Farmer, and Horticultural Journal,* for example—indicate the overlap in interests. Not until the

1830s, however, with horticulture as a separate movement firmly established, did periodicals devoted solely to horticulture become established. In 1835 the *Horticultural Register and Gardener's Magazine* appeared in Boston. It lasted only four years but was edited by such notable horticulturists as Thomas Green Fessenden and Joseph Breck. A second, longer-lived horticultural periodical was founded and edited in Boston by Charles M. Hovey, another Boston nurseryman. The *American Gardener's Magazine, and Register of Useful Arts* began publication in 1835; under a changed title, the *Magazine of Horticulture,* it existed from 1837 to 1868. Also noteworthy is the *Horticulturist,* edited by A. J. Downing from 1846 until his death six years later. All of these are useful since they include moral essays on horticulture, practical and scientific treatises, descriptions of individual horticulturists and their achievements, and news of horticultural societies. Ulysses Hedrick provides a useful survey of horticultural journalism in his *History of Horticulture,* pp. 494–98.

*Other Periodicals*

The popularity and significance of rural pursuits among elite Bostonians can be gauged from the coverage they received from general interest periodicals aimed at the elite audience. These periodicals include the *Massachusetts Magazine* (1789–96), the *Monthly Anthology and Boston Review* (1803–11), the *North American Review* (1815–), the *New England Magazine* (1831–35), and the *Atlantic Monthly* (1857–). The Unitarian periodical, the *Christian Examiner* (1824–69), also falls in this category. Many of the articles devoted to rural pursuits consist of review essays, wide-ranging commentaries that take as their starting (or sometimes ending) point a reference to, for example, an MSPA publication, an agricultural address, or a horticultural treatise. The nature and importance of agriculture in Massachusetts and the moral utility and aesthetic glory of horticulture and rural cemeteries received special attention.

*Institutional Histories*

The MSPA celebrated its hundredth anniversary by publishing *Centennial Year (1792–1892) of the Massachusetts Society for Promoting Agriculture* (Salem, Mass.: n.p., n.d.). This includes profiles of the early founders, spotty but interesting information on the society's activities, and lists of MSPA officers. Although not a formal history, the "Abstract of Records, 1792–1858," found in *Transactions of the Massachusetts Society for Pro-*

*moting Agriculture,* n.s., 1 (Boston: J. H. Eastburn, 1858): i–iv, 5–153, is a useful parallel source. The society's later history is covered in *An Outline of the History of the Massachusetts Society for Promoting Agriculture* (Boston: Meador, 1942). The Essex Agricultural Society published its own centennial history, *The History of the Essex Agricultural Society of Essex County, Massachusetts, 1818–1918,* written by Thomas Franklin Waters, in 1918.

There are two histories of the Massachusetts Horticultural Society, both commissioned and published by the society. The first, *History of the Massachusetts Horticultural Society, 1829–1878,* was written by Robert Manning, Jr., a commercial horticulturist and officer of the MHS, and published in 1880. The second, *History of the Massachusetts Horticultural Society,* was written by Albert Emerson Benson for the society's centennial in 1929. An update on the society's history, *Twenty-Five Historic Years,* was written by Edward I. Farrington and published by the MHS in 1955. Also useful for the antebellum period is H. A. S. Dearborn's "Historical Sketch of the Massachusetts Horticultural Society," in *Transactions of the Massachusetts Horticultural Society, Part III* (Boston: William D. Ticknor, 1852), pp. 61–92. In addition, there is a separate history of the early development of Mount Auburn, Jacob Bigelow's *History of the Cemetery of Mount Auburn* (Boston: James Munroe, 1860). The author, a prominent physician and Harvard professor, was a driving force behind the establishment of a rural cemetery in the environs of Boston.

# Index

Adams, Charles Francis, 213
Adams, John, 5, 36–37, 44, 106, 214; and rural pursuits, 38, 86, 213–15
Addison, Joseph, 35, 46
Agricultural reform: among the Boston elite, 108, 122–31, 125n, 174, 176, 180, 217, 231
Agricultural societies: in U.S., 1, 57n, 124; county and town, 103, 135–36, 175, 176–77, 213, 215, 225, 226; in Britain, 196. *See also* Bath and West Society; Essex Agricultural Society; Massachusetts Society for Promoting Agriculture; Philadelphia Society for Promoting Agriculture
Agriculture, attitudes toward: literary, 3, 41–43; Puritan, 3; physiocratic, 3–4; republican, 4; and theories of history, 5–6, 42; Jeffersonian, 7; among Boston elite, 41–43, 119, 121, 123–24, 187, 203; MSPA, 68
Ames, Fisher, 19, 30–31, 43–56, 58, 74, 106, 147
Appleton, Nathan, 83, 84, 142, 143, 144, 153, 170, 205
Appleton, Samuel, 142, 162
Appleton, William, 143–44
Aristocracy, attitudes toward: Jeffersonian, 17; Federalist, 17–18, 32–33; Boston elite, 17–18, 32–33, 39, 144–45, 171, 183, 185–86, 196–97, 202, 204–7, 212

Banks, Sir Joseph, 87, 88, 89
Baring, Sir Francis, 36, 38–39, 48, 218
Barrell, Joseph, 39–43, 46, 60, 106, 147, 223
Bath and West Society, 57, 61, 87, 89
Bedford, John Russell, duke of, 29, 30, 33n
Bigelow, Timothy, 215
Boston elite: and Puritan legacy, 2–3; colonial, 15, 21; formation of, 15–16, 16n;

composition of, 16–17, 84, 84n, 141; legitimacy of, 17–18, 170–71, 172, 201–2, 203, 204, 211; consolidation of, 83–84, 141, 145, 203; ethos of, 141–44, 161–62, 172, 201, 211–12; fear of class decline among, 190–91, 208, 209; postbellum, 205–12
—attitudes of, toward: commerce, 9–11, 12, 42–43, 119, 121, 130–35, 187, 203, 208; manufacturing, 9–10, 11–12, 130–37, 187; modernization, 9–12, 125–37, 192–204, 211; mercantile traits, 17–18, 142–45, 183–86, 202, 204–7, 212; merchants, 17–18, 74, 74n, 75, 121, 124, 142–45, 203; social hierarchy, 17–18, 144–45, 203–4; the South, 17–18, 81, 189; Jeffersonians, 18–19; Shays's Rebellion, 18; aristocracy, 17–18, 32–33, 39, 144–45, 171, 183, 185–86, 196–97, 202, 204–7, 212; Britain, 32–33, 39, 183, 196–97, 202, 205, 218; British merchants, 36–39, 74–77, 202; agriculture, 41–43, 119, 121, 132–34, 187, 203; farmers, 73–74, 73n, 121–35, 186–95, 198, 203, 204; rural depopulation, 123–35, 137, 186–90, 194–95; New England, 124–45, 132, 133, 134, 186–98
—involvement in: gentleman farming, 1, 24–32, 40–45, 52–56, 69, 107–19, 184–86, 195–98, 213–32; horticulture, 1, 24, 27, 27n, 40–45, 52–54, 107–19, 147–73, 176, 181, 197, 205, 207–11, 215–32; rural pursuits, 1, 12, 20, 21–22, 39, 43, 44, 45, 51–52, 55–56, 106, 107–8, 160–61, 181–86, 195, 200, 202–5, 207, 210–12; manufacturing, 11, 82–83, 83n, 135, 136, 161–62, 163, 203; commerce, 15–16, 73, 161–62, 163; stockbreeding, 24n, 27n, 92–95, 92n, 95n, 100–102, 108, 117, 118, 176,

Boston elite (*continued*)
181–82, 181n, 183, 196, 205, 207,
213–32; horse breeding, 95, 95n, 108,
108n, 181, 182–83, 207; livestock importation, 95, 95n, 100–102, 117, 175–
76, 196, 217, 231; agricultural reform,
108, 122–31, 174, 176, 180, 217, 231;
postbellum business, 206
Bowdoin, James, 215–16
Breeding, applied to human society, 171,
182, 208–10
Brooks, Peter Chardon, 84, 116–17, 142
Brown, James, 216–17
Buckminster, Joseph, 11, 58, 75–76
Bussey, Benjamin, 147–48, 217–18, 223

Cabot, George, 1, 12, 19, 21, 43, 44, 48,
49, 56, 58, 82, 106, 212
Cabot, Joseph Sebastian, 218
Cabot, Samuel, 151, 151n
Cleveland, Horace W. S., 167, 167n
Cobham, Richard Temple, Lord, 49, 51,
51n
Codman, John, 36, 38–39, 48n, 218–19
Coke, Thomas, 22n, 29, 30, 33n, 75, 96,
175, 175n
Colman, Henry, 131–32, 192–94
Commerce, attitudes toward: Puritan, 3;
physiocratic, 3–4, republican, 4–5; and
theories of history, 5–6, 42; Jeffersonian,
7; Boston elite, 9–11, 12, 42–43, 119,
121, 130–35, 187, 203, 208; literary,
42–43
Cook, Zebedee, 165, 166, 169–70, 170n,
219
Craigie, Andrew, 92n, 219–20
Crowninshield, Richard, 220
Cultivation, ideal of, 163–64, 170–72,
181–82, 184, 200, 205, 207, 210
Cushing, Caleb, 162, 191
Cushing, John Perkins, 151–52, 181n,
192

Dearborn, Henry Alexander Scammell,
112n, 163, 170, 170n, 220–21
Depopulation, rural, 122–25
Derby, E. Hasket, 60, 62, 63n, 119, 221–
22
Derby, E. Hersey, 62, 119, 120, 178
Dexter, Aaron, 58, 96, 222
Downer, Samuel, 222
Downing, Andrew Jackson, 164, 167,
167n

Elite, use of term, 15n
Essex Agricultural Society, 135, 136, 176–
77, 186–87, 191, 211, 225
Essex Junto, 19–20, 43–55, 60, 74, 82
Everett, Edward, 11, 84, 117, 142, 171

Farmers, practical: in republican theory, 4;
in historical theory, 6; in Jeffersonian ideology, 7; in Jacksonian ideology, 9; and
MSPA, 60n, 62n, 64–66, 68–71, 73–74,
98–105, 177–80, 202–3; criticism of
MSPA, 70–71, 99–105, 178–80, 180n;
viewed by Boston elite, 73–74, 73n,
121–35, 186–95, 198, 203, 204; criticism of Boston elite, 119
Federalist ideology, 17–20, 32–33, 46, 50–
51, 54–55, 71–72, 81, 81n, 104–5
Federalist party, 16, 17–20, 81–82

Gardner, John Lowell, 222–23
Gardner, Samuel Pickering, 222–23
Gentleman farming: among Boston elite, 1,
24–32, 40–45, 52–56, 69, 107–19,
184–86, 195–98, 213–32; in Britain,
24–33, 69n, 75, 87, 89; and MSPA, 63,
69, 98, 99–102; criticized, 119; defended, 120–21
Gill, Moses, 72
Goddard, Benjamin, 223
Goddard, Nathaniel, 223
Gore, Christopher: 27–32, 39n, 43, 44,
48, 54, 55, 58, 106, 118, 196
Gray, John Chipman, 165, 168–69, 223–
24
Great Britain: aristocracy of, 22, 22n, 33,
33n, 34, 202; country estates of, 22, 33–
39, 48n, 218, 227–28; gentry of, 22n,
33, 33n, 35, 202; Agricultural Revolution in, 24–26, 26n; gentleman farming
in, 24–33, 69n, 75, 87, 89; horticulture
in, 24, 24n, 25, 87, 89, 230; landed merchants of, 34–40, 48n, 202; rural retirement in, 45–46, 49–50, 50n

Hagley, 36, 49, 50n, 51n
Harvard College, 16, 58, 63, 64, 83, 84n,
91, 113, 127, 170, 179n
Higginson, Stephen, 19, 36, 43, 60
History, theories of, 5–6, 5n, 42, 163
Hobhouse, Sir Benjamin, 87, 89
Holkham, 29, 33n, 96
Holmes, Oliver Wendell, 95n, 190, 210n

Horse breeding, 95, 95n, 108, 108n, 181, 182–83, 207

Horticultural Society of London, 87, 89, 112, 157–60, 169, 169n

Horticulture: among Boston elite: 1, 24, 27, 27n, 40–45, 52–54, 107–19, 147–73, 176, 181, 197, 205, 207–11, 215–32; in Britain, 24, 24n, 25, 87, 89, 230; in U.S., 155, 164; and materialism, 162–72, 211; class associations of, 168–70, 171–72; and cultivation, 170–72, 181, 210; and breeding, 171

Hunnewell, Horatio Hollis, 153–55, 172

Ingersoll, Nathaniel, 1, 12, 212, 224

Jackson, Charles, 152, 224
Jackson, James, 223, 225–26
Jackson, Jonathan, 19, 43, 60, 74, 82
Jackson, Patrick Tracy, 82, 224
Jefferson, Thomas, 5, 17, 20, 51, 63n, 72
Jeffersonian ideology, 7, 17, 19, 38, 50–51, 102

King, Rufus, 29, 31, 32n, 43, 48
Knight, Thomas Andrew, 89, 90, 112, 157, 157n

Lawrence, Abbott, 83, 142, 163, 192
Lawrence, Amos, 83, 143, 205
Lawrence, Amos Adams, 184–85
Lee, Francis Lowell, 184, 184n
Lee, George, 152–53, 153n
Lee, Henry, 83, 94–95, 153
Lee, Joseph, 152
Lee, Thomas, 148, 152
Lettsom, John Coakley, 36, 75, 75n, 76
Livestock importation, 95, 95n, 100–102, 117, 175–76, 196, 217, 231
Loring, George Bailey, 181n, 191, 225
Lowell, Francis Cabot, 82, 136
Lowell, John (1743–1802), 19, 43, 58, 59, 66, 70, 82, 108
Lowell, John (1769–1840): impressions of Europe, 46, 108, 110–11; and MSPA, 58, 85–86, 89–91, 92n, 96–105, 174; Federalist, 85, 86, 113; and horticulture, 89, 111–13, 111n, 112n, 147, 157, 157n, 160–61, 222; on agriculture, 93, 95, 100–102, 120, 121, 126–31, 147, 198; and gentleman farming, 107, 111–13; as lawyer, 108–13; mercantile outlook of, 108–14, 198; on rural depopulation,

123, 132; on manufacturing, 130, 135–37; mentioned, 82, 116, 144

Lyman, George W., 181n
Lyman, Theodore, 22–24, 24n, 27, 106, 118, 147, 181n, 215, 225
Lyman, Theodore, Jr., 225–26
Lyttleton, Lord, 49, 50n, 51n

Malthus, Thomas, 137
Manufacturing, attitudes toward: Puritan, 3; physiocratic, 3–4; Boston elite, 9–10, 11–12, 130–37, 187
Massachusetts: modernization in, 129, 130–31; rural depopulation in, 122–35
Massachusetts Horticultural Society (MHS): formation of, 155, 219; and Horticultural Society of London, 156–59, 169, 169n; composition of, 157–58, 169, 169n; and practical horticulturists, 157n, 158, 159, 169n; and MSPA, 158, 159, 159n, 160; and gender, 165–66, 210–11; postbellum, 208, 208n, 210–11, 227
—activities: library, 158; publication, 158; seed and plant distribution, 158–59; exhibitions, 159–66, 197, 218, 222–23, 229; premiums, 159, 159n; dinners, 159–71, 197
Massachusetts Society for Promoting Agriculture (MSPA): function of, for Boston elite, 56, 67–69, 105, 202–3; formation of, 57–58; leadership of, 58, 60, 72, 86, 89–90, 114–19, 174, 178, 213–32; mercantile outlook of, 58–61, 60n, 71, 72–76, 135–36, 203; membership of, 60, 60n, 75, 87, 89, 92n, 175n, 213–30; and practical farmers, 60n, 62n, 64–66, 68–71, 73–74, 98–105, 177–80, 202–3; and European agriculture, 61; and Bath and West Society, 61, 66n, 87, 89; stated goals of, 63, 66, 67, 71, 103; and gentleman farming, 63, 69, 98, 99–102; criticism of, 70–71, 99–102, 103–5, 177–80, 180n; ineffectuality of, 76–77, 85–86; and MHS, 158–60
—activities: publication, 61, 89–90, 89n, 174; library, 61n, 89; premiums, 61–63, 92–102, 117, 118, 159n, 174, 176, 224, 232; botanical garden, 63–64, 76, 90–91, 102, 174; seed and plant distribution, 63, 65, 91–92, 92n; agricultural tool acquisition, 63n, 92, 93, 177; surveys, 66, 67, 86–87; encouragement of local societies, 86–87, 86n; stockbreed-

MSPA (*continued*)

ing, 92–95, 92n, 100–102, 175–76, 181, 182, 217; livestock importation, 95, 95n, 175–76, 217; Brighton cattle show, 95–103, 117, 118, 123, 132, 159, 174, 176, 177–78, 224, 228, 232; Mount Auburn Cemetery, 159–60, 161, 166, 167

Materialism, 8, 142, 162–72, 211

Merino sheep, 30, 62, 92–95, 117, 128, 216, 220, 228

Modernization, attitudes toward: republican, 4–5; Jacksonian, 6–7; Jeffersonian, 7; postrevolutionary liberal, 7–8; antebellum, 8–9; Boston elite, 9–12, 125–37, 192–204, 211

Motley, Thomas, Jr., 181n, 217–18

Mount Auburn Cemetery, 159–60, 161, 166, 167, 179n, 218, 220

Newhall, Cheever, 226

New World: degeneration in, 10n; regeneration in, 170n

Olmsted, Frederick Law, 167, 167n

Otis, Harrison Gray, 82, 106–7, 113

Parkman, Francis, 144, 207–10, 208n, 226–27

Parsons, Gorham, 63n, 101, 117–18, 177–78

Parsons, Theophilus, 19, 74, 74n

Pastoral ideal, 3, 6n, 41–43, 45–49, 48n

Peck, William Dandridge, 62, 63–64, 90, 91

Perkins, James, 148

Perkins, Samuel Gridley, 89, 148, 157, 157n

Perkins, Thomas Handasyd, 1–2, 12, 84, 95n, 129, 148–51, 152, 161, 172, 173, 205, 212

Philadelphia Society for Promoting Agriculture, 57n, 124

Physiocracy, 3–4

Pickering, Timothy: Federalist, 19; and rural pursuits, 43–45, 60, 101, 128; on manufacturing, 135, 136; mentioned, 114, 214, 215, 222

Pickman, Benjamin, 221, 227–28

Pomeroy, Samuel W., 62, 92n, 118, 135

Pope, Alexander, 46, 49, 50, 51n

Prince, John, 228

Puritans, legacy of, 2–3

Quincy, Josiah, 1, 12, 58, 114, 116, 126–31, 135, 147, 178, 212

Republican theory, 4–9

Repton, Sir Humphrey, 23, 24, 25

Roscoe, William, 36, 37, 76

Rural cemetery movement, 166–68, 218, 220. *See also* Mount Auburn Cemetery

Russell, George R., 143, 187–88

Russell, Henry S., 181, 182

Salem, 15, 119, 136, 218, 220–21, 228

Sargent, Charles Sprague, 229

Sargent, Ignatius, 228–29

Shays's Rebellion, 18, 60–61, 67, 71

Sinclair, Sir John, 30, 37, 214

Smithfield market, 96, 97

Stickney, Josiah, 229

Stockbreeding, 24n, 27n, 92–95, 92n, 95n, 100–102, 108, 117, 118, 176, 181–82, 181n, 183, 196, 205, 207, 213–32

Story, Joseph, 166, 192

Stowe, 22, 36, 49, 50, 51, 51n, 227–28

Sullivan, Richard, 58, 116, 119, 123, 126, 131–35

Taylor, John, 123–24

Thomson, James, 46, 47, 49, 50n, 51n

Thorndike, Israel, 19, 95, 101

Tudor, Frederic, 126, 154, 155

Unitarianism, 16, 84n, 113, 205

Virtue, 4, 8, 9, 17, 67–69, 202–3

Warren, John, 230

Warren, John Collins, 230

Webster, Daniel, 11–12, 191–99, 230–32

Welles, John, 223, 232

Whig party, in Massachusetts, 141, 170n

Wilder, Marshall Pinckney, 155, 156, 161, 172, 179–80, 181n

Winthrop, John, 201

Woburn, 29, 30, 33n, 36

Wolcott, Oliver, 43, 44, 48, 55

Young, Arthur, 29, 30, 33n, 75